Introduction to the World's Major Religions

CONFUCIANISM AND TAOISM

Volume 2

Randall L. Nadeau

Lee W. Bailey, General Editor

GREENWOOD PRESS
Westport, Connecticut • London

Library of Congress Cataloging-in-Publication Data
available on request from the Library of Congress.

British Library Cataloguing in Publication Data is available.

ISBN 0–313–33634–2 (set)
    0–313–33327–0 (vol. 1)
    0–313–32724–6 (vol. 2)
    0–313–33251–7 (vol. 3)
    0–313–32683–5 (vol. 4)
    0–313–32846–3 (vol. 5)
    0–313–33590–7 (vol. 6)

First published in 2006

Greenwood Press, 88 Post Road West, Westport, CT 06881
An imprint of Greenwood Publishing Group, Inc.
www.greenwood.com

Printed in the United States of America

The paper used in this book complies with the
Permanent Paper Standard issued by the National
Information Standards Organization (Z39.48–1984).

10 9 8 7 6 5 4 3 2 1

Introduction to the World's Major Religions
Lee W. Bailey, General Editor

Judaism, Volume 1
Emily Taitz

Confucianism and Taoism, Volume 2
Randall L. Nadeau

Buddhism, Volume 3
John M. Thompson

Christianity, Volume 4
Lee W. Bailey

Islam, Volume 5
Zayn R. Kassam

Hinduism, Volume 6
Steven J. Rosen

CONTENTS

SET FOREWORD

This set, *Introduction to the World's Major Religions,* was developed to fill a niche between sophisticated texts for adults and the less in-depth references for middle schoolers. It includes six volumes on religions from both Eastern and Western traditions: Judaism, Christianity, Islam, Hinduism, Confucianism and Taoism, and Buddhism. Each volume gives a balanced, accessible introduction to the religion.

Each volume follows a set format so readers can easily find parallel information in each religion. After a Timeline and Introduction, narrative chapters are as follows: the "History of Foundation" chapter describes the founding people, the major events, and the most important decisions made in the faith's early history. The "Texts and Major Tenets" chapter explains the central canon, or sacred texts, and the core beliefs, doctrines, or tenets, such as the nature of deities, the meaning of life, and the theories of the afterlife. The chapter on "Branches" outlines the major divisions of the religion, their reasons for being, their distinctive doctrines, their historical background, and structures today. The chapter on "Practice Worldwide" describes the weekly worship practices, the demographic statistics indicating the sizes of various branches of religions, the global locations, and historical turning points. The chapter on "Rituals and Holidays" describes the ritual practices of the religions in all their varieties and the holidays worldwide, such as the Birth of the Buddha, as they have developed historically. The chapter on "Major Figures" covers selected notable people in the history of each religion and their important influence. A glossary provides

definitions for major special terms, and the index gives an alphabetic lo-
cator for major themes. A set index is included in volume 6 (to facilitate
comparison).

In a world of about 6 billion people, today the religion with the greatest
number of adherents is Christianity, with about 2 billion members, com-
prising 33 percent of the globe's population. Next largest is Islam, with about
1.3 billion members, (about 22 percent). Hindus number about 900 million
(about 15 percent). Those who follow traditional Chinese religions number
about 225 million (4 percent). Although China has the world's largest population, it is officially Communist, and Buddhism has been blended with
traditional Confucianism and Taoism, so numbers in China are difficult
to verify. Buddhism claims about 360 million members (about 6 percent
of the world's population). Judaism, although historically influential, has
a small number of adherents—about 14 million (0.2 percent of the world's
population). These numbers are constantly shifting, because religions are
always changing and various surveys define groups differently.[1]

Religions are important elements of the worldview of a culture. They
express, for example, the cultural beliefs about cosmology, or picture of the
universe (e.g., created by God or spontaneous), and the origin of humanity (e.g., purposeful or random), its social norms (e.g., monogamy or polygamy), its ways of relating to ultimate reality (e.g., sacrifice or obedience
to law), the historical destiny (e.g., linear or cyclical), life after death (e.g.,
none or judgment), and ethics (e.g., tribal or universal).

As the world gets smaller with modern communications and global
travel, people come in contact with those of other religions far more frequently than in the past. This can cause conflicts or lead to cooperation, but
the potential for hostile misunderstanding is so great that it is important
to foster knowledge and understanding. Noting parallels in world religions
can help readers understand each religion better. Religions can provide
ethical guidance that can help solve serious cultural problems. During war
the political question "why do they hate us?" may have serious religious
aspects in the answer. New answers to the question of how science and
religion in one culture can be reconciled may come from another religion's
approach. Scientists are increasingly analyzing the ecological crisis, but the
solutions will require more than new technologies. They will also require
ethical restraint, the motivation to change the destructive ecological habits
of industrial societies, and some radical revisioning of worldviews. Other
contemporary issues, such as women's rights, will also require patriarchal
religions to undertake self-examination. Personal faith is regularly called

into consideration with daily news of human destructiveness or in times of crisis, when the very meaning of life comes into question. Is life basically good? Will goodness in the big picture overcome immediate evil? Should horrendous behavior be forgiven? Are people alone in a huge, indifferent universe, or is the ultimate reality a caring, just power behind the scenes of human and cosmic history? Religions offer various approaches, ethics, and motivations to deal with such issues. Readers can use the books in this set to rethink their own beliefs and practices.

NOTE

1. United Nations, "Worldwide Adherents of All Religions by Six Continental Areas, Mid-2002," *World Population Prospects: The 1998 Revision* (New York: United Nations, 1999).

INTRODUCTION

CHINESE RELIGION AND THE WORLD'S RELIGIONS

Confucianism and Taoism are the two major religious traditions of China. They represent the religious foundations of one of the oldest civilizations in the world, with origins predating the Roman Empire and the founding of Christianity. Over the centuries, Confucianism and Taoism spread to other countries of East Asia: Confucianism was adopted by the Korean and Japanese civilizations as a model for governmental organization and as a basic orientation toward the self and the world, and Taoist influence on those cultures can be seen in the form of Son/Zen Buddhism. Today, despite a tumultuous century of civil war and rebuilding, and despite tremendous political, economic, and social influence from the West, Confucianism and Taoism remain the most abiding cultural systems of China. Moreover, Confucianism and Taoism are increasingly recognized as viable religious alternatives among non-Chinese in the West.

Can Confucianism and Taoism be included among the religious traditions of the world? What makes them distinctive? These questions will be examined in this Introduction:

1. Are Confucianism and Taoism religions in the same way that Judaism, Christianity, Islam, Hinduism, and Buddhism are religions?
2. Are Confucianism and Taoism world religions; that is, do they enjoy a worldwide following?

In addition, the basic characteristics of Chinese culture, in particular its language, will be examined, and the stylistic conventions and methodological orientations of this book will be addressed.

CONFUCIANISM AND TAOISM AS RELIGIONS

In many respects Confucianism and Taoism are different from the other traditions of major world religions. As will be seen:

- Confucianism and Taoism do not have a specific founder or date of founding, even though Confucianism appears to be named after a single individual, Confucius. In Chapter 3, it will be seen that Confucius was not the founder of Confucianism. The purported founder of Taoism, Lao-zi, was not an historical person at all.
- They do not profess belief in God. In fact, a major stream of Confucianism denies the existence of gods altogether, and Taoism, while admitting the existence of gods and other spiritual beings, asserts the superiority of Taoist priests and mystics to gods.
- They venerate or respect ancestral spirits without worshipping them. It is a common mislabeling of Chinese religion to describe it as "ancestor worship."
- They generally see religious *belief* as having less importance than religious *practice.* Both Confucianism and Taoism emphasize orthopraxy (right action) over orthodoxy (right belief).
- They have an open canon. Confucian and Taoist texts continue to be written and to be incorporated into their respective canons.
- They lack a specific institutional identity. There is no Confucian or Taoist pope, no religious headquarters or governing body.
- They have no fixed religious services and can be practiced anywhere, from shrines and temples to private studies and mountain peaks.

In light of these features, some scholars have argued that Confucianism and Taoism should not be classified as religions at all—and these include some scholars from within the Confucian and Taoist traditions themselves. Why is this? Clearly, it depends greatly on how the word *religion* is used or defined, and what constitutes a religion.

Traditionally, scholars have defined religion as belief or a system of beliefs. In particular, religion is thought to be the belief in spiritual beings of some kind—whether God or gods, or other kinds of spiritual entities, such as demonic spirits, ghosts or souls, nature deities, ancestral spirits, saints, and so on. In this sense, Judaism and Christianity are prototypes of what people think a religion should be—the belief in gods (in the case of Judaism and Christianity, one God) and lesser spirits. But there is a problem: first, religions do not limit themselves to belief alone. Belief is certainly one element of all religions, but religions also include many other defining, essential aspects:

- prayer, worship, sacrifice, and other kinds of religious ceremony;
- mythologies and cosmologies;
- biographies of prophets, saints, or saviors;
- institutional organization, churches, synagogues, mosques, or other structures, priests, rabbis, imams, or other religious leaders;
- artistic expression: music, art, and architecture; and
- meditation, physical exercises, such as yoga and dance.

Religion is never limited just to certain beliefs about gods or spirits.

A second problem is that not all religions profess a belief in gods. Obviously, not all religions profess a belief in the God of Judaism, Christianity, and Islam (the so-called Abrahamic traditions, named after their common ancestor). The Buddha is purported to have denied the existence of any eternal, all-knowing, unchanging being, including Brahman, the God or Over-Soul of his native Hindu tradition. Some people—including some within the Buddhist tradition itself—therefore describe Buddhism as a kind of atheism. In the Chinese context, there are Confucian intellectuals who have also denied the existence of any "spiritual reality," seeing the belief in "gods, ghosts, and ancestors" as the superstitious religion of the common people—useful as a way of controlling the people morally and ethically, but superstitious nevertheless. With regard to the spiritual world, Confucianism is parallel to the Western materialist or secular orientation. The Taoist attitude toward spiritual beings is more complicated. Taoist priests do believe in gods, but see themselves as being superior to them. Taoist priests are able to manipulate and control the gods, and to master god-like power within themselves. So, if the definition of *religion* is limited to "the belief in gods" (and, in particular, belief in the superiority, omniscience, and omnipotence of one God), then Buddhism, Confucianism, and Taoism would have to be excluded as religions altogether.

Certainly, Buddhism, Confucianism, and Taoism *are* religions, so there must be a definition of religion that will be inclusive of all seven traditions addressed in this series. Various scholars have come up with a number of sophisticated definitions of religion, but it may be more useful to think of religion not in terms of *what it is,* but rather in terms of *what it does* for religious followers; that is, the function of religion in individual and social life.

An inclusive definition is: "Religion is a means of ultimate transformation" (Streng, 190). Religion brings about change: cosmic, social, or individual transformation. Christians sometimes call this transformation "salvation," but most religions focus more on social or universal transformation, not just individual conversion. Religious transformation is not minor or incidental change, but rather *ultimate* change, addressing the very foundations of individual or social identity.

As a means of ultimate transformation, religions make two fundamental assumptions: first, that there is something wrong with the way things are in their nonreligious state, and second, that the means exist to change those conditions. Many religions teach that the ordinary way of viewing the world is fundamentally mistaken—that people have misperceived who or what they are in relation to reality *as it really is,* and that they need to be corrected in their understanding of themselves and their world. And virtually all religions teach that a new, religious perception of people and their world will have a transformative effect: religious knowledge will propel them to "change reality," to create a new self or a new world. Finally, religion gives people the means to act upon that knowledge—the means to achieve ultimate transformation.

Religion as a Means of Ultimate Transformation

- Religions teach that the ordinary way of viewing reality is mistaken.
- Religions show reality "as it really is."
- Religions show that reality in its nonreligious (nontransformed) state is wrong or unsatisfying.
- Religions provide the means to change reality fundamentally.

One scholar of comparative religion has described this process as providing a "model of" and a "model for" reality (Geertz, passim). Religion is a "model of" reality: it corrects people's misperceptions and describes reality "as it really is." Religion is a "model for" reality: it gives people the means to create a new, more perfect self, community, and cosmos. To use a medical metaphor, religion has diagnostic and prescriptive functions. A doctor first determines the cause of an illness (the diagnosis) before suggesting treatment (the prescription). As a diagnosis, religion provides insight into people's true condition; as a prescription, religion instructs them on how to treat the condition, how to transform themselves and their world.

These two functions of religion will be examined in more detail. First, religion is a "model of" reality in the sense that it provides people with an *accurate description* of reality, often contradicting their ordinary, commonsense, or unenlightened perceptions. For example, Hinduism teaches that people are fundamentally mistaken in viewing the world as multitudinous and differentiated; they fail to see the underlying unity of reality. Or, some Christian denominations teach that people mistakenly see themselves as knowing and powerful, and that they fail to see their fundamentally sinful nature, which limits human understanding and ability. Seeing themselves as they really are opens people to the possibility of transformation through redemption. In these cases and others, religion provides a more accurate description of the way the world really is, or the way humans really are.

The means by which religions provide a correct "model of" reality are various; they include scriptures and commentaries (the teachings of gods or sages), creeds, preaching, testimonial, religious education, myths and legends, and so forth—the intellectual content of religious belief.

Second, religion is a "model for" reality, providing followers with the *means* to change the world and to model themselves upon the religious orientation of the tradition. As a model for reality, the religion projects a new possibility (a new model) for the way things *ought to be*, not just the way things *actually are* at present. The "model for" aspect of religion goes beyond mere description to directive, instruction, and prescription, showing how religious persons can bring about the ultimate transformation that is at the heart of religious belief and practice.

The means by which religions provide a "model for" reality include ethical norms (moral law), rituals of worship or thanksgiving (sacrifice, prayer, and so on), and exemplary stories (stories of heroic figures within the tradition, for ordinary people to imitate or follow). Religions tell their followers not only "what life is," but *how to live,* specifically, how to live a *religiously transformed* life.

Based upon this definition, Confucianism and Taoism are clearly two of the world's great religions, serving as a "model of" reality and a "model for" the ultimate transformation of their followers and communities.

- Both teach that the ordinary or unenlightened way of viewing life is mistaken.
- Both describe reality "as it really is," based upon the teachings of the Confucian and Taoist sages.

- Both show that the nonreligious state of existence is unsatisfying and nonharmonious.
- Both provide the means to change reality fundamentally and to create conditions of social and cosmic harmony.

CONFUCIANISM AND TAOISM AS WORLD RELIGIONS

World religions are religions that cross national boundaries. Some world religions are *missionary* religions, aiming for the conversion of other persons to the faith, including persons of different national or ethnic origins. This is true of Buddhism, Christianity, and Islam, for example, which have spread by conversion since the second or third century of their founding. In other cases, a religion originally associated with a particular people or culture becomes a world religion by virtue of voluntary or forced *migrations*. Such was the case of Judaism at various times in its history, from the fall of the First and Second Temples in the sixth century B.C.E. and the first century C.E. to the forced expatriation from Nazi-occupied Europe in the twentieth century C.E. Some traditions remain closely tied to their culture of origin, such as Shinto (which is limited to Japan, both culturally and geographically, and therefore cannot be classified as a world religion), while others are associated primarily with a particular culture but have been adopted or appropriated by people in other parts of the world. Hinduism, for example, was connected primarily to India until American and European intellectuals began converting to Hinduism in the nineteenth and twentieth centuries.

In what sense can Confucianism and Taoism be classified as world religions? Like Judaism, the spread of Confucianism and Taoism can be attributed partly to the migrations of Chinese throughout the world. Beginning as early as the Han Dynasty (around the time of Jesus), Chinese began to settle in other parts of Asia (including present-day Korea, Vietnam, Malaysia, and Myanmar). Today, ethnic Chinese live in every corner of the world and are vital contributors to the economic, social, and political life of many countries. Chinese is the world's most widely spoken language, not only because China is the world's most populous country, but also because Chinese retain their cultural, religious, and linguistic identity even after several generations as citizens of other countries. Chinese immigrants have preserved their language, and they have also preserved their Confucian and Taoist values, which underlie Chinese cultural identity, as well as the practice of ancestor veneration, artistic expression, physical exercise, traditional Chinese medicine, and so on—all having roots in China's religious traditions.

Confucianism and Taoism also can be classified as world religions because people from other cultures have voluntarily appropriated their teachings. This was true of Korea at the beginning of the Yi (Choson) Dynasty (fourteenth century, though Confucian influence was known before); of Japan during the Tokugawa Shogunate (seventeenth century); and, to a lesser extent, of Europe and the United States in the twentieth century. In this sense, Confucianism and Taoism are more like Hinduism: associated primarily with the country of origin, but exerting a profound influence among converted nations or individuals. Today, Japan and Korea are thoroughly Confucian in their social values and religious practices, and a number of non-Chinese Americans and Europeans have begun to identify themselves as Confucian or Taoist.

It is impossible in modern times to think of one's own religious identity in isolation from the fact of religious pluralism in the world. In the last century, the growth of intercultural communication has led Chinese to see their Confucian or Taoist identity in contrast to other world religions. This has inspired an increase in comparative studies and interreligious dialogue between Chinese and Western intellectuals. Confucians in particular have examined their tradition in light of religious and philosophical insights from India and the West. The New Confucianism of the last century is explicitly comparative, and often syncretic—bringing insights from Buddhism or Western religion and philosophy into creative synthesis with Confucian thought. Chinese are no longer Confucian or Taoist simply by virtue of their cultural upbringing, but as a conscious choice from among the pluralistic alternatives of the world's religions.

Though they remain primarily Chinese, Confucianism and Taoism are not exclusively Chinese religions. The worldwide impact of Confucianism and Taoism will be examined in Chapter 4.

WHAT IS CONFUCIANISM?

People in the West tend to identify religious traditions with their founders. Christianity is thought to have been founded by Jesus of Nazareth, Islam by the Prophet Mohammed. The word *Confucianism* suggests a tradition that was "founded" by Confucius, who lived two thousand five hundred years ago. However, Confucianism does not refer simply to one man or one collection of scriptures. The ideals, values, and behaviors that are called Confucianism actually predated Confucius by at least one thousand years.

The English word *Confucianism* is a relatively late invention (one scholar has found no use of the term before 1687 C.E.), and Confucius himself was not known in Europe until Jesuit missionaries visited China in the 1600s. The Christian missionaries saw a strong link between the cultural values that they observed among Chinese officials and the classical texts attributed to Confucius and his followers, so they named this tradition Confucianism.

Interestingly, the word *Confucianism* does not exist in the Chinese language. This is largely because Confucian values and behaviors predate Confucius himself; Confucius's contribution was to collect, organize, and highlight the beliefs and practices that were definitive of his culture. Confucius is recorded as saying, "I transmit but do not create. I place my trust in the teachings of antiquity." As a "transmitter" or "systematizer" of values, Confucius was certainly important, but the values and behaviors of Confucianism were central to Chinese culture even before the beginning of recorded history, some one thousand years before Confucius. Neither Confucius nor his followers considered the First Sage to be a religious founder.

The terms that are equivalent to Confucianism in Chinese are *Ru jia, Ru jiao,* or *Ru xue*—the *Ru* school, the *Ru* tradition, or *Ru* studies. In Confucius's time, the *Ru* were scholars, but at a much earlier time (1000 B.C.E. or before), the Chinese character *Ru* referred to religious priests or shamans

Temple to Confucius, Guangzhou, China. Courtesy of the author.

who were ritual experts—masters of religious music and dance—especially skilled in summoning good spirits, exorcising evil spirits, and bringing rain and other blessings. By the time of Confucius, the *Ru* were also historians, because the shamanic rituals of the past had fallen into disuse and were known only in the historical records. Confucius was an exemplary *Ru* scholar as he was especially interested in cultural history (the history of music, dance, and other arts) and in ritual. One of his major contributions was to codify and advance the ritual traditions of the early Zhou Dynasty. Consequently, Confucianism refers to all of the values and practices of the *Ru* tradition, not simply to the religion of Confucius.

What, then, is the *Ru* tradition, and how should Confucianism be defined in this book? For Chinese, Confucianism is the general term for the *religious and ethical ideals, values, and behaviors* that have shaped Chinese culture for the past three to four thousand years. These include

- the veneration of ancestors;
- education in history and culture (poetry, music, painting, and calligraphy);
- the cultivation of harmonious, hierarchical relations in one's family and social life; and
- the grounding of moral teachings and ethical principles in a religious or cosmic reality.

These are Confucian behaviors and values in the sense that Confucians value them, not because Confucius invented them.

Confucianism can be defined by its Chinese equivalent, *Ru jiao*, a system of values and practices originating in China's prehistory, but codified by Confucius and developed by the Confucian tradition.

WHAT IS TAOISM?

Taoism is an even more complicated term. In English, the word was coined two to three centuries after Confucianism, appearing in book titles as *Taouism* in 1839 C.E., as *Tauism* in 1855 C.E., and finally as *Taoism* in 1879 C.E. The term was used to translate the Chinese *Dao jia* and *Dao jiao*, which mean "school of the Dao" and "religion of the Dao." Though there is no historical evidence of a school of the Dao prior to the Han Dynasty (206 B.C.E. to 220 C.E.), Taoists themselves trace their origins to the mythical *Lao-zi*, a name meaning "Master Old" or "Old Infant," the supposed author of the *Dao de jing* (*Scripture of the Dao and Its Power*). Myths tell of personal encounters between Confucius and Lao-zi, so this so-called reli-

gious founder is purported to have lived, like Confucius, in the Spring and
Autumn Period of the Zhou Dynasty (770–476 B.C.E.). Legends relate that
while in human form, Lao-zi was a recluse or hermit who was disgusted
with the ways of the world and only deigned to share his wisdom when he
departed China for the mystical mountains of the West. Beseeched by a
gatekeeper at the far western pass that separated China from the barbar-
ian wilds of the West, Lao-zi agreed to recite his lessons in "five thousand
words"—this explains why the *Dao de jing* is often called in Chinese the
"Five Thousand Character Classic." According to some schools of Taoism,
Lao-zi was a seer and magician, capable of physical self-transformation,
and is now a transcendent deity or "pure spirit."

Like Confucianism, however, Taoism is not limited to the teachings of
one sage or one book. Taoists believe that the Dao itself originated in a far
more distant past: it is a cosmic "Way" (the literal meaning of *Dao*) that
formed, or began to form, before the existence of all individual "things." As
the *Dao de jing* relates, "Before there was a 'two' and a 'three,' there was the
'One.'" This Cosmic One describes the original unity of the universe, an undifferentiated energy that "gave birth" to the "ten thousand things." The Dao
continues to exist. In fact, it is eternally evolving or "coming into existence"
and is "never complete." It is an energy that permeates the universe and can
be "tapped" as a source of health, vitality, long life, and supernatural power.
The Taoist religion is an historical transmission of texts and rituals that attempt to explain, harness, create, and re-create that cosmic energy.

Until recently, Western historians of China limited Taoism to a school
of philosophy—set out abstrusely in the *Dao de jing* and elaborated by the
sages Zhuang-zi (dates uncertain, but he lived between 368 and 289 B.C.E.)
and Lie-zi (an historical figure only known by a book appearing in his name,
dating anywhere from 300 B.C.E. to 300 C.E.). These three thinkers were
said to be the authors of a philosophy that was distinctly "anti-Confucian":
rebelling against education, against government service, against the moral
and ethical codes of social interaction, and against the norms and rules
that govern everyday life. These Taoists advocated instead a life of "free and
easy wandering" (a chapter title from *The Book of Zhuang-zi*), unbounded
by the norms of society, or even by the constraints of language and logic.
This is one reason that these books are often so confusing—they are meant
to be. The teachings of Lao-zi, Zhuang-zi, and Lie-zi are the heart of this
philosophical tradition, as described in Chapter 2.

But this is only one part of the story of Taoism. Whereas historians used
to limit Taoism to these thinkers and their reclusive philosophy, it is now

known that Taoism continued to evolve and develop and came to include not just philosophical texts, but also church-like institutions, rites and ceremonies (with hundreds if not thousands of ritual instruction manuals), a rich tradition of physical and hygienic practices with the goal of long life or immortality, a pantheon of terrestrial and celestial deities, and mythologies of their lives and heavenly existence. Of course, historians have been aware of these religious elements for a long time—and all of these beliefs and practices continue to exist—but in the past they were denigrated as superstition or folk religion. Nor was it recognized that these highly elaborate, intellectually sophisticated, and ritually complex elements are part of the Taoist tradition. Taoism, therefore, includes much more than the teachings of Lao-zi and his immediate followers. It is rather a religious tradition with certain identifiable features, including

- a priesthood, composed primarily of ritual specialists;
- rituals that benefit individuals or social communities by "tapping into" the power of the Dao; and
- a canon of religious texts (one of the most voluminous canons in the world's religions, including hundreds of scriptures, commentaries, treatises, and manuals).

Taoist priests making offerings. Courtesy of the author.

The beliefs and values underlying this religion extend far beyond the formal aspects listed, and many Chinese today exhibit Taoist characteristics apart from these institutional forms. Just as Confucianism describes a system of values and behaviors that permeates Chinese society, most Chinese are Taoist to one degree or another, perhaps even unaware of the religious origins of their thinking and habits. The Taoistic strains of everyday life will be explored throughout this book, but in brief they can be summarized as follows:

- the sense that reality extends beyond the observable realm and includes spiritual power that has physical effects and manifestations but is not limited to the physical world;
- the belief in *harmony,* not only among persons, but between persons, the natural world, and the cosmos;
- the practice of meditation and physical exercises that emphasize the unity of an individual's psychological, emotional, physical, and spiritual identity; and
- the belief that internal and external harmony has practical benefits, from social welfare to individual health and longevity.

Most Chinese today, even after a century of Western influence (not to mention half a century of Communist rule), would consider these things common sense, and although the institutional forms of Sect Taoism are now (perhaps temporarily) in eclipse, Taoism as an approach to life is still very much alive.

CHINESE LANGUAGE AND CULTURE

The Chinese written language has been the great unifier of Chinese civilization for more than three thousand years. Because it is pictographic in origin, written Chinese does not depend upon a common spoken language. In fact, Chinese characters were adopted by other cultures and integrated into their linguistic systems. Written Japanese, for example, contains Chinese characters (*kanji*) in addition to Japanese phonetic symbols; classical forms of Korean, Vietnamese, Tibetan, and Burmese also make use of Chinese characters. As Chinese characters can be pronounced in many ways, they are not dependent upon a common spoken language.

There are more than thirty dialects of spoken Chinese, with eight major linguistic groups:

Dialect	Where spoken
Cantonese	In the south, mainly Guangdong, southern Guangxi, Macau, Hong Kong
Hakka	Widespread, especially between Fujian and Guangxi
Xiang	South central region, in Hunan
Kan	Shanxi and southwest Hebei
Mandarin	A wide range of dialects in the northern, central, and western regions. North Mandarin, as found in Beijing, is the basis of the modern standard language
Northern Min	Northwest Fujian
Southern Min	The southeast, mainly in parts of Zhejiang, Fujian, Hainan Island, and Taiwan
Wu	Parts of Anhui, Zhejiang, and Jiangsu

These dialects of Chinese have common Tibetan-Sinitic linguistic roots, but from a practical standpoint they are so different as to be mutually unintelligible. A Chinese man from Taiwan who speaks the Taiwanese or Southern Min dialect and travels on business to Hong Kong, where Cantonese is spoken, finds it impossible to understand what he hears on radio, television, or in personal conversation. Nor can he make himself intelligible to others. But the same individual, remarkably, is able to read the *Daily Standard,* a leading Hong Kong newspaper. Based upon the pictographs and ideographs that make up Chinese characters, the Chinese written language can be read using any number of pronunciations—from Mandarin to Cantonese (and even including Japanese and Korean pronunciations, as Japan and Korea make use of Chinese characters in their own written languages).

Various Chinese governments have attempted to standardize the spoken language. Today, most Chinese are able to speak the Mandarin dialect. The word *Mandarin* means "official": Mandarin is the dialect of the capital (Beijing) and was established as the official dialect in the Qing Dynasty (1644–1911 C.E.), with limited success. In the last century, this effort at linguistic standardization has accelerated both in the People's Republic of China (Mainland China) and the Republic of China on Taiwan, but there are still many Chinese, both in China and abroad, whose first language is a dialect other than Mandarin.

Given this diversity, China's primary means of communication has been the written text—a linguistic innovation that accounts for a cultural continuity that has lasted for some three thousand years. Regardless of how they are pronounced, Chinese characters have a stable meaning; even today educated Chinese are able to read texts that were composed in the Zhou Dynasty two thousand five hundred years ago. Unlike India, which is oriented toward oral communication and the three-dimensionality of sound (India's primary artistic expression is sculpture and architecture, which is believed to "resonate" with divine sounds), Chinese culture is visually oriented, and its primary artistic expressions are two-dimensional: pen and ink drawing, landscape painting, and calligraphy. Politically, the advantage of written communication over oral pronouncements is the fact that texts can be copied or printed. They can cross both spatial and temporal boundaries: texts can be transmitted to persons in different places and different times. As a result, the Chinese are the world's greatest bibliophiles, and the textual tradition is core to Chinese religion, both Confucian and Taoist.

CHINESE CHARACTERS

It is impossible to fully understand a culture or a religious tradition without immersion in the language of that tradition. In the Chinese case, this is especially true of the written character. In this book, the written forms of several key concepts, as a way to unlock their meanings and implications, will be looked at in detail.

Chinese characters express meaning, not just sound. So, to understand the meaning of a word or concept, it is essential to look at it—to see how it is written or drawn. In antiquity, the characters looked more like what they represent, but even today the relationship between the meaning of the character and the appearance of the character on the page can be seen.

Chinese characters are *pictographic* depictions of their meanings. The earliest forms of the words for "man," "woman," "sun," "moon," "rain," "cauldron," and "well" clearly *look like* the objects they are drawn to represent.

The ancient Chinese attached an almost mystical significance to their written language. According to legend, a minister to the Yellow Emperor by the name of Cang Jie "discovered" what came to be the Chinese written text in bird prints on the ground. The character for "culture" or "civilization," pronounced *wen*, is a pictograph of these bird prints. For Chinese, the written language is not a human invention, but is literally "nature's imprint" upon the world.

Modern Chinese includes four kinds of character: pictographs, ideographs, lexigraphs, and phonetic lexigraphs.

Pictographs are characters that look like the things they represent, though less so today than in antiquity. Originally, these characters looked even more like pictures, such as the characters for "sun," "moon," "mountain," and so on.

Ideographs are characters that represent an abstract idea, such as the characters for the numbers one, two, and three; the characters meaning "above" or "below"; or the characters meaning "concave" and "convex."

Lexigraphs are characters that are composed by combining two or more characters together. The combination of characters into a single character creates a new meaning. A vast majority of Chinese characters are of this kind, and it is especially helpful to know the various components of a character—like the etymologies of English words—to better understand the implications of the character's meaning.

Finally, *Phonetic Lexigraphs* combine two or more characters, one of which indicates the character's pronunciation rather than its meaning. Based on its phonetic component, it is possible at times to pronounce characters that one has never encountered before.

Chinese characters, which are pictographic, are represented in English, which is phonetic, through romanization. In this book, Chinese characters are romanized using a system called *pin yin romanization,* developed in the People's Republic of China. All romanizations in this book reflect the pronunciation of the Mandarin dialect.

There are many excellent translations of the Confucian and Taoist texts discussed in this book; they will be cited in the Further Readings section for each chapter and in the Selected Bibliography at the end of the book. All quoted passages in this book are the author's translations.

Two other conventions in this book should be mentioned here. First, all Chinese and Japanese names will appear in their proper order, surname followed by given name; second, all dates will appear in the form B.C.E. (Before the Common Era, corresponding to the Euro-American B.C.) and C.E. (Common Era, corresponding to the Euro-American A.D.).

FURTHER READINGS

The definition of religion adopted in this book is derived primarily from two scholars: Frederick Streng and Clifford Geertz. Streng's book, *Understanding Religious Life,* is an especially readable introduction to the concept of religion and its various manifestations.

For the history of the labels Confucianism and Taoism as names for the indigenous religions of China (as well as the history of the names of all the world religions), see Wilfred Cantwell Smith's *The Meaning and End of Religion.* A recent study of the Jesuit encounter with Chinese religion suggests that the Jesuits invented Confucianism itself. This more radical thesis is put forward in Lionel Jensen's *Manufacturing Confucianism.* In a similar vein, J. J. Clarke has written a fascinating book on Western encounters with Taoism: *The Tao of the West: Western Transformations of Taoist Thought.* Both of these books offer critical perspectives on labeling Chinese religions.

For an introduction to the Chinese language, Raymond and Margaret Chang's *Speaking of Chinese* is recommended. The classic Chinese-English dictionary of Chinese characters is that of Bernard Karlgren, which provides background on the etymological origins of Chinese graphs.

Chang, Raymond, and Margaret S. Chang. *Speaking of Chinese.* New York: Norton, 1978.

Clarke, J. J. *The Tao of the West: Western Transformations of Taoist Thought.* New York: Routledge, 2000.

Geertz, Clifford. "Religion as a Cultural System." In *The Interpretation of Cultures.* New York: Basic, 1973.

Jensen, Lionel. *Manufacturing Confucianism: Chinese Traditions and Universal Civilization.* Durham, NC: Duke University Press, 1997.

Karlgren, Bernard. *Grammata Serica Recensa.* Edited by Tor Ulving. *Dictionary of Old & Middle Chinese: Bernard Karlgren's "Grammata Serica Recensa" Alphabetically Arranged.* Philadelphia: Coronet, 1997.

Smith, Wilfred Cantwell. *The Meaning and End of Religion.* Minneapolis: Fortress, 1962.

Streng, Frederick. *Understanding Religious Life.* Encino, CA: Dickenson, 1976.

TIMELINE

c. 2200–1600 B.C.E.	Xia Dynasty.
c. 1600–1100 B.C.E.	Shang Dynasty: production of "oracle bones" on sheep's bones and turtle shells.
c. 1100–249 B.C.E.	Zhou Dynasty: great age of Chinese philosophy.
551–479 B.C.E.	Kong-fu-zi (Confucius), the First Sage of Confucianism.
372–289 B.C.E.	Meng-zi (Mencius), the Second Sage of Confucianism.
	Lao-zi, the first mythical Taoist sage and legendary author of the *Dao de jing*.
368–289 B.C.E.	Zhuang-zi, the second Taoist sage.
313–215 B.C.E.	Xun-zi, the Third Sage of Confucianism.
221–206 B.C.E.	Qin Dynasty: burning of the books, suppression of Chinese philosophical tradition.
206 B.C.E.–9 C.E.	Former Han Dynasty.
???–c. 178 B.C.E.	Zhang Dao-ling, founder of the Way of the Celestial Master Taoism.
195 B.C.E.	Han Emperor Gao-zi stops in Lu to make a great offering of ox, sheep, and pig to Confucius, establishing Confucianism as a state cult.

184 B.C.E.	The Yellow Turban Uprising venerates Lao-zi as a god.
25–220 C.E.	Later Han Dynasty: establishment of the Confucian Grand Academy, emergence of Religious Taoism, introduction of Buddhism to China.
59	Offerings to Confucius made compulsory throughout the empire.
220–581	Period of North-South Division: Confucian tradition in relative eclipse, expansion of Taoism and Buddhism.
fl. c. 300	Ge Hong, founder of the Esoteric stream of Religious Taoism.
581–907	Sui and Tang Dynasties: Confucianism exported to Korea and Japan, Tang imperial patronage of Buddhism and Taoism, integration of Taoist ritual in village life.
640	Temples to Confucius established in all districts and counties.
768–824	Han Yü, Tang Confucian scholar.
960–1279	Song Dynasty: Neo-Confucian revival of Confucian teachings, Taoist Internal Alchemy, development of monastic Quan-zhen School of Taoism.
1130–1200	Zhu Xi, First Sage of Neo-Confucianism.
1260–1368	Yuan Dynasty.
1313	Four Books of Confucius established as the basic texts for the Civil Service Examination.
1368–1644	Ming Dynasty: second phase of Neo-Confucianism, integration of Taoism and folk religion.
1472–1529	Wang Yang-ming, Second Sage of Neo-Confucianism.
1644–1911	Qing Dynasty: Confucian School of Evidential Research, syncretistic movements influenced by Taoism.
1670	Sacred Edicts promulgated by Emperor Kang-xi, reaffirming Confucian moral virtues as the Chinese standard.

1911–present   Republic of China (Taiwan): May Fourth Movement attacks on Confucian feudalism.

1949–present   People's Republic of China (Mainland China): New Confucianism among Chinese intellectuals in China, Taiwan, and overseas Chinese communities; revival of Taoism in village communities; Confucianism and Taoism exported to the West.

1

HISTORY OF FOUNDATION

This chapter looks at the origins and development of Chinese religion from China's mythic prehistory to the present. Confucianism and Taoism did not emerge as fully developed religious traditions until the Han Dynasty, but they can trace their roots to the scriptures or classics of the Spring and Autumn Period of the Zhou Dynasty.

THE MYTHIC AND EARLY HISTORICAL PERIOD TO 770 B.C.E.: SHANG AND WESTERN ZHOU DYNASTY RELIGION

Mythic Origins of Chinese Civilization

According to early mythological accounts, the beginnings of Chinese civilization in the Xia Dynasty (2200?–1600? B.C.E.) were preceded by a great flood—a common motif in a number of the world's religions. The flood, and its control and resolution, is illustrative of the Chinese understanding of the relationship between humankind and the natural world.

In the time of Emperor Yao (dates unknown, but purported to have been the fourth of the Five Legendary Emperors in the mythic period of Chinese history), the waters reversed their natural course, flooding the middle kingdom. (The appellation "middle kingdom" is the literal meaning of the Chinese characters *zhong-guo*, "China.") Rivers overflowed their banks, the plains were covered with water, birds and beasts occupied the homes where humans were meant to dwell, and the people were forced to live in trees and caves, where birds and beasts were meant to dwell.

Table 1.1
Periodization of Confucianism and Taoism

Chinese Dynastic History	Confucianism	Taoism	China and the World
Mythic period			
Xia Dynasty (2200?–1600? B.C.E.)			
Shang Dynasty (1600?–1100? B.C.E.)			
Classical Period			
Zhou Dynasty (1100?–249 B.C.E.)	Confucius (551–479 B.C.E.)	Lao-zi (?–? B.C.E.)	
Western Zhou	Meng-zi (372–289 B.C.E.)	Zhuang-zi (370?–301? B.C.E.)	
Eastern Zhou	Xun-zi (313?–238? B.C.E.)	Lie-zi (btw 300 B.C.E. and 300 C.E.)	
Spring & Autumn Period			
Warring States Period			
Qin Dynasty (221–206 B.C.E.)	Burning of the books		
	Imperial Confucianism	**Taoist Sectarianism**	
Han Dynasty (206 B.C.E.–220 C.E.)	Confucianism becomes state orthodoxy; Grand Academy established	Emergence of Religious Taoism; the Celestial Masters, External Alchemy	Introduction of Buddhism to China
Period of North-South Division (220–581 C.E.)	Dark Learning synthesizing Confucian and Taoist thought	Imperial patronage at the Wei court; Shang-Qing School and first edition of the Taoist Canon	Buddhism expands in China

Period	Confucianism	Taoism	Export
Sui-Tang Dynasties (581–907 C.E.)	Han Yü (768–824 C.E.)	Imperial patronage at the Tang court; Ling-bao School; integration of Taoist ritual in village life	Confucianism exported to Korea and Japan
	Confucian Renaissance	**Alchemical & Priestly Taoism**	
Song Dynasty (960–1279 C.E.)	Song Neo-Confucianism Zhu Xi (1130–1200 C.E.)	Internal Alchemy	
Yuan Dynasty (1260–1368 C.E.)	Zhu Xi's annotated Four Books becomes standard for civil service examinations (1313 C.E.)	Quan-zhen School and integration of Taoism with Buddhist monasticism	
		Popular Taoism	
Ming Dynasty (1368–1644 C.E.)	Ming Neo-Confucianism Wang Yang-ming (1472–1529) School of Evidential Research	Blended movements heavily influenced by Taoism; Integration of Taoism and folk religion	
Qing Dynasty (1644–1911 C.E.)	**"New Confucianism"**		
Republic of China (1911– C.E.) People's Republic of China (1949– C.E.)	Attacks on Confucian Feudalism, emergence of modern New Confucianism		Confucianism and Taoism exported to the West: Boston Confucianism and Euro-American Taoism

3

Emperor Yao appointed his son, Kun, to control the flood. For nine years, Kun struggled, finally stealing from the gods a "swelling mold" that he used to dam up the waters. The theft of this sacred earth angered the gods, who slayed the Emperor Kun, leaving his body on a mountain peak. The swelling mold fell away in great clods of earth, swallowed up by the rising waters.

As the flood increased, a great creature emerged from the belly of Emperor Kun. His name was Yü; various versions of the myth describe him as a bear, a dragon, a turtle, or fish. Yü came down from on high to continue his father's work. He walked with a limp across the land—a walk that has been described as "the gait of Yü." His steps followed the pattern of the Great Bear in the sky, *Ursa Major*, or the Big Dipper. From high above (Yü appears to have been a gargantuan figure), he saw the river valleys and channels beneath the surface of the waters, and, rather than damming the flood as his father had done, Yü led the water into the seas by deepening the valleys and channels that already existed in the ground. He "wore the nails off his hands and the hair off his calves," and the flood receded. The water, flowing through the channels, formed the Yangze, the Huai, the Yellow River, and the Han—the four great rivers of China. The birds and beasts returned to their nests and caves, and the people of the middle kingdom were able to level the ground and live on it once more.

As a reward for his efforts, Yü was made emperor and became founder of the Xia Dynasty.

This is, of course, a myth, with no historical evidence to support it (the account first appears in a book written at least one thousand years after the purported events), but it illustrates important values of Chinese culture and religion. Some of these themes can be identified later as Confucian or Taoist, but the myth itself predates the emergence of Confucianism and Taoism and assumes no preference.

1. The flood is seen to be a natural event; it is not described as a divine punishment. The element of punishment in the myth has to do with taking from the gods what is rightfully theirs, the "swelling mold" used by Emperor Kun.
2. The proper order of things is for humans to live upon and till the earth and for birds and beasts to remain in their proper place—the two should not be confused or encroach upon one another.
3. The aggressive solution of damming the waters is improper, as it forces the water against its natural tendency (to flow in channels).
4. The more ecologically harmonious solution of channeling the waters is proper and allows the water to follow its natural course.

Some scholars see this myth as reflecting the Neolithic transition from a nomadic culture dependent upon hunting and gathering, which involves greater interaction with the animal world (either as quarry or in imitation of animal behaviors), to a culture that is settled and agricultural, where humans are more clearly differentiated from animals. Archaeological evidence indicates that by 6000 B.C.E. (at least four millennia prior to the first Chinese writing), the people of the middle kingdom lived in fixed communities, as indicated by the discovery of earthen walls, wooden pillars, and kiln-fired pottery dating to that period.

The Shang Dynasty

The first Chinese writing—and thus the beginning of recorded history—was engraved on the dried bones of sheep and oxen as well as the plastron (lower) shells of turtles dating to the Shang Dynasty (1600?–1100? B.C.E.). First excavated in the 1920s, there are now more than one hundred thousand "oracle bones" in museum collections around the world, estimated to be 5 to 10 percent of the total produced. Most are from about 1200 B.C.E. The ideograms carved into these objects are in pictographic form (about three thousand pictographs have been deciphered), and later evolved into the Chinese characters in use today.

These engraved bones and shells are known as oracle bones because the writing was used to record the results of divination. The procedure was as follows:

1. Pits were bored or chiseled on the back of the bone or shell.
2. A question was addressed to the oracle bone, often in the form of opposing alternatives, e.g.:
   - "We *will* receive the millet harvest."
   - "We *will not* receive the millet harvest."
3. A hot bronze poker was applied to the pits; the heat caused cracks to form.
4. The cracks were numbered and examined, then interpreted by court diviners as lucky or unlucky omens.
5. Records were engraved on the bones, sometimes with a verification of the accuracy of the prediction. (Keightley)

Shang religion was directed at three categories of divine being:

- *The Lord on High*: the high god ⇒ held dominion over the weather, harvests, urban settlements, warfare, sickness, the king's person (not worshipped directly)
- *Royal Ancestors* ⇒ interceded with *The Lord on High* for the king (worshipped only by the king)
- *Nature Deities* ⇒ directed the course of seasons, storms, and harvests; subordinate to the *Royal Ancestors*

These spiritual beings were served in worship and sacrifice: by burning animals or grain, pouring wine into the ground, and throwing sacred objects into rivers.

Principally, sacrifices were made to the *Royal Ancestors,* according to a rigid sacrificial schedule. If carried out correctly, these sacrifices were thought to have a constraining effect on the ancestors, forcing them to act for the king's benefit. This established ties of mutual obligation and reciprocity, and magical power over the spirit world. The king made sacrifices to his father, grandfather, and prior generations on a daily basis, reinforcing his sense of family identity and securing the blessings of the spirit world.

Even today, ancestor worship is the primary expression of Chinese religion, and certain basic beliefs have been maintained since antiquity. From the Shang Dynasty to the present, Chinese assume

- that people continue to exist after death;
- that ancestral spirits exert power over the living, influencing our everyday lives; and
- that the dead depend upon the living for care and sustenance.

The continuity of ancestor veneration, based upon these three principles, is remarkable given the span of Chinese recorded history (well over three thousand years). Ancestor veneration was adopted by the Confucian tradition as a primary emphasis but was embraced as well by Taoism and Buddhism. Today, the veneration of ancestors in the home and at the gravesite is a universal everyday practice among Chinese, both in China and overseas.

The Zhou Dynasty

Zhou peoples lived to the west of Shang and learned writing and the arts of civilization from Shang culture. In the eleventh century B.C.E. (around 1040), they sacked the capital, overthrew the Shang court, and established a new dynasty. As the inheritors of an already ancient culture, they main-

Family at ancestral tomb. Courtesy of the author.

tained many of its ways, including an ancestral cult (focused on Lord Millet, First Ancestor of the Zhou), a strict sacrificial schedule, and divination using oracle bones and stalks of grain.

The Zhou kings, who sought a religious justification for their usurpation of power, did so by appealing to *Tian,* a high god superior in power to *The Lord on High.* Zhou texts describe *Tian* in one sense as an anthropomorphic deity, directing human affairs, and in another sense as an abstract, almost mechanical principle of natural order. More and more, the emphasis was on the latter definition, and *Tian* is best translated by its literal meaning of "Heaven."

In *The Book of History* (*Shu-jing*), a work of myth and history tracing China's first five dynasties (Tang, Yü, Xia, Shang, Zhou), is recorded *The Great Declaration of King Wu,* the "military king" and Zhou Dynasty founder. In this declaration, King Wu accuses the last Shang Dynasty king of oppressing his people, failing to maintain the calendrical cycle of sacrifices to the gods and ancestors, and being "abandoned to drunkenness and reckless in lust."

> For his many crimes, the King of Shang has been punished by Heaven. Heaven is going by means of me to rule the people.

According to *The Book of History,* King Wu was succeeded by King Wen, the "civil king," whose fourth son, the Duke of Zhou, became China's greatest culture hero (esteemed in particular by Confucius). At the center of the Duke of Zhou's religious and political thought was the concept of the Mandate of Heaven. The Mandate of Heaven establishes the divine right to rule; it is conferred upon just kings and removed from unjust kings. As the Son of Heaven, a king has a divine right and duty to rule his people and to ensure their welfare. Speaking to Shang nobles, the Duke of Zhou explained:

> King Wu of Zhou possessed a mandate which said, "Destroy the Shang Dynasty." Because our actions did not go contrary to Heaven's course of action, your Royal House has come under our control.
>
> I will explain it to you. Your ruler was greatly lawless. Our house did not originate this movement against your house. It came from your own court. When I reflect that Heaven has applied such great severity to the Shang ruler, it shows that he was not upright.

So, the political overthrow of the Shang Dynasty was justified in moral and religious terms. The idea of the "moral right to rule" become central in subsequent Chinese political thought.

THE CLASSICAL PERIOD TO THE BEGINNING OF THE HAN (770–206 B.C.E.)

Zhou Dynasty Religion

As in the Shang, the Zhou empire practiced ancestor worship, divination, and ritual offerings to nature spirits and celestial deities. One feature of Zhou religion, based upon archeological evidence as well as poetry col-

Table 1.2
The Classical Period to the Beginning of the Han (770–206 B.C.E.)

Zhou Dynasty (1100?–249 B.C.E.)	Confucianism	Taoism
Western Zhou	Confucius	Lao-zi
Eastern Zhou	(551–479 B.C.E.)	(?–? B.C.E.)
Spring & Autumn Period	Meng-zi	Zhuang-zi
Warring States Period	(372–289 B.C.E.)	(370?–301? B.C.E.)
	Xun-zi	Lie-zi
	(313?–238? B.C.E.)	(btw 300 B.C.E. and 300 C.E.)

lected or reconstructed a few hundred years after the fall of the Zhou, was shamanism.

Shamanism describes the close, even intimate, interaction between humans and spiritual beings—a crossing over between the material world and the spiritual world. There are two kinds of shamans. In one case, the shaman is able to send forth his or her own spiritual nature (what might be called the "soul" or "souls") on spirit journeys to distant places in the world, galaxy, or cosmos. The second type of shaman is the "spirit medium," who is able to receive spirits (gods, nature spirits, or spirits of the dead) into his or her own body, then manifesting exceptional behaviors or displaying divine knowledge (often in the form of prognostication).

Both kinds of shamanism seem to have been central to early Zhou religion. For example, in a long prose poem entitled "Far-off Journey," shamanistic spirit journeys are described. "Far-off Journey" appears in the *Songs of Chu*, poems composed in the border regions of the south. Far removed from the royal court, where more formal ceremonies and ritual offerings were conducted, these poems reflect a mystical strain in early Chinese religion. The poems describe shamanic spirit journeys and ritualized sexual encounters between humans and spirits.

At court, another kind of shamanism was practiced. Here, the shamans—typically women or young girls—were mediums for the gods, receiving their spiritual power and using this power to exorcise evil and misfortune from the royal house. These mediumistic rites consisted of stately dances and the performance of orchestral music—using bells, chimes, woodwind and stringed instruments. Though this is still a matter of scholarly speculation, evidence suggests that women held extremely powerful positions in the early Zhou priesthood.

Religious Decline of the Spring and Autumn and Warring States Periods

After five hundred years, particularly near the end of the Spring and Autumn Period of the Eastern Zhou (770–476 B.C.E.), a mood of religious skepticism prevailed, as evidenced by the plaintive poems of *The Book of Poetry*, which mourn the powerlessness or indifference of the high god *Tian* ("Heaven"). This religious skepticism reflected the political developments of the time. The general political and religious characteristics of the later Zhou Dynasty are as follows:

- decline of the royal house (the Zhou an empire in name only);
- decline of royal ancestral rites;
- decline in the power of the royal ancestors;
- constant warfare and its attendant ills: political instability, starvation, forced and voluntary migration;
- use of religion for political purposes: to enforce alliances, protect kingdoms and their armies, and to symbolize victories and transfers of power;
- growing religious skepticism at every level of society, expressed in poetic references to Heaven's powerlessness or indifference; and
- steady decline in the number of independent states: from 1,773 original states, to 160 states by 770 B.C.E. (the beginning of the Spring and Autumn Period), and 7 states by 481 B.C.E. (beginning of the Warring States Period).

The Confucians

Though the Zhou Dynasty produced China's greatest philosophers—Confucius, Mencius, Xün-zi, Zhuang-zi, and Mo-zi, to name a few—it was a violent and uncertain time. Political life was dominated by feudatory rivalries, shifting alliances, annexation of the small by the great, assassination, civil war, bureaucratic mismanagement, starvation, and mass migration. Lu, the home state of Confucius, was invaded twenty-four times between the years 720 and 480 B.C.E.

The political uncertainties of the period contributed to the rise of a class of diplomats, administrators, and military advisors called *shi.* In earlier times, the term *shi* referred to warriors of the noble class (the same character is pronounced *samurai* in Japanese, though the age of the samurai in Japan was much later in history) attached to particular feudatory states, but in the Spring and Autumn and Warring States Periods, *shi* traveled from state to state seeking court recognition for their skills in debate, military strategy, diplomacy, and political administration. If their arguments seemed convincing, the dukes of the feudatory states adopted them as retainers. Even then, however, the *shi* prided themselves on their principled courage and independence, and a *shi* did not hesitate to abandon a state if the ruler acted against his advice.

One of the best-known of these traveling advisors was Confucius, the Latinized name of *Kong-fu-zi* (Grand Master Kong). Born in 551 B.C.E., Confucius lived at the end of the Spring and Autumn Period. He traveled from state to state, offering advice on government, virtue, and education.

Confucius. Courtesy of the author.

Though he was never hired as a retainer and lamented his inability to reform his world, he was a great teacher, gathering a loyal following, traditionally numbered at three thousand, with seventy-two primary disciples.
Confucius emphasized self-cultivation: education, high moral standards,
and a deep-felt commitment to one's family and community. He appealed
to the eminent teachers and forgotten traditions of China's cultural past,
and sought to restore the high culture of antiquity.

Confucius believed that an ideal society had once existed, under the
leadership of the Duke of Zhou centuries before. He admired the Duke of
Zhou so much that he dreamt of him, and he claimed that all of his ideas
were firmly rooted in the past. The Master said:

> I transmit but do not create.
> I place my trust in the teachings of antiquity.

Confucius's disciples called themselves *Ru*, "ritualists" or "scholars." The
Ru were often mocked as anachronistic eccentrics, attempting to restore
the ritualism of earlier times. They dressed in an archaic style that came to

be known as *Ru*-clothing, held performances of ancient court music and dance, and even spoke in an old dialect no longer in use. As scholars, they banded together in brotherhoods under esteemed masters (preferably first-generation disciples of Confucius), to whom they granted the same respect and obedience that a son grants his father.

The *Ru* supported themselves meagerly, as teachers (through patronage) and as ritualists (primarily conducting funerals). The *Ru* School ceased to exist as an institutional body with the persecutions of the Great Unifier, First Emperor of the Qin Dynasty (221–206 B.C.E.). Though Confucianism enjoyed a revival in the Han Dynasty (206 B.C.E.–220 C.E.) and exerted profound influence upon Chinese culture throughout its history, the *Ru* School existed only in Zhou times.

Two prominent Confucians of the Warring States Period (475–221 B.C.E.) deserve further mention here:

"Mencius" (372–289 B.C.E.) is the Latinized form of the name *Meng-zi,* Master Meng, renowned as the Second Sage of Confucianism. An advocate of righteous leadership, Mencius believed that the best rulers appeal to that which is best in their subjects. Because all persons are possessed of a basic goodness, any person is capable of becoming a sage. This teaching had a profound effect upon the development of the Confucian tradition and remains a fundamental principle of Confucianism today.

Xun-zi, Master Xun (313?–238? B.C.E.), is often called the Third Sage of Confucianism, but stands in contrast to Mencius for his general distrust of human nature and his advocacy of strong government, socialization of children through discipline and education, and moral persuasion using ritual as a guide to character. Maintaining a Hobbesian view of natural self-ishness (Thomas Hobbes, 1588–1679, was a British political philosopher best known for his negative view of human nature and the need for social control), Xun-zi argued that human nature could be rectified only in an environment of strict regularity, patterned upon ritual norms and the moral example of the sages. The debate between Meng-zi and Xun-zi on basic human nature raged in Confucian circles for centuries, and although most Confucians believe with Meng-zi in the inherent perfectibility of all persons, they share with Xun-zi a sense that education and personal restraint are necessary for the cultivation of sagehood.

The teachings of Confucius, Mencius, and Xun-zi will be discussed further in Chapter 3; see Chapter 6 for their biographies.

The Six Schools

Confucius was perhaps the best-known of the wandering advisors/ teachers of the Zhou Dynasty, but virtually all of the major figures of the classical period played a similar role. They were not merely political and military advisors, but also what might be called Renaissance Men, versed in the classics, concerned with universal principles of ethics, and dedicated to the restoration of peace and order. Gradually, they developed into six schools:

1. *Confucians* (known as Ritualists or Scholars): dedicated to the restoration of political and social conditions established by the Duke of Zhou centuries earlier
2. *Mo-ists*: followers of the philosopher Mo-zi who taught the doctrines of radical pacifism and universal love
3. *Realists* (or Legalists): dedicated to political power, social control, and law and order
4. *Taoists*: recluses who rejected government service, civil society, and conventional values
5. *Dialecticians* (or Logicians): dedicated to the study of language and logic, perhaps as a rejection of political engagement
6. *Yin-Yang Cosmologists*: dedicated to the study of the cosmos and its interrelations

The Taoists

Among the Six Schools, the principal rival to Confucianism was the Taoist school. Initially, the Taoists were associated with hermits or recluses, who saw no point in trying to right the world's wrongs and regarded efforts at political reform as futile. Though not yet known as Taoists, Confucius is purported to have had an encounter with two such recluses during his travels. They had gone back to nature and advocated a self-sustaining lifestyle of subsistence farming.

On another occasion, Confucius's disciple Zi-lu came across a recluse working as a city gatekeeper.

> Zi-lu was staying overnight at the Stone Gate outside the city. The gatekeeper for the morning watch asked him, "Who sent you?"
> "Confucius," Zi-lu replied.

Table 1.3
The Formative Period: Han to Tang (206 B.C.E.–907 C.E.)

	Imperial Confucianism	Taoist Sectarianism	China and the World
Qin Dynasty (221–206 B.C.E.)	Burning of the books		
Han Dynasty (206 B.C.E.–220 C.E.)	Confucianism becomes state orthodoxy; Grand Academy established	Emergence of Religious Taoism: the Celestial Masters, External Alchemy	Introduction of Buddhism to China
Period of North-South Division (220–581 C.E.)	Dark Learning synthesizing Confucian and Taoist thought	Imperial patronage at the Wei court; Shang-qing School and first edition of the Taoist Canon	Buddhism expands in China
Sui-Tang Dynasties (581–907 C.E.)	Han Yü (768–824 C.E.)	Imperial patronage at the Tang court; Ling-bao School; integration of Taoist ritual in village life	Confucianism exported to Korea and Japan

"Oh, isn't he the one who knows full well that something can't be done, but goes ahead and does it anyway?"

The best-known of these recluses was Zhuang-zi (368–289 B.C.E.), a contemporary of Mencius, who was from the state of Song in the south, and thus part of the southern tradition of Zhou shamanism. Though Zhuang-zi was probably a member of the gentry (*shi*) class, he repeatedly refused to serve as an official or to offer his advice to state rulers. On numerous occasions, his flippancy and disregard for social convention led to threats on his life.

Lao-zi, the "Old Boy," was a semi-mythical figure of an unknown time. The work ascribed to him, entitled *Dao de jing* (*The Classic of the Way and Its Power*), probably dates from the fifth or fourth century B.C.E., about the time of Zhuang-zi and Meng-zi. The *Dao de jing*, with its often cryptic images and phraseology, is concerned with a great number of issues, including aesthetics, ethics, cosmology, human nature, the natural world, sagehood, epistemology, political power, and both spiritual and practical achievement. Both in East Asia and in the West, the sayings of Lao-zi have meant many things to many people.

The third of the preeminent Taoist sages of the classical period was Lie-zi. Very little is known about the historical Lie-zi, but he appears as an heroic figure in *The Book of Zhuang-zi*. His own book did not exist prior to the Han Dynasty, however. Lie-zi championed a reclusive and hedonistic (pleasure-seeking) lifestyle, and was completely oblivious to social constraint, duty, or responsibility. A key theme of the book attributed to Lie-zi is the idea that such a lifestyle will be rewarded with long life, even physical immortality, and the book is full of references to mountain retreats or far-away islands populated with joyful immortals. The cultivation of immortality became a major goal of the Taoist tradition.

THE FORMATIVE PERIOD: HAN TO TANG (206 B.C.E.–907 C.E.)

Imperial Confucianism

The fractured Zhou Dynasty came to an end in 221 B.C.E., with the establishment of a new dynasty by the Great Unifier, Yellow Emperor of the Qin (*Qin shi huang di*). The Qin was to be China's shortest-lived empire, a mere fifteen years, but its negative effects were long-lasting, particularly for the Confucian tradition.

In order to bring unity to the empire, the Yellow Emperor of the Qin carried out a brutal program, favoring the Legalist school over the others of the Six Schools and imposing a severe, draconian rule. He gathered up the great books of the other traditions—singling out the Confucian school for especially ruthless suppression—and put them to the torch. Many of the classical texts of the Zhou were lost forever, and the Confucian Classics had to be reconstructed during the Han Dynasty (206 B.C.E.–220 C.E.).

Apart from the lasting notoriety he gained for the burning of the books, the Yellow Emperor is known for his megalomaniacal interest in creating massive monuments to himself. His goal was self-preservation beyond the grave with all of the glory of his reign. He built a magnificent tomb, burying with his crypt thousands of life-sized terra-cotta soldiers, chariots, and steeds. Recently excavated, these are now on view near Xian, in Shanxi Province. This is early evidence of a belief in immortality—or some kind of continuing existence beyond death—that was to play an important part in religious Taoism in later centuries.

Terra-cotta soldier at Qin Imperial Tomb.
Courtesy of the author.

The Yellow Emperor's reign was mercifully short-lived and inaugurated one of the most stable of China's dynasties, the Han. The Han Dynasty saw the establishment of a political meritocracy—the assignment of positions in government bureaucracy by virtue of merit, not birth—based upon classical learning. China during the Han Dynasty was the most technologically advanced, economically complex, and politically stable nation in the world. Its renown was so great that, even today, the Chinese are known as "Han people," and the Chinese language is made up of Han characters. The Han was the first of China's great empires: its political boundaries extended as far north as modern Korea and as far south as modern Vietnam.

One effect of the Han's great power was increased contact with the outside world. It was at this time that China first encountered Buddhism. Central Asian Buddhist monks traveled to the Chinese capital, bringing their scriptures and monastic regulations. They established translation centers and learned how to explain Indian cosmologies in Chinese terms. Their influence in the Han was small, but these foreign monks were the seeds of a rich intellectual and monastic tradition that grew rapidly in periods of political disunity, and Buddhism was significantly "made Chinese" within three hundred years of its arrival.

Seeking an alternative to the Legalist principles favored by the Yellow Emperor of the Qin, the Han rulers elected Confucianism as the educational and political doctrine that could settle the empire. To this end, the Han emperors established a Grand Academy, for the reconstruction of the Confucian Classics and the education of "ministers and worthies." Confucian scholars of this period interpreted the Classics in cosmic terms, "unifying Heaven, Earth, and Man" in a triad of harmonious correlations. Borrowing heavily from the *Yi Jing* (*The Book of Changes*), the Confucians developed a "correspondence theory" of natural events and human actions—seeing changes in the weather as indications of political success and failure; the lines and shapes of an individual's hands or face as indications of personal fortune and misfortune; the songs of children at play, or the calls of birds in flight, as coded language reflecting the contentment or discontent of the people. This "correlative cosmology" and its key value of *social and political harmony* was definitive of the Imperial Confucianism of the Han to Tang periods.

The close connection between Confucianism and the imperial house meant that Confucian fortunes rose or fell with the imperial state. Consequently, Confucianism flourished during periods of political unity and was eclipsed during periods of political disunity. During the Period of North-

South Division (220–581 c.e.), Confucians developed a Taoist-Confucian blended philosophy called "Dark Learning," but they had little influence at court. The Empire again in disarray, Buddhism and Taoism enjoyed a meteoric rise in influence and power and gained widespread followings among the people.

Finally, in the Tang Dynasty (618–906 c.e.), a Confucian minister named Han Yü (768–824) composed a memorial to the throne condemning Buddhists and Taoists in a statement of religious exclusivism rarely seen in Chinese history. This memorial expressed the key values of Imperial Confucianism: social responsibility, loyalty to the state, veneration of ancestors and of the great teachers of antiquity, and a hierarchical ordering of society based upon intellectual achievement (reading, writing, and knowledge of history and the arts). Han Yü accused Buddhist monks and Taoist adepts of being parasites upon the productive "four classes" of farmers, workers, artisans, and merchants; of neglecting the core Chinese (that is, Confucian) values of ritual propriety, social harmony, and moral responsibility; and of importing "foreign" or "aberrant" cultural norms. Han Yü's memorial is representative of the close links between Confucianism and the state, an association that can be traced back to the Han Dynasty and that has typified Imperial Confucianism for the past two thousand years of Chinese history.

Religious Taoism

Though it is meaningful to speak about a "school of the *Dao*" before the Han Dynasty, it had no identifiable social base or institutional organization. Religious Taoism as an *institutional* entity does not come into existence until the later Han.

In the period from the Han to the Tang, the Taoist religion was born, bringing together three diverse streams into a single religious tradition that still thrives in Chinese communities today. These three streams can be labeled as Sect Taoism, Esoteric Taoism, and Priestly Taoism.

Sect Taoism

A variety of religious groups arose at the end of the later Han Dynasty, all claiming to possess the power of the Dao, and all claiming a deified Lao-zi as the source of their revelations. One of these groups achieved a measure of legitimacy in the eyes of the state and a symbolic permanence in the subsequent development of the tradition. This was the Way of the Celestial Masters or Five Bushels of Rice Sect (named for its membership tithes) founded by the semilegendary Zhang Dao-ling. Zhang Dao-ling originated the Way of the Celestial Masters based upon revelations from the god Lao-zi on a mountaintop in Sichuan.

The Way of the Celestial Masters was highly organized, with a parish structure consisting of male-female pairs called "libationers" (named after a ritual of pouring wine into the ground as an offering to both earth gods and star gods) who governed their membership in regional groupings. The head priest of the organization was the Celestial Master, a position passed down by inheritance from one generation to the next. Even today, the highest-ranking Celestial Master is believed to be a direct descendent of the founder, Zhang Dao-ling.

Initially, the Way of the Celestial Masters existed largely on the margins of Chinese society and did not enjoy government sponsorship in the Han Dynasty. But one of the emperors of the Period of North-South Division, the Tai-wu Emperor of the Northern Wei Dynasty, who reigned from 424 to 448 C.E., established the Way of the Celestial Masters as the state religion of his small kingdom. And during the Tang Dynasty, Sect Taoism enjoyed sponsorship by a number of emperors, though it was never given the status of state religion and was generally given less support than Buddhism, which was highly favored by virtually every Tang emperor. This government backing allowed Sect Taoism to enjoy several centuries of growth and development as a church organization.

Esoteric Taoism

Unlike Sect Taoism, Esoteric Taoism is focused upon individual self-cultivation, with a goal of physical immortality attained through alchemical means.

From 364 to 370 C.E., in the early years of the Period of North-South Division, a man named Yang Xi received a series of extraordinary spiritual revelations in the Bucklebent Hills of Mao Shan. The source of these revelations was the spirit of one of the early libationers or parish leaders of the Way of the Celestial Masters, the Lady Wei Hua-cun (251–334 C.E.). These revelations were set in writing by Tao Hong-jing (456–536 C.E.), and became the foundation of the great collection of scriptures, essays, poetry, legend, and local history called the *Taoist Canon*. The sect that based itself on these teachings was called *Shang-qing*, "Highest Purity."

Lady Wei Hua-cun's revelations heralded a new development in religious Taoism: the cultivation of alchemical techniques aimed at personal immortality. These techniques are usually referred to as "Taoist alchemy"—*alchemy* is the magical transformation of "base" substances into "pure" substances, such as lead into gold, or a mortal physical body into an immortal physical body.

The Mao-shan revelations were not the first alchemical texts in Chinese history. In fact, the search for immortality can be traced to the Zhou Dynasty, where archeologists have discovered bronze vessels with the inscriptions "long life," "delay old age," and "non-death." Excavations of burial chambers from the Han Dynasty show a remarkable interest in life beyond the grave. In the tomb of the Countess of Dai (dated to 168 B.C.E.) were found food, clothing, and cash, figurines of servants and attendants. The corpse was encased in jade and multiple coffins; the body had been embalmed, and the bodily orifices sealed with jade stoppers. Clearly, mourners for the Countess must have expected her to make use of her body beyond her death. Emperor Wu of the Han, who reigned from 141–87 B.C.E., heard tales of winged beings living on an isle of immortals called Peng-lai, as well as Mount Kun-lun, said to be ruled by the Queen Mother of the West, and he sent expeditions to find them.

What was different about the teachings of the Esoteric Taoists was the belief that, instead of an afterlife, or life beyond the grave, there could be unending life—death could be avoided altogether. This could be accomplished by various means: a diet of herbs, fungi, and other medicinal plants; the transmutation of cinnabar into gold, which was then ingested into the body; gymnastic exercises and the "circulation of breath"; and the summoning and internalization of star gods to protect the organs of the body and to ward off the "spirits of ageing and decay." The Taoist Canon contains literally hundreds of alchemical books, recipes, and formulas—often illustrated—outlining these techniques. After the Mao-shan revelations, this esoteric stream of Taoism became one of its major defining features.

Priestly Taoism

A third stream that shaped the future development of Taoism placed an emphasis on community rituals. This stream of the tradition can also be referred to as "liturgical Taoism," because it is concerned with the proper steps, songs, incantations, and symbolic objects associated with religious ritual. Once again, the specific instructions for these rituals came in the form of divine revelations to a branch of the Way of the Celestial Masters called *Ling-bao*, "Spiritual Treasure." The Ling-bao revelations form another major part of the Taoist Canon, which contains hundreds of ritual manuals in addition to the alchemical texts of the Shang-qing tradition.

Priestly Taoism represents the point of contact between the Taoist religion and the popular religion of the common people. For centuries, the people had made offerings of incense, silk, wine, meat, fruits, and grain to a variety of spiritual beings, including nature deities, family ancestors, and wandering or "hungry" ghosts. Most of these religious beliefs and practices were highly localized, and the people of one village or community worshipped different gods from those of other communities. The gods were enshrined in temples built near a great tree, or they were worshipped at mounds constructed in their honor.

The Taoist religion, which had national aspirations, initially came into conflict with the local religious cults, accusing them of worshipping false gods and spirits of death, and describing their offerings as "bloody sacrifices"—in contrast to the "pure sacrifices" to the Taoist gods, which were celestial spirits or immortals. The Shang-qing tradition, for example, said that the religion of the people was tied to death while Taoism represented the power of life. Indeed, the spirits of Chinese folk religion are primarily spirits of the dead—from deified heroes killed in battle to family ancestors. The Taoist pantheon, by contrast, consists of spirits never touched by death—either human immortals or celestial Pure Ones and astral spirits, or star gods.

But the Ling-bao revelations settled these differences and created a system whereby the local cults could be integrated into the Taoist religion. The system still exists and can be observed in community temples to this day. The Taoist priest—steeped in the alchemical practices of the Shang-qing revelations, accomplished in the ritual procedures of the Ling-bao manuals—commands and controls the local gods and spirits with his shamanic power, power derived from the Pure Ones at the apex of the celestial pantheon. Establishing his altar at the local temple or shrine, the Taoist priest calls forth an army of divine generals, commanding officers, messengers, and soldiers to wage battle with the marauding ghosts of disease and dissension, healing community ills. This battle takes place within the priest's body and imagination, and exhausts his "vital breath." In this sense, the priest is making a great personal sacrifice, as the very powers he invokes to serve the community would, if retained for his own use, create an immortal, invincible body. His priestly work strengthens the community while weakening his own essence and spirit.

The basic goals and practices of Taoism outlined here still exist today, though primarily in their alchemical and priestly forms, as the sectarian organization of early Taoism has evolved into a looser structure. Today, one can still be initiated into the esoteric practices of alchemical transformation, and one can observe Taoist priests at work in the popular religious temples of Chinese communities in Taiwan, Hong Kong, and Mainland China. The basic form of religious Taoism, then, has maintained a remarkable consistency for two thousand years. Its development in the late imperial period will be addressed below.

THE CHINESE RELIGIOUS RENAISSANCE: SONG TO QING (960–1911 c.e.)

The last millennium of Chinese religious evolution has witnessed a series of creative elaborations on the major concepts and practices of the Three Traditions (Confucianism, Taoism, and Buddhism). In this period, blending was the overwhelming strategy of choice in dealing with religious diversity, and the Confucian and Taoist traditions outdid one another in developing integrative schemes, seeing the "three religions as one," though

Table 1.4
The Chinese Religious Renaissance: Song to Qing (960–1911 c.e.)

	Confucian Renaissance	**Alchemical & Priestly Taoism**
Song Dynasty (960–1279 c.e.)	Song Neo-Confucianism Zhu Xi (1130–1200 c.e.)	Internal Alchemy Quan-zhen School and integration of Taoism with Buddhist monasticism
Yuan Dynasty (1260–1368 c.e.)	Zhu Xi's annotated Four Books becomes standard for civil service examinations (1313 c.e.)	
		Popular Taoism
Ming Dynasty (1368–1644 c.e.)	Ming Neo-Confucianism Wang Yangming (1472–1529 c.e.)	Blended movements heavily influenced by Taoism; Integration of Taoism and folk religion
Qing Dynasty (1644–1911 c.e.)	School of Evidential Research	

always recognizing their own tradition as the highest organizing principle and the most perfect manifestation of the Way.

Neo-Confucianism

Though Confucianism had established itself as a politically persuasive school, lending support to the government bureaucracy, it was counterbalanced by the emergence of Buddhist and Taoist institutions in the fluid period between the Han and the Sui Dynasties (220–581 C.E.). The Sui and Tang Dynasties (581–906 C.E.) mark the Golden Age of Buddhism and Taoism in China, a period of flourishing that saw the erection of magnificent monasteries, temples, and statues as well as a significant proportion of the Chinese people (estimated to be as much as one-sixth of the total population) pursuing religious vocations as Buddhist monks or Taoist priests. It was not until the Song Dynasty (960–1279 C.E.) that Confucianism enjoyed a revival in what might be called the Confucian Renaissance, a period of tremendous intellectual innovation among Confucian scholars from the mid-Song through the Ming Dynasty (1368–1644 C.E.). It was during this period as well that Confucianism spread to other parts of Asia, particularly Korea and Japan, and had a profound impact upon both scholars and the common people; indeed it remains the primary religious and ethical orientation of the Korean and Japanese people today.

Neo-Confucianism is the general term for two schools that still dominate Confucian intellectual discussion to this day: the Rationalist School, born in the Song Dynasty and systematized by Zhu Xi (1130–1200 C.E.), and the Idealist School of the Ming Dynasty, epitomized by Wang Yangming (1472–1529 C.E.). Though both have political implications, this phase of Confucian intellectual development is more concerned with personal transformation by means of study, meditation, and ethical self-cultivation than it is with social or governmental organization.

In Chinese, the Rationalist School of Song Neo-Confucianism is described as "The Study of Principle." The idea of *Principle* was coined by the Neo-Confucian school as the essence or defining form of all things in the universe. For Zhu Xi, Principle underlies all things—it is their "original nature," meaning, and purpose. It is "heavenly," that is, endowed by Heaven (*Tian*), which means that all things in the universe—the universe itself—are naturally good. This does not mean that there is no evil or imperfection in the world, however. Principle is "expressed" or "brought into material existence" by the force of *qi*, the "vital breath." Some of the *qi* is pure and strong (this idea came from Taoism), but other *qi* is impure and weak. In individuals, feelings sometimes are expressed as "good *qi*," but sometimes as "bad *qi*." Therefore, while the underlying Principle of human nature is good (in the sense that the underlying Principle of all things is good), that nature can be expressed in either good or evil terms in the human heart and mind.

Zhu Xi concluded from his philosophical analysis of reality that in order to "discover the good," people cannot simply look within themselves. Looking within themselves, they find a heart-and-mind that may be either good or evil, but it is difficult to distinguish between them on their own. Therefore, the Song Neo-Confucians advocated a thorough "investigation of things": intense study of the external world to discover the underlying Principle of all things, including people. By studying the Principle of things, people can gain a profound understanding of Principle that they then "recognize" in themselves, strengthening the good and pure *qi*-energy of the heart-and-mind. In practical terms, this means that self-cultivation actually consists in attention to things outside the self. The "investigation of things" is what people do in school—the study of history, literature, science, great books, and great ideas. To pursue this end, Zhu Xi reedited the Confucian Classics, with extensive commentaries on the words of Confucius, Mencius, and the other Confucian sages. Zhu Xi's editions of the Classics became standard, and by 1313 C.E. were made the basis of the national examination—a standard that held until the end of the imperial period, some six hundred years later.

By contrast, the Idealist School of Ming Neo-Confucianism is described in Chinese as "The Learning of the Heart and Mind." This teaching is attributed primarily to Wang Yang-ming, who lived during the Ming Dynasty, about three hundred years after Zhu Xi. Himself a failure in the imperial examinations but profoundly steeped in Confucian learning, Wang struggled to put Zhu Xi's teachings into practice: mastering the Classics, developing his own skills in essay writing and calligraphy, and pursuing scientific investigation of nature. In the process, however, Wang became extremely discouraged and was especially disheartened to think that his "basic nature" was subject to evil or imperfection. Rejecting Zhu Xi's morally neutral stance, Wang insisted that the heart-and-mind is itself pure and good and could be known directly, through intuition, meditation, and self-examination.

The teachings of Song and Ming Neo-Confucianism represent two moral and philosophical strands that are still debated among Confucians today. What they have in common is an intense interest in the self, support for the life of the mind (through study or contemplation), and a generally optimistic view of human potential. Whereas the Rationalist School emphasizes the "corrective" benefit of study, however, the Idealist School maintains that persons are naturally good and can know this through direct personal experience. For Zhu Xi, self-improvement is based upon education and leading a disciplined life. One of the most important books he composed was a manual of family rituals to strengthen the family and to create the kind of "patterned" life that brings out the best in human nature. The book is a guide to etiquette and ceremony, from the naming of children to the conduct of funerals and ancestor veneration. For Wang Yang-ming, study and self-discipline are important, but they are incidental to recognizing the basic goodness at the center of the human heart.

Which of these views won out in late imperial and modern Chinese history? Certainly, from the perspective of political and educational leaders, Zhu Xi's Rationalist School was the more appealing, especially when Zhu Xi's definitive editions of the Confucian Classics became the standard for government examinations. Zhu's emphasis on classical learning and on self-discipline through ritual and etiquette was highly favored by the state, which sought the means to bring order to the empire. Confucian Principles were interpreted as a set of moral rules governing every aspect of daily life.

The Rationalist School was favored in the late imperial period among scholars and educators, especially the Qing Dynasty (1644–1911 C.E.) scholars who founded the School of Evidential Research. These were some of the greatest book-learners in Chinese history, producing voluminous commentaries on the classics, massive reference books including multivolume encyclopedias and dictionaries, and minute records of government directives and local histories. The image of the bespectacled Chinese intellectual with his flowing high-collared robes comes from these scholars, who were condemned by twentieth-century reformers for their antiquated, bookish ways.

Wang Yang-ming's Idealist School has also had a long-term impact, especially in Japan, where it was the dominant Confucian school and where it enjoyed a successful synthesis with Buddhism, and among contemporary Chinese intellectuals. Today, Chinese Confucians identify themselves closely with Wang Yang-ming, not only in their more optimistic view of human nature, but also in their emphasis on personal freedom and the cultivation of a holistic lifestyle, rather than one bound by the rules of "reading, writing, and ritual." The emphasis on personal religious cultivation favored by Ming Neo-Confucianism has reemerged as the defining practice of contemporary Confucians, and it has made Confucianism appealing to non-Chinese in the United States and Europe, as will be seen later in this book.

Alchemical and Priestly Taoism

The late imperial period has seen a process of both "interiorization" and "externalization" in Religious Taoism. Whereas the alchemical practices of the immortality cult were interiorized in the Song and Yuan Dynasties, the priestly functions continued to grow more widespread as Taoism penetrated the religious life of the common people.

Taoist adepts of the Song and Yuan Dynasties radically reinterpreted the alchemical treatises of the Shang-qing School. The ancient texts were now understood to be mystical, symbolic recipes, not for actual foods or chemical concoctions, but for meditative visualizations and gymnastic exercises. The various elixirs of External Alchemy—cinnabar and gold, saltpeter and mica, cinnamon and pine seeds—were read as code words for the meditative practices of Internal Alchemy. The practices undertaken involved conscious control and manipulation of one's own mind, body, and spirit, without any need for the ingestion of foreign materials. In fact, Internal Alchemy creates an ideal of total self-containment, without external intake or stimulation of any kind. Practices favored by this school include "interior vision" (visualization of celestial deities within the various "fields" and "meridians" of the body); "circulation of breath" and "embryonic breathing"; "returning the essence" (a sexual practice similar to Tantric Hinduism and Buddhism); "guiding and pushing" (gymnastics or martial arts); and "cutting off cereals" (abstinence from grain, or, ideally, a fasting diet of "saliva and air"). In all cases, the goal was a complete interiorization of cosmic energy: perpetual recirculation of the Dao within the body so that energy/life is never depleted.

At the same time that personal religious practice was more and more internalized, Priestly Taoism continued to spread among the common people, to the extent that Taoist priests were fully integrated into temple-based folk religion by the end of the imperial period. Taoism supplied ritual specialists for community festivals, ceremonies of thanksgiving and supplication, or rites of protection and exorcism. Within the priesthood, a hierarchy was established, from the Masters of the Way (descendents of the Way of the Celestial Masters) dressed in formal embroidered robes and versed in the alchemical ritual instructions of the Taoist Canon, down to the Jade

Maidens and Golden Boys (spirit mediums) of the temple courtyards and country lanes.

These ritual specialists were well known to the people. Whereas the Confucian intellectuals of the Rationalist School and the School of Evidential Research were traditionalists dedicated to the preservation of Chinese high culture, the Taoist ritual specialists were traditionalists of a different kind—preserving religious ceremonies and community rites that had been recorded in Taoist scriptures and passed down from master to disciple for nearly two thousand years.

Another major development in the Song Dynasty was the emergence of a fourth major school of Sect Taoism, in addition to the Way of the Celestial Masters, the School of Highest Purity (*Shang-qing*), and the School of Spiritual Treasure (*Ling-bao*). This was the School of Complete Reality (*Quan-zhen*), founded in the twelfth century. *Quan-zhen* Taoism was heavily influenced by Buddhist monasticism, and the sect established Taoist abbeys modeled upon Buddhist monasteries. Like their Buddhist counterparts, *Quan-zhen* Taoist monks practice celibacy, vegetarianism, and a strictly regulated lifestyle. Monastic Taoists seek to overcome physical or material desire. Unlike the Alchemical Taoists of the *Shang-qing* tradition, monastic Taoists do not attempt to cultivate physical immortality, but seek a spiritual transcendence of the material world.

Of the four major schools of Sect Taoism described in this book, only *Quan-zhen* Taoism has a visible presence today. Complete Reality abbeys still exist in China, and in fact have enjoyed a minor resurgence in the last two decades of the twentieth century. One of the most famous of these abbeys is the *Bai-yun guan* (Abbey of the White Cloud) in Beijing, dating in its present form to 1394 C.E. Today, the White Cloud Monastery is a popular tourist destination in the capital. Other *Quan-zhen* abbeys have been established throughout China.

RELIGION IN MODERN AND CONTEMPORARY CHINA FROM 1911 C.E.

The year 1911 C.E. marked the end of two millennia of imperial rule, and the creation of a tenuous parliamentary state. The past century has been tumultuous, as the Chinese people have been subjected to colonization from abroad, civil war, and internal restrictions on their civil freedoms and cultural traditions.

The late Qing Dynasty reformers, dedicated to the creation of a New China, were skeptical of China's religious traditions, believing that religious superstition had contributed to China's backwardness, to the nation's lack of resistance to the imperial aspirations of Japan and the West, and to the political despotism and stagnation of the central government. Confucianism, Taoism, and Buddhism—as well as the local folk traditions of the people—were associated with China's imperial past. Subsequently, the Nationalist government of the Republic of China (which was founded in Nanjing in the 1920s and moved its capital to Taipei, Taiwan, in 1949) and the central government of the People's Republic of China (which established its capital in Beijing as a Communist state in 1949) have placed restrictions on religious observance, especially at the local level. In Communist China, the Three Religions all suffered severe restrictions on religious education and practice. Confucianism fared better on Taiwan, which has attempted to preserve traditional culture, and many Buddhist and Taoist leaders fled Mainland China for Taiwan, Hong Kong, and the West after the Communist government took control of religious temples, monasteries, and abbeys in the 1950s. Today, traditional religion is resurgent in China, but the influence of Westernization (including Communism) has been great, and China's religious culture is threatened with extinction. At an institutional level, Buddhist monasteries and Taoist abbeys are administered by quasigovernmental religious associations answerable to political authorities. Religious institutions simply are not permitted complete freedom and autonomy, and voluntary religious associations (cults or sects) are subject to severe restrictions. Nevertheless, the Chinese people today enjoy more religious freedom than they have had in half a century, and religious observance, writing, and research is enjoying a modest recovery.

Despite this tumult, the Confucian and Taoist traditions have been invigorated by contact with other religions and worldviews, and the defining characteristic of modern-day Chinese religion is its informed responsiveness to alternative systems of thought and practice. What twentieth-century Confucians describe as New Confucianism or the Third Epoch of Confucianism has shown a great willingness to engage with Buddhism, Christianity, and Western philosophy, and even to incorporate other religious perspectives into a broader synthesis.

Another major development in the twentieth century has been the exportation of Confucianism and Taoism to the West—a second wave of foreign expansion after the first wave of Confucian expansion to Korea, Japan, and Vietnam in the fifteenth through seventeenth centuries. Taoist self-cultivation and traditional medicine are now wildly popular in the West, and Confucianism today claims non-Asian adherents for the first time in its history. This fledgling movement has been dubbed Boston Confucianism, as most of these Western Confucians are scholars and intellectuals associated with Harvard University, Boston University, and other northeastern U.S. schools.

Clearly, despite major setbacks in the past eighty or ninety years, Confucianism and Taoism still survive, following the Dao by adapting to changing conditions and defining themselves as world religions with unlimited potential for growth and expansion. Chapter 4 will examine the contemporary practice of Chinese religion both in China and abroad.

FURTHER READINGS

One of the best general works on Chinese history is by the eminent French historian Jacques Gernet, *A History of Chinese Civilization.* For the history of the Shang Dynasty, and the religious meaning and significance of oracle-bone inscriptions, see David Keightley's *Sources of Shang History: The Oracle-Bone Inscriptions of Bronze Age China.* Another insightful book by a French scholar, *China in Antiquity,* written by Henri Maspero, presents a wealth of background on China's mythic past.

For the religious history of the Zhou Dynasty, consult the works above, as well as the introduction to and translations of the *Chu-ci* (*Songs of Chu*) by David Hawkes. The best general introductions to the classical philosophers of the Six Schools are by Fung Yu-lan and A. C. Graham. Wing-tsit Chan's book of selected translations of Chinese philosophy from the Zhou Dynasty to the present is a comprehensive source.

There are many books on Confucius and his social, political, religious, and philosophical background. One of the most readable is by Japanese scholar Shigeki Kaizuka. His book, *Confucius,* can be found in English translation. On Lao-zi and the early history of Taoism, there are, again, many good books (not to mention many translations of the *Dao de jing,* more or less true to the Chinese original). Recommended is a book originally written in French, Max Kaltenmark's *Lao Tzu and Taoism.*

For the history of Taoism during its formative period, see Isabelle Robinet's *Taoism: Growth of a Religion.* For a more general introduction to Taoism, both its history and its beliefs and practices, an excellent and readable choice is Eva Wong's *The Shambhala Guide to Taoism.* Recommendations for translations of *The Analects* of Confucius and of the *Dao de jing* appear at the end of Chapter 2.

The best and most recent book on Confucianism is Xinzhong Yao's *An Introduction to Confucianism*. Focusing more on Confucianism as a scholarly tradition is another recent book, John Berthrong's *Transformations of the Confucian Way*.

Julian Pas has collected a series of articles on religion in contemporary China: *The Turning of the Tide: Religion in China Today*. For Western Taoism and Confucianism, see J. J. Clarke's *The Tao of the West* and Robert Neville's *Boston Confucianism*.

Berthrong, John. *Transformations of the Confucian Way*. Boulder, CO: Westview, 1998.

Chan, Wing-tsit. *A Source Book in Chinese Philosophy*. Princeton: Princeton University Press, 1963.

Clarke, J. J. *The Tao of the West: Western Transformations of Taoist Thought*. New York: Routledge, 2000.

Fung Yu-lan. *A History of Chinese Philosophy*. Translated by Derk Bodde. Princeton: Princeton University Press, 1952.

Gernet, Jacques. *A History of Chinese Civilization*. Translated by J. R. Foster and Charles Hartman. Cambridge: Cambridge University Press, 1996.

Graham, A. C. *Disputers of the Tao: Philosophical Argument in Ancient China*. La Salle, IL: Open Court, 1989.

Hawkes, David. *The Songs of the South: An Ancient Chinese Anthology of Poems by Qu Yuan and Other Poets*. New York: Penguin, 1985.

Kaizuka, Shigeki. *Confucius*. Translated from the Japanese by Geoffrey Bownas. New York: Macmillan, 1956.

Kaltenmark, Max. *Lao Tzu and Taoism*. Translated from the French by Roger Greaves. Stanford, CA: Stanford University Press, 1969.

Keightley, David N. *Sources of Shang History: The Oracle-Bone Inscriptions of Bronze Age China*. Berkeley: University of California Press, 1978.

Maspero, Henri. *China in Antiquity*. Translated by Frank A. Kierman, Jr. Amherst: University of Massachusetts Press, 1978.

Neville, Robert Cummings. *Boston Confucianism: Portable Tradition in the Late-Modern World*. Albany: State University of New York Press, 2000.

Pas, Julian. *The Turning of the Tide: Religion in China Today*. New York: Oxford University Press, 1989.

Robinet, Isabelle. *Taoism: Growth of a Religion*. Translated from the French by Phyllis Brooks. Stanford, CA: Stanford University Press, 1997.

Wong, Eva. *The Shambhala Guide to Taoism*. Boston: Shambhala, 1997.

Yao, Xinzhong. *An Introduction to Confucianism*. Cambridge: Cambridge University Press, 2000.

2

TEXTS AND MAJOR TENETS OF THE CLASSICAL PERIOD

THE TEXTS AND TEACHINGS OF CLASSICAL CONFUCIANISM: SOCIAL HARMONY

The Confucian Classics

The classical Confucian canon consists of the Five Classics and Four Books. The Five Classics were said to have been edited by the Master himself. They certainly predate Confucius, but scholars today are doubtful that he had a hand in composing them. Nevertheless, their importance to Confucius and his followers cannot be understated, and Confucius urged his students to commit the Classics to memory.

The Five Classics

1. *Yi-jing* (*The Book of Changes*)—a divination manual based upon *yin-yang* cosmology
2. *Shi-jing* (*The Book of Poetry*)—a collection of 305 Zhou Dynasty poems
3. *Shu-jing* (*The Book of History*)—a history of the Xia, Shang, and Zhou Dynasties
4. *Li Ji* (*The Book of Rites*)—a ritual manual of Zhou court ceremonies
5. *Chun Qiu* (*The Spring and Autumn Annals*)—a commentary on historical events

Confucius believed in the moral power of education: in his mind, an educated person was by definition a good person. Today, education is not associated with moral virtue. But for Confucius, to be educated meant not simply to have mastered intellectual skills and knowledge, but also to have been personally transformed by one's studies. Education shapes one's character, not just the mind.

Confucian education is broad, but it begins with reading and study. In traditional times, this meant committing the Classics to memory. There are profound lessons to be learned by studying the Classics:

- the mutual correspondence between humans and the cosmos (what might be called ecology), as taught in *The Book of Changes;*
- the underlying unity of basic human feelings, as taught in *The Book of Poetry;*
- the importance of tradition or collective memory, aided by the study of *The Book of History;*
- the means for maintaining community through social norms, as taught by *The Book of Rites;* and
- the principle of learning from errors of the past and from the positive example of the sages of antiquity, as taught in *The Spring and Autumn Annals.*

This is more than mere book learning. It is study that leads to the development of character through moral and religious insight.

The Four Books

The Four Books were the primary works of the early Confucian tradition after Confucius.

1. *Lun-yü (The Analects)*—the conversations and sayings of Confucius
2. *Da Xue (The Great Learning)*—an essay on the cultivation of leadership
3. *Zhong Yong (The Doctrine of the Mean)*—an essay on the cultivation of sagehood
4. *Meng-zi (The Book of Mencius)*—the essays of the Second Sage of Confucianism

Within two or three generations of Confucius, his teachings were assembled by some of the students of his own direct disciples in a collection of sayings. This collection was called *Lun-yü*, literally "Conversations" or "Dialogues" (the meaning of *lun)* and "Pronouncements" or "Sayings" (the meaning of *yü).* The work, often called *The Analects* in English, is in twenty sections and 496 chapters. About half of the book seems to reflect the actual words of Confucius.

The Great Learning and *The Doctrine of the Mean,* also attributed to Confucius's immediate disciples, are brief texts of a few hundred characters and were used for centuries as primers for school children on proper cultivation of the self in relation to the social and cosmic world. *The Great Learning* introduces Five Phases cosmology and is probably a product of an editing process not completed until the Han Dynasty, but *The Doctrine of the Mean* is certainly representative of the early Confucian vision. One oft-quoted passage in particular states succinctly the profound interrelationship between personal moral cultivation and universal social harmony:

> In order to illuminate their illustrious virtue for all the world to see, the ancient sages regulated their states.
> But before regulating their states, they first ordered their families.
> Before ordering their families, they first cultivated their own behavior.
> Before cultivating their own behavior, they first corrected their thinking.
> Before correcting their thinking, they first made their intentions sincere.
> Before making their intentions sincere, they first extended their knowledge.
> The extension of knowledge is found in the investigation of things.
> Investigate things; only then can your knowledge be extended.
> Extend your knowledge; only then can your intentions be sincere.
> Make your intentions sincere; only then can your thinking be correct.
> Correct your thinking; only then can your behavior be well-guided.
> Guide your behavior; only then can your family be well-ordered.
> Order your family; only then can your state be regulated.
> Once the states are regulated, there will be peace in the world.

This statement is characteristic of the Confucian vision, beginning with education and self-cultivation as the means to social harmony. It is perhaps the most succinct overview of the Confucian program for life, demonstrating the link between improving oneself and improving the world. From a Confucian point of view, it is impossible to attend to one without attending to the other.

Proper Ordering of Confucian Cultivation, According to The Great Learning

1. the "investigation of things": study of history and the natural world
2. the "extension" of knowledge: applying what one has learned to new situations and phenomena
3. "sincere intention": moving from knowledge to moral action

4. becoming "mentally correct": avoiding temptation, applying moral virtue to all of one's thoughts

5. becoming "physically cultivated": applying moral virtue to all of one's actions

6. the well-regulated family: harmony within the home

7. the well-regulated state: harmony within the community

8. peace and harmony "all under Heaven"

Finally, *Meng-zi*—the last of the Four Books—is a collection of essays attributed to the Second Sage of the Confucian tradition, Mencius. The teachings of Mencius will be discussed in Chapter 3.

The Teachings of Classical Confucianism

The emphasis on education is one of the hallmarks of Confucianism, a legacy of excellence in learning that persists to the present day. Troubled by the chaotic social and political strife of his day, Confucius believed that the only hope for his state was not stronger armies and more efficient armaments, but the restoration of *wen*, "culture" or "civil society." The character *wen* means specifically "writing," which shows that the highest cultural expression in Chinese history is found in written texts, but Confucius emphasized the study of all the arts in his curriculum—music, dance, and painting—as well as history and literature.

The Jün-zi

Though Confucius lived in a time when women could not leave the home, and thus his own disciples were confined to men, he would accept any student, regardless of ability to pay. "Where there is teaching," he said, "there should be no discrimination according to class." His admissions test was simple: "I will take any student," he said, "who, if shown one corner of a square, can give me the other three." He was also a great student himself and believed that one can learn from any situation and any person. "If I see three persons walking, one could be my teacher." The goal of education is to create men of broad learning and culture, which he called *jün-zi*, "gentlemen."

Prior to Confucius, the word *jün-zi* was a designation of class. A good translation of the pre-Confucian *jün-zi* was "nobleman," or, more literally, "son of a nobleman," which, in a feudal society, means the same thing, as one's class status depended entirely upon the class of one's parents. This meant that one was born either as a *jün-zi* or as a commoner, with the accompanying rights, privileges, and duties of one's class identity.

Though the word *jün-zi* indicated status by birth prior to Confucius, the Confucian sense of the term indicated status based on learning and character. The Confucian redefinition of the term means something more like the English word *gentleman*, the conventional translation of *jün-zi*. "Gentleman" is a good English equivalent, because, like *jün-zi*, the word once indicated status based upon birth into a high-class family, but later came to refer to any man of character, a man displaying sophistication and politeness, regardless of class. Any man can be a gentleman if he so chooses, and this democratic idea of the *jün-zi* was fundamental to the Confucian program of individual self-cultivation.

The Confucian curriculum was quite broad, the goal being to create a cultured *jün-zi* with wide abilities. The ideal *jün-zi* was a Renaissance man skilled in debate, composition, ritual performance, the arts, and athletics.

The Confucian Curriculum

- Ritual studies
- History and Political Science
- Literature
- Philosophy
- Arts: music and dance
- Physical Education: gymnastics, archery, charioteering

In his reinterpretation of *jün-zi*, Confucius showed how he worked: taking what was best from the past but reinterpreting it in light of modern conditions and his own humanistic inclinations. No longer a symbol of high birth, the *jün-zi* was for Confucius a title of honor, indicating high moral and educational standards—a goal accessible to anyone who was willing to make the commitment. Education and character: these were the twin goals of Confucian self-cultivation.

As individualistic as this curriculum may appear to be (it depends entirely upon personal resolve and individual effort), Confucius believed that the *jün-zi* would "rise to the top" of Chinese society and serve as a model for the world, just as the "sage kings" did in antiquity. His ultimate goal was social transformation through cultural restoration, but this could only be accomplished one individual at a time. For Confucianism, there is no fundamental disharmony between individual excellence and social improvement; in fact, the two are inseparable. The *jün-zi* leads by example, "like the wind blowing the grass ... like the pole star around which all the other stars revolve." So, to change society, one need not be a powerful military leader or a wealthy scion of society, but simply a learned, morally upright individual—leading by example and inspiration.

This is the starting point of Confucianism: the moral perfectibility of the individual who is dedicated to changing himself or herself and thereby improving the world. But how? What does it mean to live in the world? And what is the ideal human environment in which to cultivate the self and improve the society?

Li

The model or analogy for all of the major teachings of Confucius is *li*— ritual—specifically the court sacrifices and ceremonies of the early Zhou. The character for *li* is illustrative of its meaning: on the left is an element common to all characters having to do with religion, and on the right is a stand supporting a bowl half-filled with rice, in which two sticks of incense have been placed. Etymologically, *li* means a ritual of "sacrifice" or "offering."

Li

Due to the social strife of the late Spring and Autumn Period, the *li* of the early Zhou Dynasty had long fallen into disuse. With dynastic power dispersed among the various states, the court no longer had the resources or the political power to sponsor grand ceremonies. Confucius knew of them only through his careful study of the *Li Ji* (*The Book of Rites*), a detailed ritual manual that was one of the Five Classics of the Confucian curriculum. The ancient ceremonies were elaborate and very impressive. They featured thousands of musicians, playing panpipes, plucked stringed instruments, woodwind organs, drums, and hanging brass gongs struck with hammers or mallets. In addition, dancers by the hundreds, arrayed in rows and columns, wearing long pheasant-feather plumes and sashes with jade pendants moved in unison to the harmonious sounds of the orchestra in the temple courtyard. Sacrifices of oxen and sheep were made by burning them on an altar, the smoke rising to the heavens, while wine was poured from ritual vessels into a hole bored into the courtyard grounds.

No one loved the old-time religion more than Confucius.

> Zi-gong wanted to do away with the sacrificing of the lamb at the ceremony held at the beginning of each month to report to the ancestors. The Master said, "Zi-gong, you are reluctant to give up the lamb, but I am reluctant to give up the ceremony."

Why did Confucius love *li?* Part of the reason was aesthetic. Again and again, he tells how much he is moved by descriptions of *li.* One passage in *The Analects* tells us that he was so moved by a performance of ancient ritual music that for three months he was not conscious of the taste of food. His nostalgia for the ancient *li* was deeper than mere aesthetic appreciation, however. He believed that the early Zhou was China's Golden Age, that it was a time of peace, of leadership by sage kings and loyal ministers, and of cultural achievement, dignity, and beauty. The ancient *li* were symbolic of a civilized society. Imagine a state that was so harmonious that it could afford to put its resources in music and dance, rather than soldiers and armaments. Imagine a society that modeled itself upon the grandeur, order, and harmony of the great ceremony. Confucius was not interested simply in the restoration of the *li,* but more important, in the re-creation of a civilization that cherished the *li.* Such a society had its priorities straight: culture, tradition, and the harmony of humans and cosmos. This was the first reason that Confucius talked often about *li.*

Confucius made ritual the cornerstone of his philosophy. He advocated a "return to *li,*" meaning literally the restoration of the ancient ceremonies. But, like the word *jün-zi,* he redefined the term for ritual, *li,* and gave it an expanded, symbolic meaning. For Confucius, the word *li* refers not only to religious rites or ceremonies, but symbolically to all "ceremonial" behavior. *Li* refers to *the proper patterns of action for every situation, in a living human context.* Religious rituals are models for *li* but do not exhaust its meaning. In a Confucian sense, *li* means both *ceremony* and *ceremonial living.* It is a word whose meaning even in modern Chinese includes "ritual, etiquette, propriety, and decency"—in short, the traditional norms of social interaction.

It was crucial to Confucius that *li* should not become ritualistic in the negative sense: mechanical, fake, or hypocritical. He believed that ritual should be performed with sincerity and emotion:

> The Master said, "Unless I take part in a sacrifice with all my heart and mind, it is as if I did not sacrifice at all."

And he believed that *li* as an abstract principle, representing the sincerity and reverence and religious awe of the sacrifice, should be the basis for moral self-cultivation and self-understanding in every context:

> The Master said, "Do not look at what is contrary to *li*. Do not listen to what is contrary to *li*. Do not speak what is contrary to *li*. Do not act in any way that is contrary to *li*."

To quote his greatest disciple, Mencius, "Every motion, every stance precise in the performance of *li*: this is the highest virtue." This means that *li* should not just be a set of actions, or rules, but a *principle* of conduct—one might even say an "attitude" toward how one lives one's life. There can be no true *li* without sincerity.

Ren

The second key term of Confucius's philosophy is *ren,* variously translated as

- love
- benevolence
- compassion
- human-heartedness
- perfect co-humanity
- goodness

To be *ren* (kind, "co-human") is to be sincere, modest, compassionate, and transparent, in the sense that one's thought and behavior are completely unified. A man who is *ren* sees himself as the member of a community and identifies himself with others. He practices *li*—he is considerate and polite—because he wants to do so, because he knows that his own happiness depends upon harmony, respect, and warmth within his family, community, or circle of comrades and friends.

A person who is not *ren* is described in *The Analects* as a "small" or "petty" person. A petty man is concerned with appearances. He does things for show. He has a quick wit and a quick tongue, manipulating conventions for his own purposes. He places himself before others. He seeks wealth and fame above all else. He is never serious about his commitments or his destiny, yet in other respects, he is overly anxious about himself and his future. The person who is not *ren* is "disconnected," not only from others but also within himself.

By contrast, the man who is *ren* (in Confucian terms, a gentleman) is "well integrated"—he does the good because he wants to, not because he has to. He would rather be with his friends or family than alone, because his very identity is dependent upon these relationships.

Ren is based on *li.* The basic meaning of *ren* is "the emotion engendered in a sacrifice." Confucius extends the scope of this definition to include the feelings that should underlie proper social interaction.

> The Master said, "To master oneself and return to *li* is what is meant by *ren*. If for a single day a man could return to the observance of *li* by mastering himself, then the whole world would consider *ren* to be his. However, the practice of *ren* depends on oneself alone, and not on others."

Ren has an almost mystical quality. It is internal, and therefore, very close. "As soon as I want it," Confucius says, "there it is right by me." And yet, Confucius admitted that he had never seen a man who "really loves *ren*" and was never able to achieve it himself . It is a principle of reverence and love at once close to the heart and yet difficult to attain.

Ren

One can think of *ren* as a feeling, but it is not "private" in the sense that people in the West ordinarily think of feelings.

This is a remarkably simple character: on the left is an element common to all characters referring to "persons" or "humans," and on the right is the number two. The literal meaning of *ren*, then, is something like "co-human." This represents the fact that *ren* is personal, but not private: it is shared with others. It might be said that *ren* is the profound, deeply felt sense that one is a "social being," an individual-in-community. One's participation in a social network—of family, friends, and community—is fundamental to one's basic identity. A sense of "co-human" existence is the most deep-seated emotion that any person can experience. The Second

Sage Mencius went so far as to say that it was impossible to conceive of a person who was not *ren*. In other words, *ren* is the basic criterion of being human.

Sociability is probably the most fundamental value of Confucianism, a value that we see in both *li* and *ren*. To many Westerners, this value sounds trite, especially as they tend to think of religion as a very private matter. But from a Confucian point of view, being human means *living in community*, and doing so with sincerity and with constant attention to one's own words and gestures. The story is told of Confucius encountering a pair of hermits in his travels:

> The hermits Chang-ju and Jie-ni were pulling a plow. Confucius was passing by and sent his disciple Zi-lu to ask them where he could cross the river... Jie-ni asked, "Aren't you a disciple of Confucius of Lu?"
>
> "Yes, I am."
>
> Jie-ni said, "The world is as chaotic as a flood. Who can change it? Instead of following someone who avoids certain particular men, why don't you become a disciple of someone who avoids society altogether?" He went back to his hoeing.
>
> Zi-lu reported this conversation to Confucius. Impatiently, Confucius said, "Men cannot flock with birds and beasts. If I do not associate with men, with whom should I associate? The world has a certain *Dao*—who am I to change it?"

Clearly, for Confucius, that *Dao* is the Way of social engagement.

From *ren* emerges all of the other Confucian virtues, which might be defined as applications or manifestations of *ren*:

- filial piety: showing reverence toward one's parents; filial piety is the source of all relational roles, and thus, of personhood
- devotion: single-minded commitment to fulfilling one's responsibilities
- sincerity: the correspondence between one's outward behavior and inner feelings
- vigilance: concentration, reverence
- empathy: internalizing the needs and interests of others as one's own; reciprocity, mutuality
- trustworthiness: doing what one has planned or promised

The value in this list that deserves further elaboration is empathy. *Empathy* is an important element of *ren*, because it indicates that the feelings associated with *ren* are common to all human beings. A man knows how to treat others because he knows how he would like to be treated; he knows what words or behaviors would be harmful to others because he knows what words or behaviors would be harmful to him.

> Zi-gong [a favorite disciple of Confucius] asked: "Is there one word that could serve as a guide for my whole life?" Confucius said: "The word is *empathy:* do not do to others what you do not want others to do to you."

Confucius believed that people should not find it difficult to understand one another. So, it is possible to "take oneself as an analogy" for others (a good definition of empathy).

> Confucius said: "A man of *ren* helps others to establish what he wishes to establish for himself, helps others to attain what he wishes to attain for himself. To be able to take what is near to oneself and make it an analogy for the treatment of others—that is the way of *ren.*"

This can be seen in the definition of *ren* that appears in the Han Dynasty *Huai nan zi:*

> *Ren* means the enjoyment that one feels in one's innermost heart in loving others. It is the feeling of joy at the good luck of others, and the feeling of sadness at their misfortune.

The idea is that people are generally alike: they have the same basic feelings, reactions, or emotional responses to the things that other people say and do. This common feeling is possible in a society that is united by common values, and at the same time, it helps to *create* such a society. Again, *ren* appears to be "inner" or "personal," but it is fundamental to Confucian *social* life.

The Five Constant Relationships

The central importance of *li* and *ren* suggests that humans are fundamentally social or relational. Quoting Mencius, "To be human is to be co-human" (in Chinese, the word for *human* and the word for *co-human* are homonyms, both pronounced *ren* though written differently). This relationality is made concrete in the actual relationships that people experience over the course of a lifetime: relationships within the family, the community, and the state. These relationships are not static. They need to be nurtured and cultivated. There are duties and responsibilities appropriate to each.

The *Meng-zi* (*The Book of Mencius*) discusses concrete relationships in specific terms: the Five Relationships. These are the fundamental relationships of life:

1. parent-child
2. ruler-subject
3. husband-wife
4. old-young
5. friend-friend

Before discussing the particular characteristics of each, note first that these relationships are regarded as permanent, and second, that they are hierarchical. They are permanent in the sense that they are (or should be) binding, even extending beyond death. The relationship between parents and children continues throughout one's lifetime, and children nurture their parents in old age just as the parents nurtured their children in infancy and youth. This relationship continues after death in the form of ancestor veneration. The relationship between husband and wife should be permanent as well, and Chinese to this day are reluctant to divorce. This relationship continues after death in the form of fidelity in widowhood. Friendship, too, should be binding and permanent—even today, Chinese do not take friendship lightly; they are even hesitant to use the word *friend* except when referring to someone with whom they expect to have a lasting connection.

The Five Relationships are hierarchical in two senses. First, they are hierarchal from top to bottom: the parent-child relationship is most important, with priority over every other.

> The Duke of Shê told Confucius: "In my country, people are upright. If a father steals a sheep, his son will testify against him."
>
> Confucius said: "In my country, 'being upright' has a different meaning. A father shields his son, and a son shields his father. That's what we mean by being upright."

What Confucius is saying is that the blood relationship between parent and child should take precedence over the political relationship between ruler and citizens. The family takes precedence over the state. Ideally, the ruler "acts like a father," and indeed, the parent-child relationship should be a model for the others.

The second way in which the Five Relationships are hierarchical is from left to right: the left side of each pair takes precedence over the right. Age plays a role in three of these relationships (parent-child, older sibling-younger sibling, older friend-younger friend); gender in one (husband-wife); and political status or achievement in the other (ruler-subject). Because the relationships are hierarchical, expectations differ as to the roles played by each party. In particular, the lesser party must show deference and respect. This can be seen in the moral responsibilities that are assigned to each:

1. The child's duty toward the parent is *filial piety.*
2. The subject's duty toward the ruler is *righteousness.*
3. The wife's duty toward the husband is *fidelity.*
4. The younger sibling's duty toward the older is *respect.*
5. The younger friend's duty toward the older friend is *reliability.*

Just as the parent-child relationship takes precedence over and serves as a model for the other four relationships, the child's duty of filial piety is the highest concrete virtue and serves as a model for the other virtues. *The Analects* says, "*Filial piety* is the foundation for *ren.*"

The duties and responsibilities that are performed in everyday life should be backed by real intention, just as *li* should be accompanied by *ren* if "ceremonial living" is to be honest and sincere. The duties listed above are not simply ways of acting, but, more important, they are ways that should be nourished as deeply felt emotions.

> When he was asked about *filial piety,* Confucius said: "Nowadays, 'filial piety' means having the ability to support one's parents. But even our dogs and horses receive our support! Without *reverence,* what is the difference?"

Confucius is lamenting "nowadays" what he observes to be a cynical and superficial application of filial piety: simply giving one's parents material support in their old age. But such a performance of duty does not go far enough. It must be accompanied by real feeling.

If the hierarchical nature of the Five Relationships were the whole story, then Confucianism would be oppressive and autocratic. But the higher party also has duties and obligations toward the lower:

1. The parent's duty toward the child is *kindness.*
2. The ruler's duty toward the subject is *benevolence.*
3. The husband's duty toward the wife is *affection.*
4. The older sibling's duty toward the younger is *guidance.*
5. The older friend's duty toward the younger friend is *humane concern.*

Moreover, the higher party is not exempt from respectful criticism.

> Confucius said: "When serving your parents, you may criticize them gently.
> If they do not follow your advice, you may press further, but you should be
> even more respectful. Never let your efforts lead to anger."

It is a common misreading of Confucianism to see it as tyrannical. This is
partly because of the historical fact that Confucianism has tended toward
a hierarchical rigidity that sometimes fueled dissension and revolt. The imperial state in particular at times imposed harsh measures in the name of
Confucianism. With the overthrow of the dynastic system in the twentieth
century, Confucianism was condemned as the value system supporting imperial oppression. But the Confucian vision itself is hierarchical without
being autocratic, assigning rights and responsibilities to both sides of the
fundamental human relationships and grounding all relationships in the
values of humaneness and empathy.

> Confucius said: "A *jün-zi* who rejects *ren* is not worthy of the name *jün-zi*.
> A *jün-zi* does not violate *ren* even for a moment. Even when he is in a hurry,
> this is so. Even when he is in a difficult situation, this is so."

If the ruler acts in accordance with moral principles, he does not need to
impose his authority or resort to punishments.

> Confucius said: "If the ruler himself is upright, the people will act accordingly,
> even without the use of commands. If the ruler is not upright, the people will
> not obey him even if he commands them to do so."

The ruler commands the respect of his people, not by autocratic orders and
punishments, but by virtue of his own exemplary behavior. Like a *jün-zi*
lacking *ren,* a ruler who is not upright is not worthy of the title. "Let the
ruler be a ruler, the subject a subject, the father a father, the son a son," Confucius said, in what came to be known as "the rectification of names." Individuals should not merely fill a role, but they should identify themselves in
terms of their relationships and their reciprocal responsibilities. Far from
permitting tyranny, the Confucian tradition is, at its best, a profoundly
egalitarian political philosophy. When asked if it was justified for a subject
people to overthrow a corrupt leader, despite his status as king, Mencius
replied, "I do not call such a person 'king.' I call him 'tyrant.'" Though the
people should not overthrow a king, it is justifiable to overthrow a tyrant;
the name *king* (as well as any other honored name: parent, elder, friend)
must be deserved.

Tian

Confucius grounded his moral philosophy in religion: in particular, the religious rites of antiquity (*li*), which he generalized to describe all moral action. In another specific sense, Confucius based his life upon religious belief. In *The Analects*, Confucius refers frequently to a high god named *Tian* ("Heaven") as a personal protector and divine arbiter of justice.

There are seventeen passages in *The Analects* referring to *Tian*. Confucius was described as a kind of prophet, "a bell with a wooden clapper" reminding people of Heaven's intention. Confucius believed he had been given a task by Heaven to restore the early Zhou ideal of social harmony and order. *Tian* intended that Confucius should restore the ritual culture of the past, and that his teachings should spread far and wide. His brief autobiography expresses his confidence in a personal mandate from Heaven:

> The Master said, "When I was fifteen years old, I became serious about my studies. When I was thirty, I took my stand in *li*. When I was forty, I was no longer uncertain about right and wrong. When I was fifty, I learned the will of Heaven. At sixty, I heard the will of Heaven with an obedient ear, and at seventy, I could do whatever my heart desired without overstepping proper bounds."

Especially when threatened, Confucius fell back on his belief in Heaven's support:

> Confucius was threatened with his life in the state of Kuang. He said: "King Wen is dead, but his legacy lives on here [in me], does it not? If *Tian* intended for civilization to die out, it would not have been preserved for later generations. But if *Tian* does not intend for civilization to die out, what can the people of Kuang do to me?"

A similar incident occurred when a feudal lord named Huan Tui, enraged with Confucius's meddling in state affairs, sent men to put him to death. Hearing of this,

> The Master said, "Heaven engendered the virtue that is in me. What can Huan Tui do to me?"

Frequently in *The Analects*, Confucius laments his lack of recognition. Heaven alone understands him:

The Master said, "Alas! No one understands me. By studying things on a lower level, I reach to a higher level. The one who understands me is *Tian*."

Tian is clearly anthropomorphized: Heaven knows, commands, intends, punishes, and responds to men. Most important, Heaven is the final judge and authority for morality and virtue. Confucius appeals to Heaven as the ground of his ethical convictions.

Confucius interpreted his own life in explicitly religious terms—appealing to the belief in a Heavenly mandate and grounding moral action in religious ritual.

Confucian Values and Behaviors

In summary, these are the key principles of classical Confucianism:

1. education in history and culture (poetry, music, painting, and calligraphy)
2. the cultivation of harmonious, hierarchical relations in one's family and social life
3. the importance of *ren*—human-heartedness—in all social interaction (*ren* as the basis for *li*)
4. the underlying unity of all persons, expressed as "empathy" or "recip-rocity"
5. the veneration of ancestors
6. the grounding of moral teachings and ethical principles in a religious or cosmic reality (*Tian*)

In later centuries, Confucians have expanded and elaborated upon these principles, but they are still fundamental. In this sense, the basic values and ideals of Confucianism have remained constant for more than two millennia.

THE TEXTS AND TEACHINGS OF CLASSICAL TAOISM: NATURAL HARMONY

The Taoist Classics

The major classics of the School of the Dao were the *Dao de jing* and the *Zhuang-zi.*

The *Dao de jing* was compiled in its present form later than the *Zhuang-zi,* but tradition places Lao-zi before Zhuang-zi, and much of the work dates to 480–360 B.C.E., so Lao-zi will be examined first. The book, whose title means "The Classic of the *Dao* and Its Power," consists of sayings and poetic aphorisms that were probably compiled by a group of individuals rather than being written by a single author. These sayings are brief, cryptic, and imagistic, and therefore, subject to many interpretations. It is no wonder that the *Dao de jing* is the source of well over one hundred English translations, often so different from one another that it is hard to believe that they are translations of the same work.

The discussion below will look at some of the principal ideas of the *Dao de jing*. It should be noted, however, that these ideas are often expressed in symbolic or imagistic hints. The language of the book is vague and perplexing, suggestive of a mystical or shamanistic orientation toward the cosmos. For example, the predominant images employed to describe the *Dao* are "mother," "ancestor," or "storehouse." The ideal person is likened to an infant, a young girl, or an old man. The goal of life is to imitate or resemble water, a mirror, a valley, or an "uncarved block."

Reconstructing the community that composed the *Dao de jing* is extraordinarily difficult. Modern scholars think that the book was a compilation of images, ideas, and sayings that were current among a group of individuals who were seeking alternatives to the more predominant values of the early Warring States Period (475–221 B.C.E.). One scholar, Michael LaFargue, has helpfully identified "targets" of the Lao-ist critiques, as well as "stances" that are suggested (they are rarely made explicit) in the *Dao de jing*. These themes, as well as the images employed to express the Lao-ist orientation, will be examined in the discussion to follow.

Table 2.1
Targets and Stances of the Dao de jing

Targets	Stances
• vs. exciting and "desirable" things • vs. the cultivation of "showy" personal qualities • vs. status-seeking by self-assertion • vs. impressive and strict rule • vs. problem-solving by force and confrontation • vs. social improvement programs, whether material or educational	be content with what one already has true substance often appears unimpressive or negative self-effacing people gain the most true esteem a deferential and flexible attitude wins the allegiance of the people war, even in victory, is "unlucky" organic goodness and social harmony will be present without conscious intervention

Source: Michael LaFargue, The Tao of the Tao Te Ching, Albany: State University of New York Press, 1992.

What is known of Zhuang-zi (Master Zhuang) is derived from a book in thirty-three chapters by the same name, seven of which can accurately be ascribed to Zhuang-zi or his immediate contemporaries. These seven are known as the Inner Chapters:

1. Floating and Wandering
2. A Discussion of the Sameness of Things
3. Principles of Caring for Life
4. In the Human World
5. Powerful Charms
6. Great Ancestor-Teacher
7. Countering Political Authority

Though they share the same basic orientation, the *Lao-zi* and *Zhuang-zi* books have a very different style and tone. Whereas the *Dao de jing* consists of brief and often obscure verses, the *Zhuang-zi* is a book of stories, anecdotes, quips, queries, and conversations. It is written in a more fluid style than the *Dao de jing,* more like prose than poetry.

Zhuang-zi was not a system-builder. His was an attitude of toleration, pointing out the relativity of all distinctions and hierarchies, and offering new perspectives to a society made sick by competition, entanglement, anxiety, and futility. Yet Zhuang-zi's solution to these social problems is not social, but individual and attitudinal. The trap people are in is of their own making; life itself is free, peaceful, and joyful, and people realize this by retiring from worldly affairs and "sitting in forgetfulness," contemplating the universal Dao.

The Teachings of Classical Taoism

Dao

Both Confucianism and Taoism emphasize *harmony.* But whereas Confucianism seeks harmony within social relations, the classical Taoists strove for harmony between humans and the natural world. If for Confucius the central image or standard of life is ritual and court ceremony, the Taoists base themselves on the "Way of Nature": the *Dao.*

Though the *Dao* is associated with the Taoists (*Dao* and *Tao* are the same character in Chinese), they were not the only school to make use of the term. Confucius, too, uses the word *Dao,* but his is a moral and social *Dao,* the *Dao* of "Right Action" or "Righteousness." Thinking of the *Dao* as a path, Confucius advocates following the Path of the sage kings, who ruled with wisdom, justice, and benevolence. In this sense, one is either on the path or off it, either living as a self-cultivated *jūn-zi* or living as a self-interested "small man." To live in accordance with the *Dao* is to follow the path of righteousness and virtue.

The Confucian *Dao* is the path of service. It is a Way that helps people to care about others and not solely about themselves:

> Confucius said: "Wealth and high status are what every man desires, but if they are attained in violation of the *Dao,* they should not be kept. Poverty and low status are what every man hates, but if they are avoided in violation of the *Dao,* they should not be avoided."

Confucius's *Dao* is straightforward. There is nothing mystical about it. It is also completely human:

> Confucius said: "It is persons who make the *Dao* great, not the *Dao* that makes persons great."

This is to say that the *Dao* is not something outside human affairs. In fact, it is principally a product of human activity. It is a Way of giving, and of sacrificing personal self-interest for the benefit of others.

By contrast, Lao-zi's *Dao* is a metaphysical abstraction. He calls it

- "the One"
- "the nameless"
- "non-being"
- "mother"
- "ancestor"
- "the great form"

The *Dao de jing* describes the *Dao* as the ultimate source of all existence, most evident at the beginning of time, before the division of reality into the "ten thousand things." Because the world is now differentiated—"many" rather than "One"—it is difficult to perceive or "know" the *Dao.* Lao-zi can "point to it" but can never "pin it down." It is "invisible," "inaudible," "vague," "elusive," "profound," "distant," "vast." It is indeterminate. It cannot be described. In fact, it can hardly be named:

> The *Dao* that can be spoken is not the Eternal *Dao.*
> The name that can be spoken is not the Eternal Name...

We look for it but do not see it; its name is "Invisible." We listen for it but do not hear it; its name is "Inaudible." We reach for it but do not find it; its name is "Minute." These three cannot be further understood, and they dissolve into one. Above, it is not bright; below, it is not dark. Unravelled, it cannot be given any name.

It returns to non-being.

This is called "the shapeless shape, the insubstantial form." It is called "Indistinct." From the front you cannot see its front. From the back you cannot see its back.

Grasp the *Dao* of old in order to guide things in the present. Then you will know the primeval birth. This is called "the weave of *Dao.*"

Nature and Spontaneity

The model of the *Dao* is nature (*zi-ran*), a process of *non-intentional self-evolution.* Nature is "being-in-itself," at once changing and yet unchanging; passive, unobtrusive, and weak, and yet also moving, creative, and powerful. In Chinese, the word *zi-ran* means literally "self so-ing" or "self-becoming." Nature comes into existence and grows by virtue of its own inner dynamics; it is not coerced or manipulated from the outside.

The Way of Nature is cyclical. The seasons succeed one another, the heavens revolve around the earth, death returns to life. And this theme of return and recovery is central to the *Dao de jing.*

> There is a thing, formed by chaos, born prior to Heaven and Earth, silent and shapeless! It stands alone, unchanged by exterior forces. Its motion is circular, and it never tires. It is capable of being the Mother of everything under Heaven. I do not know its name, but if forced to, I'll call it "*Dao*"; if forced to, I'll name it "Great."
>
> Great, it is flowing.
> Flowing, it becomes distant.
> Distant, it returns ...
>
> Reversion is the way the *Dao* moves.
> Weakness is what the *Dao* employs.
> The 10,000 creatures under Heaven were born from Being,
> And Being was born from Non-Being.

Lao-zi emphasizes the "changelessness" of the *Dao.* Zhuang-zi, by contrast, emphasizes its "constant change." According to Zhuang-zi, the enlightened individual accepts change—even identifies with change and celebrates the process of change. One who accepts change without anxiety has no desires, attachments, or strong emotions. Such a person has no need for intellectual knowledge, which "pins things down" with linguistic labels. And one who accepts change has no particular fear of death, but meets death with equanimity and peace of mind. In one of the more famous parables of the *Zhuang-zi* book, Zhuang-zi is found singing joyfully and beating on a drum at his wife's grave, celebrating the unending process of change. To be "at ease" with change is to be "attuned" to the *Dao.*

The proper response to a changing world is spontaneity: responding to change and flowing with it. "Spontaneity" is the "natural" response; in fact, both *nature* and *spontaneity* can be used to translate *zi-ran.* To live spontaneously is to live in the spirit of the *Dao*, and Zhuang-zi describes this as acting effortlessly, moving purposelessly, going where there is least resistance, responding to a shifting situation. He illustrates such a life with the tale of a famous butcher, Cook Ding, who is so attuned to the oxen he cuts that he has not sharpened his knife for nineteen years. By "placing the knife, which has space, into the spaces between the joints, which have no space, my knife plays in emptiness." His employer is so impressed by Cook Ding's skill that he sees it as a model for life itself. Cook Ding works without effort because he has achieved a natural harmony.

Non-Action and Uselessness

Confucianism upholds intention, deliberation, and action. But for the Taoists, the Way of the *Dao* is natural and non-purposive. Lao-zi describes this naturalness as *wu-wei,* "non-action"—meaning non-purposive or non-manipulative action. *Wu-wei* can be defined as

- taking no artificial action
- non-interference
- letting things take their own course
- spontaneous transformation
- non-ado

In practical terms, it means responding to a situation rather than trying to create or mold a situation, respecting natural inclinations rather than repressing them, nourishing what is natural rather than building artificially, dredging and widening existing channels rather than digging new ones.

Paradoxically this "non-active action" accomplishes more than deliberate, manipulative behavior. Lao-zi says, "*Wu wei er wu bu wei*": "Do nothing, and there is nothing that is not done." A number of passages in the *Dao de jing* illustrate this principle:

> The most marvelous things are like water. Water can benefit the 10,000 creatures without competing, and settle in places most people despise. In these ways it is like the *Dao.*
>
> The weakest things under Heaven ride like a stallion over the hardest. The things which have no substance enter the places which have no space. Because of this, I understand the advantage of *wu-wei.* Few have the capacity to reach an understanding of the wordless teaching or of the advantage of *wu-wei.*
>
> Under Heaven, there is nothing softer or weaker than water. Yet, in attacking what is stubborn and strong, nothing can surpass it. That is why nothing can replace it. Everyone knows that the soft overcomes the stubborn, and the weak overcomes the strong, yet no one can put this into practice.

The sage understands the value of weakness and quiescence, and "acts like water" by retreating into "places that most people despise."

> He is whole because he's crooked, straight because he's bent, full because he's hollow, new because he's worn; he has because he lacks, he is amazed because there is so much.
>
> This is why the sage embraces the One and becomes the model of the universe. He does not show himself, and so he is luminous. He does not consider himself right, and so he is revered. He does not claim credit, and so he is rewarded. He does not boast, and so he endures.
>
> It is because he does not compete with anyone that no one under Heaven competes with him. When the ancients said, "He is whole because he is crooked," those were not empty words. Truly, he is whole to the end.

Zhuang-zi's interpretation of this "purposelessness" is *wu-yong zhi yong,* "the usefulness of the useless." To be useless in practical terms frees the individual to grow naturally and live long. Zhuang-zi emphasizes the universality and immanence of the *Dao.* The *Dao* is present all around, and if people can free themselves from social restraint, intellectual pride, worry, and the fear of death, they can become one with the *Dao* in a spirit of purposelessness and play.

He illustrates this by telling stories. One story he tells is about a carpenter who sees value in trees purely in terms of their material worth. He cuts them down and uses their wood for houses, boats, and coffins. Coming upon a tree with gnarled branches, poisonous leaves, and a rotted trunk, he scorns it and walks on by. But Zhuang-zi points out that because the tree is "useless" from a conventional point of view, it has grown to a magnificent size and has lived for hundreds of years. "Take it easy, and have a nap under it," he advises. "Axes will not shorten its life, nothing will ever harm it. It is because it has never been put to use that it has not suffered injury or harm." The carpenter is enlightened by Zhuang-zi's words. "Most people would consider it unlucky," he admits," but it is these same qualities that the sage recognizes as very lucky indeed!"

In addition to gnarled, rotting trees, Zhuang-zi lionizes "useless men"—cripples, hunchbacks, and madmen. Because they are not subjected to conscription and military service, they are able to "live out the years that Heaven granted them." Zhuang-zi turns conventional values upside down: what the world finds useful is destroyed in the process of being used. It is better to be useless.

Zhuang-zi concludes: "Everyone understands the usefulness of usefulness, but few understand the usefulness of uselessness!"

The Uncarved Block

According to the *Dao de jing*, the goal of life is to resemble, in one image, an "uncarved block." In keeping with the idea of a return to an original condition, the Taoists advocate reverting to a precivilized state of simplicity ... without schools, government, or institutions. Quoting Lao-zi:

Reduce the size of the state and the population. Let the weapons of war never be used. Let the people stay close to home because they do not take death lightly. Even if there are ships and chariots, there is no place to ride in them. Even if there are weapons and armor, there is no place to display them. The people revert to the use of knotted cords, they regard their food as sweet and their clothing as beautiful, and they are content in their homes and happy with their everyday lives. Though neighboring states can see one another, and the sounds of chickens and dogs can be heard from one to the other, yet the people of each state will grow old and die without ever having had contact with one another.

In such a simple, basic state, there is no need for offices and courts, or books and schools—no need even for words and numbers. The kind of wisdom and knowledge praised by the Confucians is anathema to the

Taoists. "Abandon sageliness, wisdom, humanity, righteousness, skill, and profit!" Lao-zi cries, and "recover the origin" by returning to infancy and ignorance. Lao-zi, whom many regard to be a great sage, called himself an idiot.

> Stop learning! You'll stop worrying.
> Is there really that much difference between "yes" and "no"? Is there really any difference at all between "good" and "evil"?
> People are drunk with pleasure, as they are when eating a great feast or ascending a tower in the spring. I alone am quiet. I have left no sign, like an infant who has not yet smiled. I am weary, like a man with no home to return to.
> Most people have more than they need. I alone seem to have too little. Mine is the mind of a fool—it's empty!
> Common people show off their clarity. I alone am floating in the dark.
> Common people are committed to their investigations. I alone am all mixed up.
> I'm as calm as the sea, drifting with the wind.
> Most people have a purpose. I alone am aimless and uncouth. I alone am different from other people, and value being fed by the Mother.

Lao-zi makes fun of knowledge—and language itself—because words mark distinctions and obscure the fundamental unity of persons, things, and Dao.

> One who knows does not speak; one who speaks does not know.

Lao-zi mocks Confucius and the Confucian values of benevolence, righteousness, and propriety; indeed, he goes so far as to call them symptoms of decline.

> When the Great *Dao* declined, the doctrines of "benevolence" and "righteousness" appeared. When "knowledge" and "wisdom" emerged, there was great hypocrisy. It is only when relatives can't get along that they talk about "filial children" and "loving parents," only when the state is in disorder that there are "loyal ministers."
> Abandon "sageliness" and "wisdom," and the people will benefit a hundredfold. Abandon "benevolence" and "righteousness," and the people will again be deferential to their parents and loving towards their children. Abandon clever words and profit, and there will be no more thieves or robbers. Those things [which should be abandoned] are good in appearance, but insubstantial. So, let the people have something they can follow:

manifest simplicity;
embrace the uncarved block;
reduce selfishness;
have few desires.

Lao-zi's virtues are not power and accomplishment, but emptiness and tranquility.

For Zhuang-zi, the way to become an "uncarved block" is to recover ignorance. This is reflected in many passages in which Zhuang-zi makes fun of knowledge and elegant speech. The only kind of knowledge that Zhuang-zi admires is knowledge that comes from experience or intuition. As can be seen from the story of Cook Ding, Zhuang-zi is a great admirer of skill: the skill of a butcher, a woodsman, or a craftsman. All of these skills involve "knowing *how*" to do something by experience and feel—but Zhuang-zi has nothing but disdain for the kind of rational, intellectual knowledge one gets from books and teachers.

Zhuang-zi points out that most of the assumptions, customs, habits, and deeply held beliefs of humans are relative to their limited perspective. Here is one example from Chapter 2 of the *Book of Zhuang-zi,* entitled "A Discussion of the Sameness of Things."

Humans don't sleep in marshes or trees, but leeches and monkeys do—who is to say which is the "proper place" to live? Humans don't eat grass, snakes, or mice, but deer and hawks do—who is to say which has the "proper taste"? Humans admire "classic beauties," but "if fish saw them they would dive to the bottom of the stream, if birds saw them they would fly away, and if deer saw them they would run off"—who is to say what is "true beauty"? "From my point of view," he concludes, "the standards of 'benevolence and righteousness' and the paths of 'true and false' are knotted and confused. How would I know which is which?"

The human perspective is narrow, socially and historically conditioned, and species-specific. The *Book of Zhuang-zi* opens with the mythic account of a great fish, whose name is *Kun* or "fish roe" (a humorous name, as this gigantic creature has a name describing fish eggs, which are small). Kun morphs into a bird, whose name is *Peng.* Peng's wingspan is so great that the sky appears to be covered with clouds. Peng flies off to the Lake of Heaven in the Southern Darkness.

Looking up at this magnificent creature, a cicada and a morning dove laugh incredulously. Content with their own skips and hops, they cannot see why anyone would want to fly "ninety thousand miles to the south." Zhuang-zi comments: "What do these two tiny creatures know? Petty knowledge cannot approach great knowledge. The short-lived cannot approach the long-lived."

Zhuang-zi is hinting that a broader perspective *is* possible, that wisdom *is* attainable—but not based upon traditional social standards and expectations. Conventional knowledge is relative and petty, like the limited perspective of the cicada and morning dove.

The human perspective is relative, and so too is language. Language is merely arbitrary sounds, without any real connection to the realities that they designate. Language, terms, names, and categories all are relative, and the best way to approach life is to dispense with them entirely.

> We say that some things exist and others do not; some statements are "true" and others are "false." If we deem them non-existent, we don't see them. If we deem them existent, we say we "know" them. So, what's non-existent depends upon what's existent, and what's existent depends upon what's non-existent. We can say that they give birth to each other, just as "life" and "death" give birth to each other, and "possible" and "impossible" give birth to each other. Because there is "true," so there is "false." Because there is "false," so there is "true."
>
> But the sage does not see things in this way, and illuminates all things with a heavenly gaze. For him, as soon as there is "this," there is "that." As soon as there is "that," there is "this." "This" has its "true and false," and "that" has its "true and false." There really is no difference between them. Isn't it better to say that there is no "this" or "that" at all? If we can reach a point of non-discrimination, I call that "the axle of the Dao." When the axle is in the center, the wheel spins without stopping.

What Zhuang-zi seems to be saying is that conventional values and judgments depend upon a language of "this and that," "right and wrong." But if one can dispense with that language, one can attain a higher perspective, the overarching viewpoint of the Peng bird, whose "heavenly gaze" is vast and all-inclusive. From such a perspective, there is no need for the petty discriminations of people like the Confucians, whose perspective is short-sighted and whose lives are short-lived.

The Sage

The only non-relative perspective is that of the Dao itself. And this is theoretically possible for the enlightened sage, the *zhen-ren* or "Perfected

One." The character *zhen* means "perfected" or "true." Etymologically, it shows a figure standing tall, beneath a character meaning "to see or survey," beneath another character meaning "transformation." So, the Perfected One stands above the rest, surveying the spontaneous transformations of the universe. The *zhen-ren* is like the Peng bird, with an expansive vision, a mind of equanimity and imperturbability, and a lifespan rivaling the oldest living creatures in the world.

The *Book of Zhuang-zi* describes the Perfected One in this way:

- The sage has no fear of poverty, and takes no pride in wealth.
- The sage has no fear of "failure," and takes no pride in "success."
- The sage makes no plans, but acts naturally and spontaneously.
- The sage "does not dream in sleep, does not wake with a start."
- "His breathing is deep and steady, and comes from his heels."
- The sage can "climb up high without being frightened, enter water without getting wet, enter fire without being burned."
- The sage lives out his Heaven-appointed years; his life is not cut short— and yet, the sage "does not understand loving life or fearing death."

The Perfected One has "a mind like a mirror" and sees things simply for what they are, not as objects of knowledge or tools for use. This is only possible by letting go of egotistical concerns, such as power, wealth, and self-preservation. This "mirror-like mind" is achieved by "emptying oneself of self" (Zhuang-zi says, "his mind forgets"), and adopting a perspective of indifference or "disinterestedness." Thus, one achieves mystical unity with the Dao.

How can an ordinary person reach such a sublime state? Zhuang-zi explains how to become "perfected":

Focus your will. What cannot be heard with your ears can be heard with your mind. What cannot be heard with your mind can be heard with your vital spirit (*qi*)... The spirit is empty and waits on all things. Only the Dao can gather this emptiness. Emptiness is the fasting of the mind.

The fasting of the mind means forgetting the Confucian values of benevolence (*ren*) and righteousness (*yi*), forgetting the Confucian practices of ritual (*li*) and music, and, further still, "sitting down and forgetting everything." Zhuang-zi summarizes this as "sitting in forgetfulness"—perhaps a kind of meditation in which the practitioner empties the mind of thoughts and images.

For Lao-zi as well, sagehood is attained through meditative practices, practices later elaborated by the Taoist tradition, as will be seen in Chapter 3. Lao-zi describes meditation in this way:

Can you carry the soul and embrace the One without letting go?

Can you concentrate your *qi* [breath, vital energy] and attain the weakness of an infant?

Can you polish the mirror of mystery so as to make it spotless?

Can you practice *wu-wei* [non-action] in loving the nation and governing the people?

Can you adopt the role of the female when the gates of Heaven open and close?

Can you abandon all knowing even as your intelligence penetrates the universe?

To give birth and to rear, to give birth but not to possess, to act but not to depend on the outcome, to lead but not to command: this is called "mysterious power."

Lao-zi says revert to infancy, the uncarved block, the empty mirror. This is the way to act non-aggressively, and to realize the mysterious power of non-being.

Taoist Values and Behaviors

The values and practices of classical Taoism can be summarized as follows:

1. the sense that reality extends beyond the observable realm and includes spiritual power;
2. the rejection of conventional values and behaviors, including those associated with Confucius and his followers;
3. the practice of meditation and physical exercises that reinforce the unity of an individual's psychological, emotional, physical, and spiritual identity;
4. the belief in harmony between persons, the natural world, and the cosmos; and
5. the belief that harmony has practical benefits, from social welfare to individual health and longevity.

COSMIC HARMONY: YIN-YANG COSMOLOGY

A third strand of classical Chinese religion is *yin-yang* cosmology. Though fully developed much later than Confucius and Zhuang-zi, its roots are very ancient, and the basic elements of *yin-yang* thought were taken for granted by all Chinese, including the Confucians and Taoists.

By *cosmology* is meant the theory of how the "cosmos"—both physical and non-physical reality—is structured. This includes myths of the origins of the universe, sometimes called "cosmogonic" myths.

According to a seminal Han Dynasty book, the universe has evolved in this way:

> In the beginning, before the "ten thousand things" had come into existence, there was nothing but a steaming, roiling, churning sea.

In Chinese, this condition of existence—unformed, undifferentiated, disorderly, insubstantial—is called *hun-dun*, "chaos." The characters *hun* and *dun* include the water element, showing the liquid, flowing, form-free nature of primordial existence. (In the Cantonese dialect, the same characters are pronounced *won-ton*, so the soup one orders from Chinese restaurants is "chaos soup.")

> Arising from the waters was the cosmic breath, so thick and cloudlike that it blanketed the world.

This breath is called in Chinese *qi* (sounds like "chee"), a word meaning "energy," "pneuma," "vital spirit," "air," or "breath." *Qi* is the vital energy that is formed by the activity of creation. In Chinese cosmology, all things in existence are the manifestations of this originally formless energy.

> The *qi* moved and changed, with the airy, lighter *qi* rising upwards to form the heavens: the sun, stars, and fiery planets. The heavenly *qi* made up the spiritual realm: gods, ghostly beings, the souls of the living and spirits of the dead. The heavier, more turbid *qi* congealed and solidified, falling downwards to form the earth, the moon, and the waters of the earth. The earthly *qi* made up the physical realm: the earth and the physical aspects of living human beings (their organs and bones).

The heavenward expanding, rising, and moving of *qi*-energy is called *yang*. The earthbound congealing, sinking, and solidifying of *qi*-substance is called *yin*. *Yin* and *yang* describe not things, but the way that *qi* moves and develops: the movement of expanding (*yang*) or congealing (*yin*), rising (*yang*) or sinking (*yin*), moving (*yang*) or solidifying (*yin*). They are like breathing ("breath" is a common translation of *qi*): *yin* is inhalation; *yang* is exhalation.

> The *yin* and *yang* movement of *qi* is oscillating, similar to the movement of breath. Over time, this cycle of movement formed the seasons in alternation, with the expanding, fiery, hot, and verdant energy of summer (*yang*) moving gradually to the receding, icy, hibernating, dormant energy of winter (*yin*), then evolving back to summer, in an endless rotation of creation, rest, and renewal.

This pattern, or path of existence, is called *Dao,* the cosmic Way.

This chapter will look more closely at the various components of this cosmogonic myth—*Dao, qi, yin* and *yang*—in greater detail below, but here are a few essential elements.

1. Despite the diversity and multiplicity of the "ten thousand things" that make up existence, the world is essentially constituted of a single substance or *energy* (*qi*).
2. This single energy has two fundamental ways of being, or patterns of motion, called *yin* ("congealing," "solidifying," "sinking") and *yang* ("expanding," "spreading," "rising").
3. Just as breath cannot exist without both inhalation and exhalation, energy—and therefore the cosmos itself—cannot exist without both *yin* and *yang.*
4. The cosmos is eternally in the *process* of "coming into existence," as the oscillating pattern of inhalation and exhalation is unending; thus, the *Dao* itself is "never complete," ever evolving.

The Book of Changes

Both Confucianism and Taoism trace their origins to the classical period and its seminal texts: particularly *The Analects* of Confucius; the *Dao de jing,* attributed to Lao-zi; and the *Book of Zhuang-zi.* However, both traditions claim a common source in an earlier text. This text figures prominently in both the Confucian Classics and the Taoist Canon. It was said to have been edited by Confucius himself, or, alternatively, to have been revealed by astral deities to Taoist masters. Confucians and Taoists both regard it as descriptive of the cosmological origins of the universe. Today, people worldwide employ it as a manual of divination and prognostication. That text is the *Yi Jing* (often romanized *I Ching*) or *The Book of Changes.*

The *Yi Jing* that survives today was probably a product of a later period (the Han Dynasty if not later still), but was certainly based upon a cosmological system that predates the Confucian and Taoist schools. Confucius refers to the text by name, and the books of Lao-zi and Zhuang-zi allude to its teachings. All claim it as their own. So, the story of the origins of Confucianism and Taoism in the classical period must include *The Book of Changes.*

The Book of Changes and its commentaries (particularly the Han Dynasty Great Appendix) describe the origins and structure of the universe. Like modern physics, which has discovered that it is not *matter* but *energy* that is the basic building block of the universe, the *Yi Jing* teaches that all things in existence are composed of the same cosmic "breath," or *qi.* It is important to think of *qi* in terms of energy rather than matter because *qi* is characterized by change, alternation, and fluidity in motion. *Qi* is never fixed or static. Nor is it exclusively material. Unseen or immaterial "things," such as gods, ghosts, and spirits, are also composed of *qi*, and, as discussed in Chapter 4, human beings themselves are a material-spiritual continuum, with the "body" and the "soul" equally composed of *qi*—not a mind *and* body, or soul *and* flesh, but rather a human spiritual-psycho-physical whole that grows and develops through the movements of energy/breath.

It is helpful to think of *qi* in a verbal rather than a nominal sense—as moving and acting, rather than being. Often, *qi* is translated as "breath," but it is more accurate to think of *qi* as "breathing," that is, as the "activity" of breath. The activity of breath, of course, is *inhalation* and *exhalation.* In Chinese cosmology, there can be no matter without energy, no thing without motion, in the same sense that it is inconceivable to think of breath without its activity of breathing—breathing in (inhalation) and breathing out (exhalation). *The Book of Changes* describes inhalation as *yin* energy/motion, and exhalation as *yang* energy/motion.

The various constituents of the universe come into existence by means of the *activity* of *qi:* expanding and rising (*yang*) produces the heavens, fire, and the sun; and congealing and sinking (*yin*) produces the earth, water, and the moon. All other things and activities—the four seasons and the ten thousand things that are themselves produced by the seasons—are made up of a combination of *yin* and *yang* energies, the inhaling and exhaling of *qi.*

Qi

Qi in its natural state—prior to the existence of the heavens, earth, and ten thousand things—is amorphous, undifferentiated, vaporous, or cloud-like. It is spiritual energy. One translation of *qi* is the Greek word *pneuma,* which, according to the *Oxford English Dictionary,* means "wind, breath, or spirit, or something that is blown or breathed." Etymologically, the character for *qi* shows the steam or vapor produced when cooking rice. It is a pictograph of rice in a pot: the intense pressure of the cooking causes the heavy lid of the pot to jump and rattle. It is notable that the cosmic origins of the universe are associated in the Chinese imagination with food. (Remember the primordial soup of preexistence: *hun-dun,* or *won-ton.*) Just so, *qi*—originally the vapor of cooked rice—is the cosmic energy "feeding" or sustaining all things.

Qi is the cosmic breath, vapor, steam, energy, *pneuma*. Its motion brings the heavens and earth, the sun and the moon, the four seasons, and myriad things into existence. That motion is alternately rising and expanding (*yang*) or sinking and congealing (*yin*). In *The Book of Changes, yin* and *yang* are represented by broken and unbroken lines, respectively. They are combined in groups of three (trigrams), in eight possible permutations read from bottom to top.

These trigrams are then combined to form sixty-four hexagrams (each trigram paired with the other eight: 8 x 8 = 64), which forms the structure of the *Yi Jing* as a divination manual.

What the *Changes* illustrates are fundamental principles of the universe and its operations: the fluctuation of *qi*-energy in combinations of *yin* and *yang*, the consonance or symmetry of natural forces and human affairs, and the potential for mastering and manipulating these forces for personal and social benefit.

Two of the most important characteristics of *yin* and *yang* have already been presented. First, *yin* and *yang* are not things; they are not substantial. Rather, they are the "activities of *qi*": processes of change and movement. Second, *yin* and *yang* literally cannot exist without each other. They contrast, but do not conflict, just as inhalation and exhalation, though opposite, are both necessary for the sustenance of life. This does not mean that things possess *yin* and *yang* in equal measure, however. Examining the sixty-four hexagrams, it can be seen that most are weighted one way or the other. The extremes are Hexagram #1, in the upper right-hand corner, called *qian*, and Hexagram #2, immediately to its left, called *kun*. *Qian*, consisting of six *yang* lines, is associated with masculinity; *kun*, consisting of six *yin* lines, is associated with femininity. These are exceptional, however: all of the other hexagrams—the vast majority of things and forces in the universe—are made up of both *yang* and *yin* to a greater or lesser extent.

陽　　　　　　　　　　　　　　　　　陰
Yang　　　　　　　　　　　　　　　　　Yin

The etymology of the characters for *yin* and *yang* is again illustrative of their meaning. Notice first that the characters have a common element: on the left side is a symbol meaning "mound, hill, or mountain." *Yin* and *yang*

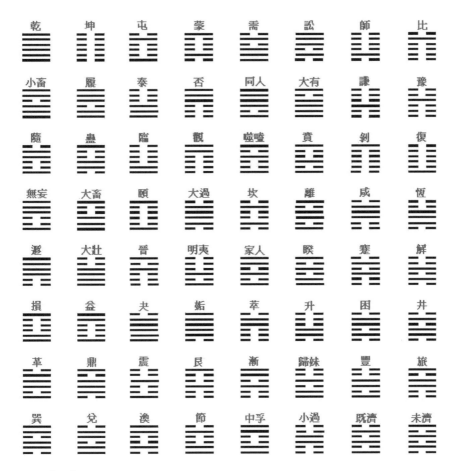

Sixty-four hexagrams.

refer first to natural, topographical features of the landscape. Recall that *yang* energy produced the sun. The character for *yang* has the sun as a constitutive element (the upper right-hand corner of the character); below the sun is a symbol that is more difficult to decipher but is thought by scholars to represent either the rays of the sun or, more likely, an ancient astrological instrument that was oriented toward the sun, like a sextant. As a whole, the original meaning of *yang* is "the sunny side of a mountain." The right side of the character for *yin* represents something covered (as by a roof), cloudy or shaded. It can be thought of as "the shady side of a mountain."

Trigrams of the Diagram of the Great Ultimate (*Yin-Yang*).

What is the relationship between the topographical symbolism of the characters for *yin* and *yang* and the inhaling and exhaling of *qi?* The key similarity is their complementarity, the idea that the one cannot exist without the other. There can be no sunny side without a shady side, just as there can be no exhalation without inhalation. Shade is evident only on a sunny day, and sun without shade would be only possible in a flat and featureless landscape—a landscape unimaginable to the ancient Chinese, whose country is full of mountains, valleys, forests, and lakes. Clearly, for the Chinese, *yang* and *yin* are as natural as the four seasons, the sun and the moon, and the mountains and the rivers.

From this beginning, it is possible to generate all of the concepts associated with *yin* and *yang*. Again, it is more helpful to think of *yin* and *yang* as forces or potentialities—qualities of existence—rather than thinking of them as forms of matter. Put grammatically, *yin* and *yang* are more like verbs or adjectives than nouns.

Yin	*Yang*
shady	sunny
watery	fiery
still	active
cold	hot
dormant	fertile
inhaling	exhaling
earthbound	heavenly
human	god-like
female	male
receptive	aggressive
emotional	rational
responsive	initiating

Yin and *yang* describe qualities of existence, tendencies, or potentialities; they are not things in themselves.

It was pointed out that the vast majority of things in the universe are composed of both *yang*-energy and *yin*-energy. Very few are exclusively one or the other, and, at the same time, few are perfectly balanced. Moreover, all things in the universe are characterized by movement and flux; the proportions of *yin* and *yang* energy, like the oscillations of breath, are con-

The Diagram of the Great Ultimate with signs of the Chinese zodiac.

stantly expanding and contracting. The familiar *yin-yang* diagram (called *tai-ji* in Chinese, "the Diagram of the Great Ultimate") should be seen as a representation of fluid motion.

The Diagram of the Great Ultimate shows that existence is fluid and changing, like the progression of the seasons. Even at the height of *yin,* there is the kernel of *yang,* and at the height of *yang,* there is the kernel of *yin.*

The Five Phases

How do the forces of *yin* and *yang* produce the "ten thousand things" of the world? Like the theory of forms of the ancient Greeks, the Chinese cosmologists of the Han Dynasty elaborated a system of Five Elements or Phases. Some scholars have equated these Five Phases with the "elements" of Greek thought (later elaborated as the atoms or molecules of modern science):

- wood
- fire
- earth
- metal
- water

This rendering of the Five Phases is misleading, however, as it ignores the dynamic quality of Chinese cosmology. The Five Phases are better understood as follows:

- the *growing* of wood/vegetation
- the *burning* of fire
- the *nurturing/enveloping* of earth
- the *hardening/fusing* of metal
- the *moistening* of water

The Five Phases interact with one another (nothing in Chinese cosmology is self-contained), manifesting *yang* and *yin* movement.

Yang interaction is generative: water (moistening) produces wood (growing), just as rain allows vegetation to grow; vegetation provides the fuel for fire; fire (such as volcanic activity and other natural forces of fusion) produces the earth; the pressure of the earth produces metal; and from the depths of the earth (where metal is found) come springs that replenish the rivers and lakes. *Yin* interactions are suppressive: moisture overcomes fire, fire smelts metal, metal cuts through vegetation, vegetation penetrates the earth, earth forms in natural and man-made dams to impede the flow of water.

Thus, all of existence is seen in terms of *processes* and *interactions*, rather than the static elements or objects of Western science and cosmology.

In the Song Dynasty, a Neo-Confucian scholar named Zhang Zai wrote a *Commentary on the Supreme Ultimate* (*Tai ji tu shuo*) with the diagram pictured below.

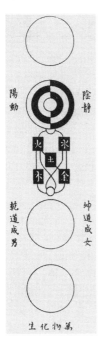

Zhang Zai's diagram of the Great Ultimate.

The inscriptions read as follows:

- beneath the lowest empty circle (bottom four characters of the whole diagram): "the ten thousand things are born through transformation"
- left of the second empty circle: "the Way of the *Qian* Hexagram matures into masculinity"
- right of the second empty circle: "the Way of the *Kun* Hexagram matures into femininity"
- center of the diagram: the Five Phases—wood, fire, earth, metal, water

- left of the *yin-yang* diagram at the top (appearing here in somewhat different form): "activity of *yang*"
- right of the *yin-yang* diagram: "quiescence of *yin*"

The empty circle at the bottom of the diagram is *wu-ji* ("Ultimate Non-being"), the inexpressible source and culmination of all existence.

Dao

There is one more key concept of ancient Chinese cosmology to examine, and it has implications for both Confucianism and Taoism: the *Dao*. The character for *Dao* once again has naturalistic origins emphasizing motion, change, and interaction. It shows a horned animal running, and it has the basic meaning of "way" or "path." Picture a natural path discovered in a forest. It is likely to have been used by a number of animals, and the hoof prints and paw prints of chipmunks, squirrels, rabbits, deer, boars, goats, sheep, and cattle can be seen. Perhaps it is a path leading to a spring or pond, and as the animals make use of the path, it becomes more and more well defined. Unlike a path made by humans (such as a road that is graded and tarred before handling traffic), the natural path of the forest animals is never finished or complete—as soon as another animal uses it, it becomes more of a path. Just so, the *Dao* is always "coming into existence"—it is characterized by incompletion, evolution, fluidity, and change.

The *Dao* is the oscillating path of *yin* and *yang*. It is active and fluid, not static and fixed; it is creative and natural. The *Dao* is found within the world, and yet it is not limited to the world, as its potential is infinite. In Chinese cosmology, the *Dao* is the unfolding of the inexhaustible generative energy of the universe. Though the *Dao* is not personified in Chinese religion, it plays a role analogous to the Creator God of Western religious traditions: bringing things into existence, underlying all of reality, present at the origin as well as within the infinite extent of reality.

FURTHER READINGS

A brief account of the major texts and teachings of the classical period is no substitute for reading the full translations. Of the innumerable translations of *The Analects* of Confucius, two new ones that are both readable and well annotated are recommended: the translations by Simon Leys and by Roger Ames and Henry Rosemont.

Turning to the Taoists, the *Dao de jing* by Michael LaFargue is recommended; his introduction and appendices are especially helpful. The standard translation of the *Zhuang-zi,* and still the most readable, is by Burton Watson. He has an edition of selected passages (*Chuang Tzu: Basic Writings*) from the text that gives a very good sense of the work as a whole. From a scholarly point of view, A. C. Graham's translation of the Inner Chapters is probably the best.

Ames, Roger, and Henry Rosemont, Jr., trans. *The Analects of Confucius: A Philosophical Translation.* New York: Ballantine, 1999.

Graham, A. C., trans. *Chuang-tzu: The Seven Inner Chapters and Other Writings from the Book of Chuang-tzu.* Boston: Allen & Unwin, 1981.

LaFargue, Michael, trans. *The Tao of the Tao Te Ching: A Translation and Commentary.* Albany: State University of New York Press, 1992.

Leys, Simon, trans. *The Analects of Confucius.* New York: W. W. Norton, 1997.

Watson, Burton, trans. *Chuang Tzu: Basic Writings.* New York: Columbia University Press, 1964.

3

BRANCHES

Neither Confucianism nor Taoism has splintered into distinct institutional branches, as is found in Judaism, Christianity, or Islam. This is due significantly to a tolerance for "complementary opposites" grounded in *yin-yang* cosmology, a theme further explored in Chapter 4. Nevertheless, there are streams of Confucianism and Taoism that have created a remarkable diversity of beliefs and practices in the Chinese religious landscape.

MAJOR FIGURES AND MOVEMENTS OF THE CONFUCIAN TRADITION

Streams of Confucianism

Confucianism and Religion

Though the separation was never formalized institutionally, there was a division within Confucianism—two streams—within the first few generations after Confucius. The first division was between a *religious* orientation, which affirms the reality of spiritual beings, and a *secular* orientation, which denies the reality of spiritual beings though admitting the social utility of religious participation. The first view was expressed in *The Analects* of Confucius, as seen in the discussion of *Tian* in Chapter 2, and was elaborated by the Second Sage of the Confucian tradition, Mencius. The more secular view was first expressed by Xun-zi, the Third Sage.

Table 3.1
Streams of Confucianism

Dynastic Period	Religious Confucianism	Political Confucianism
Zhou Dynasty (1100–249 B.C.E.)	Meng-zi (Mencius) (372–289 B.C.E.)	Xun-zi (313–238? B.C.E.)
Han Dynasty (206 B.C.E.–220 C.E.)		Confucianism becomes state orthodoxy; Grand Academy established
Period of North-South Division (220–581 C.E.)		
Sui-Tang Dynasties (581–907 C.E.)		
Song Dynasty (960–1279 C.E.)	Song Neo-Confucianism Zhang Zai (1020–1077) Zhu Xi (1130–1200 C.E.)	
Yuan Dynasty (1260–1368 C.E.)		Four Books become standard for official examinations
Ming Dynasty (1368–1644 C.E.)	Ming Neo-Confucianism Wang Yangming (1472– 1529 C.E.)	
Qing Dynasty (1644–1911 C.E.)		School of Evidential Research
Present day	New Confucianism Boston Confucianism	Confucianism and autocratic states

To understand the internal debate on divine beings, it is necessary to look once more at the Zhou Dynasty background of early Confucianism.

The early Zhou Dynasty developed a theory of divine kingship based upon a belief in a high god called *Tian,* "Heaven." *Tian* had replaced the ancestral gods of the prior Shang Dynasty, which the Zhou had overthrown. Part nature deity, part divine judge, *Tian* was first and foremost the protector of the empire, especially the semidivine person of the emperor, "Son of Heaven" (*Tian-zi*). The emperor was thought to have received a divine command to rule, called "the Mandate of Heaven" (*Tian-ming*).

With the social and political decline of the later Zhou, the people began to question the power or motivations of *Tian.* If *Tian* loved the people, why

Tian

was He not powerful enough to overcome the forces of chaos? If *Tian* was all-powerful, why was He punishing the people with war and starvation? Many poems of *The Book of Poetry* express skepticism and disillusionment about *Tian*, even going so far as to question the god's very existence.

As part of his "restoration project," Confucius expressed an almost anachronistic belief in *Tian* and showed great confidence in Heaven's power and benevolence. The Mandate of Heaven had inspired Confucius to "restore the culture of the early Zhou," and Confucius believed that Heaven was the direct recipient of religious offerings.

Tian is clearly anthropomorphized. That is, Heaven is given human-like qualities and characteristics: Heaven sees, wills, rewards, punishes, protects, gives, and receives. For the early Zhou, as well as for Confucius, *Tian* was a personal God who overlooked the world and responded—or failed to respond—to sacrifice and prayer.

Still, many modern-day scholars see Confucius as a humanist or rationalist whose religious beliefs were incidental to his principal teachings. These interpreters cite three passages in *The Analects:*

1. When asked about wisdom, Confucius said: "Be earnest in your duties to the people. Revere the ghosts and spirits, but *keep your distance.* This may be called wisdom."

In this statement, Confucius does not deny the existence of ghosts and spirits, nor does he repudiate religion. Clearly, though, he emphasizes "duties to the people" over religious practices. Moreover, he seems to favor some kinds of religious practices over others: he says one should "revere" divine beings, but not "get too close" to them. This interpretation makes sense given Confucius's emphasis upon *li*, the stately court ceremonies of an earlier era. He endorses formality in religious ritual, just as he advocates a "ceremonial attitude" toward everyday life. He does not approve of the kind of shamanistic intimacy with spirits that was practiced by Taoists. "Keep your distance. This may be called wisdom."

2. Zi-lu [a disciple] asked about serving ancestors and spiritual beings.

Confucius said, "If you cannot yet serve men, how can you serve the ancestors?"
  "May I ask about death?"
  "If you still do not understand life, how can you understand death?"

Here, Confucius once again prioritizes "this-worldly" concerns over "other-worldly" concerns. He also prioritizes a life of action over a life of speculation. This is not to say that one should not be thoughtful or reflective, but if one is wrapped up in speculation about abstract philosophical issues, how can one act ethically and effectively in the world? One's first task is "serving others" and "understanding life." The rest can come later.

   3. The topics the Master did not speak of were anomalies, power, disorder, and spiritual beings.

This last statement is too brief to be completely clear, but it would seem to indicate that Confucius was again reluctant to speculate about religious matters. By "anomalies" were meant strange natural occurrences that could be explained only by resort to supernatural causes. Confucius would not talk about them. Nor would he talk about ghosts and spirits. This does not mean that he did not believe in them, but it suggests once again an ordering of priorities. It is interesting that these two religious topics are paired with military power and social disorder, both of which Confucius clearly disliked.

   None of these statements proves that Confucius did not believe in gods and spirits. But they do suggest a reluctance to talk about them, and a prioritizing of the human realm over the sacred realm. Perhaps Confucius was simply too humble to speculate about things that he could not be certain of. Perhaps Confucius found certain kinds of religion distasteful—such as the orgiastic intercourse with spirits practiced by shamans in southern China—and thought that religious expression should be confined to the traditional ceremonies.

   The Book of Rites expresses the same view when it commands:

> Do not sacrifice more than usual.
> To do so shows lack of respect.
> Do not sacrifice less than usual.

To do so is negligent, and leads to forgetfulness of the spirits.

> Therefore, the *jün-zi* follows the *Dao* of Heaven, in the spring performing the *di* [planting] sacrifice, in the fall, the *chang* [harvest] sacrifice.

The Confucian view with regard to sacrifice (and to religion) is that it should be dignified, stately, and not excessive. Also, it is right to say that

Confucius emphasized the human side of religion—the inner state of the ritual participant, the psychological impact of the ceremony, and the moral lessons to be inferred from it—rather than the operative effects of religious ceremonies on gods and spirits. For Confucius, the most important result of religious ritual is its moral impact on the ritual participant.

Confucius had the clear sense that *Tian* is a god-like being who demands moral virtue and the restoration of culture. At the same time, Confucius's primary concern is moral cultivation and social reform, which is supported by religious practice.

What came of Confucius's belief in Heaven? The religious conception of Heaven was relatively short-lived, and, among Confucians, the anthropomorphizing of Heaven is almost peculiar to Confucius. By the end of the Warring States Period, that is, within three hundred years of Confucius's death, *Tian* was no longer anthropomorphized and no longer viewed as a god. Rather, late Zhou Dynasty Confucians de-mythologized Heaven, interpreting *Tian* as a mechanistic process of nature, or, simply, as "the heavens" (the sky).

Warring States Interpretations of Tian

1. the Creator
2. absolute principle of virtue
3. Fate, destiny
4. the heavens, physical sky
5. Nature

One of the best examples of the more agnostic view of *Tian* was elaborated by Xun-zi, the Third Sage of Confucianism known for his negative evaluation of human nature. Xun-zi was a strong advocate of Confucian *li* (ritual)—both in religious ceremony and in everyday life—but he did not share Confucius's belief in Heaven as a divine being and he did not see anything more than social benefits in religious performance.

Xun-zi was a religious skeptic. He argued against commonly held beliefs in ghosts and spirits, omens, and fortune-telling based on individual physical characteristics, that is, palmistry or physiognomy (palm-reading and face-reading). He rejected the popular beliefs of his time that omens could be read in acts of nature, such as storms, earthquakes, river currents, eclipses or movements of the moon and stars. He refused to acknowledge unseen causes of natural events or political upheaval or to admit any connection between strange natural events and the success or failure of human endeavors. The greatest wisdom, he said, is to see that the *social* realm, the realm of the *heavens,* and the realm of the *earth* are completely distinct (they form a triad): only the first of these can be understood and only human action has moral significance. In his essay entitled "A Discourse on Heaven" (*Tian-lun*), Xun-zi discusses strange events including falling stars, whistling trees, eclipses of the sun and moon, and untimely winds and rains. Such events were interpreted by diviners as having profound significance for the state, but Xun-zi observed,

> Never in history has there been a time when such things did not occur.... Marvel at them, but do not fear them!... Among all the unusual occurrences, the ones to fear are the man-made disasters.... Marvel at them, and fear them as well!

Earlier Confucians (including Confucius himself) thought of *Tian* in anthropomorphic terms, as guiding human life, rewarding and punishing the people, delighting in or detesting human acts. Xun-zi described *Tian* simply as the order of nature, independent of human behavior in its processes and activities. *Tian,* he said, is impartial, speechless, natural, spontaneous, purposeless, indifferent, unconscious, irrational, and unknowable. "So, a person of depth does not attempt to contemplate it."

This is not to say that Xun-zi rejected ceremony or religious ritual, however. He simply rejected an interpretation of religious ritual as true or efficacious:

> You pray for rain and it rains. For what reason? I say there is no reason. It is as if you had not prayed for rain and it rained anyway.

Yet, as Xun-zi argued, religious ritual has its positive effects if it is seen for what it truly is—the ordered expression of human emotion and a model of social harmony. Xun-zi describes the function of religion as "ornamental" (*wen*), a word that connotes order, pattern, emotional and aesthetic balance—the same word that Confucius used to describe "culture" or "civilization." "Ornament" creates models or paradigms for human life, and religion is part of the general molding process of education. Religious rituals (*li*) give emotion an appropriate outlet and help the people to overcome their naturally selfish expression of desire. But there is no question of spiritual efficacy.

So, the gentleman regards the *li* as ornamental, the common people as divine. To see them as ornamental is fortunate; to see them as divine is unfortunate.

Xun-zi's view of religion has enjoyed a long legacy and might even be said to be the prevalent Confucian view. Many Chinese today share the suspicion that spiritual beings (gods, ghosts, ancestors, saints, souls, and so on) do not actually exist, and that religious practices—prayer, worship, and offerings, religious services, and other activities sponsored by churches and temples—have no religious efficacy at all. Rather, they have a social utility. They bring people together, teach them proper standards of behavior and encourage artistic expression. All of these activities are socially meaningful and are worth preserving, but they have no religious significance. For this reason, the ancestral cult of modern-day China, which can be identified as a Confucian tradition, is better thought of as ancestor veneration rather than ancestor worship—it is a valued tradition and has persisted longer than any other ritual practice because of its social importance, but most Chinese are agnostic as to the religious effects of their offerings.

Confucian Orientations toward Human Nature

Within two hundred years of Confucius's death, a second debate raged concerning basic human nature. The question was, "Are humans basically good?" That is, are they inclined to be kind, generous, and sociable? Or are humans basically evil, tending toward selfishness and competition? A number of views were developed by the early Confucians.

Early Chinese View of Human Nature:

1. neither good nor evil (Gao-zi)
2. good (Mencius)
3. evil (Xun-zi)
4. equal parts of good and evil
5. some persons good, some persons evil

Mencius's View: Human Nature Is Good

Representative of the view that humans are basically good is the Second Sage of the Confucian tradition, Mencius.

Mencius is the Latinized form of Meng-zi (371–289 B.C.E.), a contemporary of the Taoist philosopher Zhuang-zi. Though *The Book of Mencius* is rich in philosophical insight—especially in the area of political theory—Mencius is best known for his theory of human nature. Defending his point of view against the lesser-known Gao-zi (who held that human nature is essentially neither good nor evil), Mencius declared that human nature is inclined toward the good. Every human has the natural inclination to do good, and this natural inclination is identified with the Confucian concept of *ren* (benevolence, "co-humanity").

The Book of Mencius has a number of illustrations demonstrating the innate presence of *ren* in the human heart. For example, he says, anyone who suddenly sees a child about to fall into a well will have a spontaneous feeling of alarm and distress. Quoting Mencius:

> All persons have feelings such that they cannot bear to see the suffering of others. The ancient kings had such feelings and therefore they created a government that could not bear to see the suffering of the people. When a government that cannot bear to see the suffering of the people is conducted from feelings that cannot bear to see the suffering of others, governing the empire will be as easy as making something go round in the palm.
>
> When I say that all persons have feelings which cannot bear to see the suffering of others, my meaning can be illustrated in this way: If a person saw a child about to fall into a well, he would immediately have a feeling of alarm and distress—not to gain friendship with the child's parents, nor to seek the praise of his neighbors and friends, nor because he dislikes the reputation of callousness if he did not rescue the child.

There is, in other words, no external motivation that governs the initial feeling of alarm and distress. Any person would be worried and concerned about the child. Some persons will not act to save the child, but even those persons would be alarmed by the sight of the child in danger. It is that initial, unreflective reaction that Mencius emphasizes, and it shows a natural propensity for benevolence and compassion.

Mencius argues, then, that *ren* is a feeling, and he goes on to say that this feeling has four aspects or kinds:

1. the feeling of *compassion* and commiseration
2. the feeling of *shame* (i.e., for wrong-doing)
3. the feeling of *modesty* or deference (keeping oneself back to make way for others; putting others first)

4. the ability to *judge* between right and wrong, and the inclination to approve of the one and disapprove of the other

For Mencius, these qualities or feelings are natural, not learned. Moreover, they are definitive of humanity: lacking them, one is nothing more than a beast. Mencius calls them the Four Beginnings or Four Seeds, out of which the major Confucian virtues sprout and grow:

1. compassion gives rise to *ren* ("benevolence")
2. shame gives rise to *yi* ("righteousness")
3. deference gives rise to *li* ("propriety")
4. judgment gives rise to *zhi* ("wisdom")

Returning to the example of the child at the edge of the well, Mencius writes:

> From such a case, we see that a person without the feeling of compassion is not really a person; a person without the feeling of shame is not a person; a person without the feeling of deference and compliance is not a person; and a person without the feeling of right and wrong is not a person.
>
> The feeling of compassion is the beginning of benevolence; the feeling of shame is the beginning of righteousness; the feeling of deference and compliance is the beginning of propriety; and the feeling of right and wrong is the beginning of wisdom. Persons have these Four Beginnings just as they have their four limbs.
>
> Now, having these Four Beginnings but saying that you cannot develop them is to destroy yourself. If you say that your ruler cannot develop them, you destroy your ruler. If anyone with these Four Beginnings knows how to give them the fullest extension and development, the result will be like a fire beginning to burn or a spring beginning to flow. When they are fully developed, they will be sufficient to protect all people within the four seas. If they are not developed, they will not be sufficient even to serve one's own parents.

It is important to recognize the developmental nature of this process. For the classical Chinese philosophers, "human nature" (*xing*) is not merely what is innate or given at birth (though these ideas are certainly present in the idea of *xing*), but also what is natural to the development of the person. *Xing*, "human nature," is etymologically related to *sheng*, "life"—the course of life, not only its beginnings. So, *xing* represents the natural development of a person over the whole course of life.

Mencius uses the organic metaphors of nurturing and growth to describe the development of human nature. The Four Seeds, he says, are "part of one's native endowment, not welded on to me from the outside." This is not to say that a person cannot be corrupted to neglect or even abuse this innate goodness, but, writes Mencius, "given the right nourishment there is nothing that will not grow." Evil, in other words, is the neglect or abuse of the inner feelings of good, like the denuding of a mountain by axes and hatchets, or—in Mencius's most famous example—the over-eager exertions of a foolish farmer:

> Do not be like the man of Song. There was a man of Song who was sorry that his corn was not growing, and so he pulled it up. Tired out, he went home and said to his family, "I'm exhausted. I have helped the corn to grow." When his son ran out to look at it, the corn had already withered and died.

It is natural for persons to be good, just as it is natural for mountains to be forested. Evil is as unnatural as a cross-cut hill. But, as the story of the farmer of Song illustrates, one must nurture goodness like the growth of corn, and not uproot the good by forcing it.

Mencius shows his Confucian colors by emphasizing the importance of education. Education is the form of nurturing that allows the Four Seeds to become the four full-flowering virtues described earlier. But education does not instill virtue; it merely encourages it.

On the basis of innate goodness, anyone is capable of becoming a sage. To become a sage, one recognizes the goodness that exists within all persons. "The sage," says Mencius, "is simply the first to discover this common feeling in his heart." Mencius's belief in human perfectibility sometimes leads him to speak in mystical terms of the "vast, flowing vital spirit" of the human heart. He writes, "If you go to the bottom of your heart, you will know your own nature, and, knowing your own nature, you will know Heaven (*Tian*) ... All the ten thousand living things are found within you. There is no greater joy than to look into yourself and find this to be true."

Xun-zi's View: Human Nature Is Evil

Xun-zi said, "Human nature is evil; goodness is acquired." For Xun-zi, the natural inclination of a person is the satisfaction of personal, usually selfish, desires. "At birth, there is the tendency toward self-benefit." Xun-zi agreed with Mencius that humans are basically feeling-oriented, but he did not describe feelings in the same morally positive terms. Mencius had argued that all persons possess morally positive feelings, including the feelings of "compassion," "shame," and "deference." But Xun-zi equated feelings simply with the emotions: love, hate, pleasure, anger, sorrow, and joy. In response to outside stimuli, these feelings manifest themselves as desires (desiring the things that one loves, or that give one pleasure and joy), the satisfaction of which is basically selfish and antisocial. Because human desires are inexhaustible, their natural expression is chaotic and competitive. If persons indulge their feelings without restraint, the result will be wrangling and strife, violence and crime, licentiousness and wantonness.

Whereas for Mencius the natural development of basic human feelings produces virtue or "goodness," Xun-zi maintains that the natural development of feelings produces suffering or "evil." Acts of virtue (benevolence, trustworthiness, filial piety, loyalty to the state, and so on) "are all contrary to a person's nature and run counter to the emotions." Humans tend to be self-interested, animalistic, and unrestrained, and must acquire the ability to harness and control their natural inclinations.

Despite his view that human nature is evil, Xun-zi was thoroughly Confucian in his conviction that humans are perfectible, that "any man can become a sage." This can be accomplished by the guidance of rulers and teachers, the implementation of universal standards of behavior, and the proper ordering of society. "Goodness is acquired," he said, through a process of gradual accumulation of models of behavior from the outside.

The key word employed by Xun-zi in this context is *wei*: to "contrive," "manipulate," or "create"; to "deliberate"; and, as a noun, "activity," "construct," "artifice," or "ornament." Goodness is not natural, but artificial. It is a human construct, invented by the sage kings of the early Zhou in the form of laws and rites. These standards of goodness are passed on from rulers to subjects and from teachers to students and can be cultivated within individuals through education. Xun-zi concluded from his negative evaluation of human nature that education is fundamentally a molding process that civilizes the young, and that public ritual (*li*) is the primary means for the creation of a prosperous and peaceful culture. *Li* ("ritual and propriety") was, of course, a defining idea for Confucius, who emphasized the broader meaning of propriety and decency in all interactions, and Xun-zi's indebtedness to Confucius on this point defined him as a Confucian thinker. In Xun-zi's terms, *li* are the rules of proper conduct in both ceremonial and everyday contexts that can shape individuals to think less often of themselves. He does not deny that this is a manipulative, unnatural process. Just as straight wood can be shaped into a wheel or dull metal can be sharpened, a person can "become clear in thought and faultless in action" through education and the practice of *li*.

The distinction between the natural and the artificial also applies to the feelings and mind. Whereas feelings are natural, thought is artificial or contrived; in other words, deliberate.

> The likes and dislikes, happiness and anger, sadness and joy of the *xing* (human nature) are called "emotions." When the emotions are aroused and the mind chooses among them, this is called "thought." When the mind is capable of action on the basis of deliberation, this is *wei*.

Deliberation is an artificial molding activity that functions to harness emotions and suppress their natural, selfish expression.

This capacity for overcoming natural desires distinguishes persons from animals. It also makes social life possible, as the unchecked expression of emotion would preclude the possibility of civil society. In Xun-zi's terms, what distinguishes persons from animals is "differentiation," both as a function of rational thought and as the basis for communal existence. "We are not as strong as oxen ... yet they are used by us. Why? ... Because we differentiate among ourselves." Condemning social egalitarianism in the strongest terms, Xun-zi underscored the ideals of social hierarchy, division of labor, and clarity of roles described by Xun-zi and his Confucian predecessors as the "rectification of names." Successful statecraft involves the proper identification of duties, the creation of models and standards for behavior, and the judicious implementation of rewards and punishments. Within such an environment, goodness can be "constructed" and society made harmonious.

Two Streams of Confucianism

Political Confucianism

It appears that *The Analects* of Confucius was not the final word on the interpretation of Confucianism. Confucius appealed to religious authority (*Tian*) and religious ritual (*li*) as the foundation of his teaching, but he was noncommittal about religion itself. He believed in human perfectibility, but made no statements as to the basic good or evil of human nature. It was up to later Confucians to interpret the Master's teachings, and to define the two orientations outlined above. On the one hand, the Third Sage,

Xun-zi, expressed an atheistic skepticism about religion and a negative evaluation of human nature. On the other hand, the Second Sage, Mencius, affirmed the importance of religious belief and practice, especially in the treatment of the dead, and he affirmed the basic goodness of human nature.

Though there has never been a formal School of Xun-zi or School of Mencius, their differing orientations have defined two broad trends within Confucianism from antiquity to the present day. Here, the first will be called "Political" or "imperial" Confucianism, and the second "Religious" Confucianism or "Confucian Spirituality." Political Confucianism has been associated primarily with the imperial (dynastic) system, which made Confucianism the foundation of its bureaucratic governing structure, the imperial examination system, and public education. It also sponsored a state cult of Confucius, with the erection of temples and memorial tablets to the First Sage.

Timeline of the Development of Political Confucianism

Han Dynasty (206 B.C.E.–220 C.E.)

195 B.C.E.	Han Emperor Gao-zi stopped in Lu and made a sacrifice to Confucius, a "great offering" of ox, sheep, and pig; afterward, local officials of Lu visited the tomb before taking up their duties
59 C.E.	Offerings to Confucius were made compulsory in the Grand Academy, with spring and autumn sacrifices—this is the first-known instance of regular offerings to Confucius outside the Kong family itself
Later Han Dynasty	The Han Emperors institutionalized the worship of Confucius and his seventy-two disciples

Period of North-South Division (220–581 C.E.)

Hiatus (court interest in Buddhism and Taoism)

Sui-Tang Dynasties (581–907 C.E.)

640 C.E.	Temples to Confucius were established in all districts and counties for the first time in history (with more than two thousand erected by 1644 C.E.). The Confucian temples had names like Temple to the First Sage, Temple of Culture, and Temple to Master Kong

720 C.E.   Images of Confucius and his disciples were erected in all Confu-
                  cian temples

Subsequent Developments in State-Sponsored Confucianism

From 740 to   Sacrifices were held at court every year on the first day of spring and
   1927 C.E.   autumn at the Temple of Heaven in Beijing
1074 C.E.   Mencius added to Confucian worship

Yuan Dynasty (1260–1368 C.E.)

                  The emperor sponsored the most elaborate sacrifices to Confucius
                  in Chinese history
1313 C.E.   The Four Books of Confucius were established as the basic examina-
                  tion texts of the Civil Service Examination
1530 C.E.   Images (statues or paintings) in Confucian temples were replaced
                  by ancestral tablets

The public support of Confucianism from the Han through the Qing Dynasties—some two thousand years of Chinese history—explains in large
measure the remarkable resiliency of the Chinese state. Political Confucianism emphasizes the maintenance of social hierarchy and political stability and teaches loyalty and obedience to authority.

For example, in late imperial China (the Ming and Qing Dynasties), emperors promulgated a series of Sacred Edicts, which were printed and distributed in towns and villages all over the nation. The first Ming Emperor, Tai-zu
(who reigned 1368–1399 C.E.), issued the first set of six Sacred Edicts:

The Sacred Edicts of the Ming

1. Be obedient to your parents.
2. Respect your elders and superiors.
3. Maintain harmonious relationships with your neighbors.
4. Instruct your sons and grandsons.
5. Be engaged in your work with contentment.
6. Do not commit wrongful deeds.

These edicts were expanded to sixteen by the Qing Emperor Kang-xi
(the longest-reigning emperor in Chinese history: 1662–1723 C.E.) in 1670:

The Sacred Edicts of the Qing

1. Strengthen proper relationships as a filial son/daughter and a fraternal
   younger brother/sister.

2. Maintain harmony with your kin.
3. Prevent disputes and litigation as a harmonious neighbor.
4. Produce adequate supplies of food and clothing in farming and horticulture.
5. Practice frugality by preventing waste.
6. Emphasize education.
7. Exalt orthodox learning and avoid heterodox teachings.
8. Explain the law to those who are ignorant or obstinate.
9. Explain the principles of etiquette and deference to those who are ignorant or rude.
10. Understand and carry out your personal duty.
11. Instruct the young to prevent them from doing wrong.
12. Avoid false accusations to protect the innocent.
13. Warn those who hide criminals and deserters to avoid involvement.
14. Pay taxes in a full and timely manner.
15. Strengthen local administration to eliminate robbery and theft.
16. Dissolve feuds and respect the sanctity of life.

The Sacred Edicts clearly show the influence of Xun-zi's practical orientation: guiding the people through education and moral instruction, sponsoring community events (including religious rites) for the purpose of social control, and rewarding loyalty and citizenship.

Of the two streams of Confucianism, it was Political Confucianism that was most visible for the greater part of China's history. From the establishment of the Grand Academy and the Confucian examination system in the later Han Dynasty (second century C.E.) to the fall of the last emperor (early twentieth century C.E.), the imperial bureaucracy embraced Confucian standards of governance and social organization. The state instilled Confucian ethics in the people through education and social policy. For nearly two thousand years of Chinese history, Political Confucianism supported the hierarchical organization of Chinese society, as reflected in the Five Permanent Relationships: parent over child, ruler over subject, husband over wife, elder sibling over younger sibling, and elder friend over younger friend.

Political Confucianism was rejected by social reformers of the late nineteenth and early twentieth centuries. Confucianism was blamed for all of China's ills—the failure to modernize, the backwardness of her customs, military defeats at the hands of Japan and the European powers. And although political Confucianism is now enjoying a certain resurgence among powerful state leaders in China and Singapore, it has not been embraced by the people. Present-day expressions of Political Confucianism will be examined in Chapter 4.

Confucian Spirituality

Religious Confucianism can be traced to Mencius. His belief in the innate goodness of persons inaugurated a tradition of Confucian self-cultivation beginning with inner awareness and a positive view of basic human nature.

This orientation is labeled here as Religious Confucianism because of its commitment to transformation at a deeply personal level. This stream of Confucian spirituality is optimistic about the individual capacity for self-improvement, even "perfection." The "path to sagehood" is realizable by virtue of one's own efforts—not by means of external molding or restraint. Any person can become a sage—a fully self-realized, morally mature, and socially engaged individual—by developing virtues that are present from the start, present simply because people are human beings living in community. Religious Confucianism assumes this potential and develops the means to bring inherent virtues to fruition.

Though the basis for Religious Confucianism can certainly be found in *The Analects,* it was Mencius who elaborated upon this view and argued for it. This tradition was reinvigorated by the Confucian Renaissance of Song and Ming Neo-Confucianism, especially in the figures of Zhu Xi and Wang Yang-ming.

Neo-Confucianism extended Mencius's positive view of human nature to the belief in a potential for perfection, "the way of the sage." Mencius encouraged his followers to emulate the sages of antiquity, but the Neo-Confucians went even further, insisting that one could actually become a sage by one's own efforts.

Zhu Xi (1130–1200 C.E.) was the giant figure of this Confucian Renaissance, emphasizing the spiritual dimension of Confucian self-cultivation. It was shown in Chapter 1 that Zhu Xi advocated a discipline of study that he termed the "investigation of things." The objective of study was to realize the Heavenly Principle within all things, including the self. To reach that Heavenly Principle, it was necessary to be vigilant in correcting one's own behavior, to be conscientious in studying the Classics, and to be inquisitive about the world (what today would be called both social science and natural science).

Zhu Xi's practice included spiritual disciplines adapted from Taoism and Buddhism. In particular, Zhu Xi advocated a form of meditation that he called Quiet Sitting, a variation of Taoist "sitting in forgetfulness" and Buddhist "sitting meditation," but with a greater emphasis on moral development and self-improvement. Neo-Confucian Quiet Sitting ideally takes place in the scholar's study or a peaceful garden. Unlike the lotus position of Buddhist meditation, no particular posture is required, and Quiet Sitting is not preceded by chanting or other preparatory rituals. The frame of mind that the Confucian cultivates is "reverence," "seriousness," or "sincerity." This is a reverence for tradition, and the lessons of the sages; for the world, and the order and harmony of nature; for family and community; and for the self, because a person who is not serious about himself or herself, and the cultivation of personal character, cannot be serious about tradition, community, or the world at large.

For Zhu Xi and the Song Neo-Confucians, the focus of Quiet Sitting was the self, to be sure, but the self could only be "understood" or "rectified" by the "investigation of things" and the "extension of knowledge"—that is, by looking outside oneself. The investigation of things involves attentive reflection upon "the principles of things and affairs" through the study of books, the modeling of wise and virtuous individuals, and engagement in public service. This serves to "rectify the mind," that is, to master and control feelings or emotions that tend to selfishness or self-interest if they are not guided and cultivated by Heavenly Principle.

The second leg of this Confucian Renaissance was elaborated by Wang Yang-ming and his followers in the Ming Dynasty. The most fundamental difference between Song and Ming Neo-Confucianism, the School of Principle and the School of Mind, is in the method of self-cultivation leading to sagehood.

Wang Yang-ming (1472–1529 C.E.) rejected the idea that self-cultivation requires the discovery of external principles. Subjecting Zhu Xi's language to a different interpretation, "the investigation of things" was for Wang the *self-correcting* activity of the mind (rectification *by* the mind rather than rectification *of* the mind). This implies a fundamentally positive evaluation of feelings, which are not only natural and appropriate, but even basic to the process of self-cultivation. Whereas for Zhu Xi the feelings must be controlled by an external Principle, Wang insisted that the feelings are "self-righting" and inherently well balanced. Wang Yang-ming reaffirmed the Mencian doctrine of "incipient feelings" as the basis and origin of the cultivation of sagehood. Again and again, Wang emphasized the capacity of the seeker to realize the natural "equilibrium" or harmony of the mind, a realization that does *not* require the "investigation of external things and affairs."

In this sense, Wang distinguished natural feelings from selfish desires, which cloud the mind, including the desire for fame or profit. The extirpation of selfish desires is what Wang meant by the "investigation of things": "to eliminate what is incorrect in the mind so as to preserve the correctness of its original substance." The "original substance" of the mind is "innate knowledge," which Wang tied explicitly to the "incipient feelings" of virtue within each individual. "Innate knowledge" is the in-born capacity to know the good, and so, Wang concluded, "There is no principle outside the mind." Beginning in one's own mind, one knows what is right.

Rather than inferring from the world what is right and wrong, Wang insisted that goodness is found within the mind, and is then "extended" in action. The application of moral judgment to action is called by Wang the "extension of the innate knowledge of the good": "to do always in one's life what one's mind says is right and good." Beginning with one's natural feelings of goodness, benevolence is extended outward to family, friends, the community, and external things. So, the "innate knowledge of the good" becomes the basis of a unity between the self and the world. This is known experientially in the sense of identity one feels for all things, from children to strangers and even to tiles and stones. "Even Heaven and Earth cannot exist as Heaven and Earth without the 'innate knowledge of the good' of humankind."

Wang Yang-ming's Confucian Spirituality was a dramatic expression of the human creation of value out of the natural harmony of feelings within the mind. In contrast to the outward-looking orientation of Zhu Xi's "investigation of things," Wang was closer to an intuitionist moral philosophy. Moral value is discovered within the self and then extended outward, rather than being extrapolated from the underlying principle of external things and affairs.

Wang Yang-ming's optimistic view of the mind made him open to learning from every possible source. He was conversant with Buddhism and Taoism, consistently approaching them with a tolerant and inquisitive attitude. Moreover, he urged his students to "learn from the words of ordinary people." This is because value is derived not from the external source of knowledge, but from the inner response of the mind.

Wang Yang-ming's efforts to distinguish "feelings," which are the naturally good expression of the mind, from "desires," which cloud the "original clarity" of the mind, set the stage for the intense introspection and personal fault-finding of the Yang-ming School of Ming Neo-Confucianism. For several hundred years, Chinese intellectual history was dominated by an emphasis on self-determination, reflecting trends toward individualism and success in the social and economic spheres. Wang Yang-ming's followers advocated the natural freedom of the mind, spontaneous expression of feeling, and celebration of the common man. In practical terms, these views led to a deliberate rejection of book learning, the civil service examinations and, in some cases, of government service altogether. Even when engaged in study of the Classics, they argued, it is preferable to read them without the use of commentaries, or to compose one's own commentaries based on an intuitive response to the texts. At its most extreme, Confucian Spirituality stands in stark contrast to Political Confucianism, which insists upon external controls and restraints upon individual desires and inclinations.

New Confucianism

Today, what has been called the Third Epoch of Confucianism has enjoyed a resurgence among Chinese intellectuals. This New Confucianism attempts to take what is best from the Confucian tradition as a whole, and to see Confucianism on a par with the other great religions of the world. One representative of this trend is Tu Wei-ming, a Taiwan-educated philosopher and historian who now teaches at Harvard University. Professor Tu has inherited the religious orientation of Mencius and the Neo-Confucian tradition to articulate what he describes as an "anthropocosmic" vision of humankind. This vision regards the individual as a "center of relationships." The relationships of family, community, nation, and globe do not exhaust the self, but bring the self to fruition, as a fully realized human being. "To be religious, in the Confucian sense, is to be engaged in ultimate self-transformation as a communal act."

New Confucianism carries forward the religious stream of Confucian Spirituality rather than the stream of Political or Imperial Confucianism. If anything, the New Confucians have been critical of the Chinese government and of any form of institutionalized Confucian norms. Their prophetic voice has been stifled by autocratic regimes, from the late imperial government of the last years of the Qing Dynasty, to the Republican government in the early twentieth century, to the Communist government of the present day, all of which favored the hierarchical, socially and politically conservative standards of Political Confucianism. These voices are now permitted freer expression, and the Confucian movement is again flourishing, especially among Chinese intellectuals seeking a religious and philosophical alternative to both Chinese collectivism, on the one hand, and Western individualism, on the other. Contemporary New Confucians are defining a goal of personal transformation grounded in the teachings of Mencius and Wang Yang-ming, and social transformation attentive to the rectifying power of ritual propriety (as described by Xun-zi and Zhu Xi)—all informed by insights from Buddhism, Taoism, and Western religion and philosophy. As a modern-day elaboration upon China's rich tradition of Confucian Spirituality, New Confucianism represents one of the most dynamic movements in Confucian history.

Contemporary Confucian Spirituality will be discussed in detail in Chapter 4.

MAJOR FIGURES AND MOVEMENTS OF THE TAOIST TRADITION

Streams of Taoism

As in the case of the Confucian tradition, although there have been identifiable schools of Taoism over the centuries, these have not solidified into distinguishable branches or formal divisions. It is helpful to identify three streams of Taoism, termed here Sect Taoism, Esoteric Taoism, and Priestly Taoism. Of the three, the first has largely disappeared in the modern era, but Esoteric and Priestly Taoism are still active, and they are in fact enjoying a resurgence in Mainland (Communist) China today. Some of the main

Taoist priest before the altar, with several acolytes, at an abbey in Chengdu, Sichuan, China. Courtesy of the author.

characteristics and defining beliefs and activities of each of these streams will be examined next.

Sect Taoism

Sect Taoism is the earliest of the branches of Taoism to come into existence as a distinct religious tradition, though it emerged some centuries after Zhuang-zi and the legendary Lao-zi.

The *Tian-shi Dao* ("Way of the Celestial Masters") was one of several religious communities formed in the latter half of the second century C.E. Others included the *Tai-ping Dao* ("Way of Great Peace"), which fomented the Yellow Turban uprising in the Later Han Dynasty, and a small unnamed sect dedicated to the worship of Lao-zi, which produced a book entitled *Lao-zi bian-hua jing (The Classic of the Transformations of Lao-zi)*. The Yellow Turbans of the Way of Great Peace had ambitious political aspirations. Under a banner that read, "The blue heaven has died and the yellow heaven will be established,"

Table 3.2
Streams of Taoism

	Sect Taoism	Esoteric Taoism	Priestly Taoism
Zhou Dynasty (1100?–249 B.C.E.)		Anti-Confucian tradition of hermits and recluses	
Han Dynasty (206 B.C.E.–220 C.E.)	Celestial Masters	Search for immortality	
Period of North-South Division (220–581 C.E.)	Ling-bao revelations	Mao-shan revelations; External Alchemy	Sect Taoism encounters local cults
Sui-Tang Dynasties (581–907 C.E.)	Complete Reality School		
Song Dynasty (960–1279 C.E.)			
Yuan Dynasty (1260–1368 C.E.)			
Ming Dynasty (1368–1644 C.E.)		Internal Alchemy	Taoism integrated with folk religion
Qing Dynasty (1644–1911 C.E.)			
Present day			

the group donned yellow turbans and rose up in rebellion against the reigning Han Dynasty in the year 184 C.E. The color yellow is associated in traditional Chinese cosmology with the earth, the Yellow Emperor, and perhaps the Buddha (the "golden man from the West"). The Yellow Turbans claimed the Yellow Emperor to be their mythic founder and the first ancestor of the Chinese people. This rebellion contributed to the fall of the Han Dynasty in 220 C.E., and the Way of Great Peace was defeated only by rival forces.

Meanwhile, the grandson of Zhang Dao-ling of the Way of the Celestial Masters surrendered to the rebel leader Cao Cao in 215 C.E., and the sect was permitted to continue after the end of the dynasty. It was sponsored by the Western Jin (265–316 C.E.) as the official religion of that short-lived dynastic kingdom.

There is as yet inadequate evidence to demonstrate interrelationships among these groups, but they had a number of features in common.

Rigidly Hierarchical Political-Sectarian Organization

The Celestial Masters divided the realm into twenty-four "governances," based on astrological numerology, with an equal number of male and female rulers, called "libationers" (a libationer makes offerings of wine). Sect followers were recorded in family registers. They were called "seed people," and the family registers indicated not only membership in the sect but also divine "chosenness" as members of the religious elect. The sect adopted numerous functions of the state: administration of justice, supervision of public works, hierarchy of titles and responsibilities. One important characteristic of the early Taoist sects was their inclusiveness: they did not distinguish between men and women or between Han and non-Han Chinese (majority and minority ethnic groups).

A Messianic, Theocratic Conception of Imperial Rule

The sects were messianic, which means that they anticipated the arrival of a messiah, usually in the form of a deified Lao-zi. The sects promised either the restoration of the imperial order or the overthrow of the empire and the inauguration of a new dynastic reign. The new order, they said, would be one of harmonious balance in the cosmos forming a continuum from Heaven to Earth. Each of the sects appealed to the religious authority of the god Lao-zi, giving him exalted titles, such as Lord Lao Most High and Lord Yellow Emperor Lao.

In the *Lao-zi bian-hua jing (The Classic of the Transformations of Lao-zi)*, Lao-zi is depicted as a great cosmic divinity and first principle:

> Alone, with no companion, he wanders in the distant past,
> Before Heaven and Earth were formed.
> He leaves his hidden state and returns to it again—
> Now he simply subsists, and is primordial;
> Then he acts, and becomes human.

In the *Lao-zi bian-hua jing*, Lao-zi promises to return to establish and rule over a new empire. This was a significant development for the legitimization of Taoism in the eyes of the state, for, instead of posing a threat to the established dynasty, the later Taoist church could declare itself its ecclesiastical supporter, as seen in Kou Qian-zhi's manipulation of the Northern Wei court, and court Taoism of the Tang Dynasty. But this scripture was also a prototype for a number of later popular sects of the lower reaches of society that proclaimed the inauguration of a new order by means of a radical transformation of the world. Sect Taoism, therefore, has sometimes been a supporter of the state, but more often, it has been a threat to political authority, inspiring innumerable messianic movements.

Revelation of Sacred Texts and Amulets

Zhang Dao-ling was said to have been the recipient of direct revelations in the form of celestial records and protective charms from Lao-zi, Lord Lao Most High, and to have based his teaching and sectarian organization on this esoteric knowledge. Other revelations took the form of spirit-possession and shamanistic trance, but this was ideally controlled and removed of ecstatic emotion. The *Tai-ping* Yellow Turbans used amulets, incantations, and charmed water to protect them from harm.

Communal Healing Rites Based upon a Conception of Sin as the Cause of Illness

The Celestial Masters encouraged individuals to public confession, penitentiary confinement in "quiet chambers," and redemption by good works. Physical illness was interpreted as a sign of moral failing, and recovery from illness was interpreted as a sign of repentance and faith.

The Yellow Turbans made good or restored health a condition of discipleship within the sect, asserting that the political crisis of the times was a result of the inheritance and accumulation of sins from one's ancestors, which can be overcome by means of ritual, divine intercession, and good works.

Some of the Taoist sects required moral austerities such as vegetarianism and abstention from alcohol. Most notable among these is the School of Complete Reality (*Quan-zhen*), which came into existence in the Tang Dynasty (618–907 C.E.). This school adopted monastic practices from Buddhism, meaning that the Taoists of this sect lived together in cloisters or monasteries. Quan-zhen Taoism still exists today, though the number of practicing Taoist monks is very small.

Rites of Propitiation and Rejuvenation

These rites involved ritualized and, therefore, controlled shamanistic possession. The fully developed tradition of Sect Taoism favored civil rituals, as opposed to military, bloody, or violent rituals, substituting pure vegetarian offerings for the bloody sacrifices of the local cults.

- The purification rite enables the persons who are sponsoring the service to transfer the spiritual benefits derived from the ritual to their ancestors, usually their deceased parents. It has three stages:

  1. prayer or thanksgiving to the gods
  2. accumulation of merit in the ritual
  3. transfer of merit to the dead

- The offering rite addresses only the highest deities, enabling the priest to ascend the heavens and call the gods into the community

Though the purification and offering rites originated in the Taoist sects, today they are part of Priestly Taoism, which is practiced throughout China as an integral part of Chinese popular religion.

Of the five characteristic features of Sect Taoism described, many remain in Priestly Taoism (discussed subsequently), as Sect Taoism has largely disappeared in modern China. Today, Taoist priests still compose amulets for protection from harm; still prepare themselves before community celebrations by isolating themselves in penitentiary chambers for confession and purification; and still perform the purification and offering rituals for the benefit of their communities. Sect Taoism no longer survives, but its ritual elements still play a vital role in Chinese religious life today.

Esoteric Taoism

The Taoist Hermits

The second stream of Taoism, Esoteric Taoism, focuses on individual self-cultivation. In the earliest period, this religious practice was conducted in isolation from social life, as opposed to Confucian engagement with society and politics. The Taoist hermits saw no point in trying to reform the world from within. In fact, they argued that social reformers intensified the very problems they set out to resolve.

Zhuang-zi in particular began a long tradition of hermits or recluses, retiring from worldly affairs to pursue meditation and creative arts. The story is told of a feudal emissary sent to draft Zhuang-zi for government service. He promised Zhuang-zi a reward of great riches, including a jewel-encased tortoise. Zhuang-zi scoffed, "Do you think that your tortoise would rather be set on display, covered with jewels? Or would it rather be dragging its tail in the mud?" When the emissary stuttered his reply, Zhuang-zi rebuffed him: "Go away! I'd rather drag my tail in the mud." Zhuang-zi's favorite activities were fishing, wandering, and beating on a drum.

Some of China's greatest artists and poets were recluses inspired by Zhuang-zi and other hermits of the classical period. Without going into further detail, these are the characteristics of China's tradition of hermits:

1. indifference to worldly affairs and material wealth

    - disregard for social convention
    - belief in the uselessness of reputation, wealth, rank, fame, and social service
    - spontaneous generosity
    - nature as escape from culture

2. hedonism and material indulgence

    - spontaneous indulgence
    - not rebelling against desire
    - positive view of natural feelings and inclinations

3. love of drink

    - wine as escape from structure and order
    - equation of drunkenness with naturalness: going along with whatever happens, including emotions and desires

4. favoring life over death

- lack of concern for death or for the spirits of the dead
- avoidance of risk, including government or military service

In addition, the *Lao-zi* and *Zhuang-zi* books contain mystical elements and suggestions of the spirit-journeys of ancient shamanism. "Without feelings and intentions, annihilating body and mind, my heart like dead ashes, and form like dry wood," says the *Zhuang-zi,* "I can travel far." The Taoist sage or Perfected One is like a religiously enlightened being, "sitting in forgetfulness," at one with the principle of change.

The Pursuit of Immortality

Esoteric Taoists interpreted Lao-zi's *Dao de jing* as an immortality hand-book, with encoded messages describing breathing techniques, elixirs, and meditation exercises ensuring long life. This was the alchemical tradition of Esoteric Taoism, which was discussed briefly in Chapter 1. The earliest practices of Taoist alchemy were external, based upon the refinement of metals and the preparation of herbal diets for ingestion in the body. The later alchemical tradition was internal, with the body itself seen to be a self-sufficient "re-circulating system," without the need for a chemical, mineral, or pharmacological diet.

The attainment of immortality, though perhaps not invented by the Tao-ists, became their primary concern. As such, the immortal "winged person" or "mountain man" were models of attainment equivalent to the Confucian sage and Buddhist "enlightened being" (Buddha).

The quest for longevity and immortality (early texts do not distinguish between long or permanent life) is so ancient that it was a natural aspiration of any Chinese by Han times. As early as the Zhou Dynasty, bronze bowls were produced with inscriptions such as "long life," "delay old age," and "non-death." No one would have questioned its desirability, though certain Eastern Zhou philosophers (including Confucius, Xun-zi, and Zhuang-zi) did express a certain disdain for active attempts to cultivate it.

Generally, the soul was thought to be unhappy after death, desiring some means to enter fully once more into the world and the affairs of the living. Pre-Han texts do not portray it in much detail, but the *Zuo-zhuan* (a historical work of the fourth century B.C.E.) describes a "Yellow Springs" where souls resided after death; it is portrayed as a miserable place.

External Alchemy

By "external alchemy" is meant the cultivation of immortality through a dietary regimen, including medicinal plants, chemicals, and minerals. Ideally, the diet was prepared with a crucible and kiln, for mixing and firing the raw materials. Minerals were subjected to intense heat, liquefying the substance. While still in molten form, the material was shaped into tiny ball-shaped pills, which, after hardening, were swallowed with tea, water, or wine. Or they were formed into spoons and other eating utensils. It was believed that the transformation that occurred in the process of production would create a corresponding transformation within the human body. For example, the alchemical transformation of lead into gold was replicated in the body, as the "base" organs were transformed into "immortal organs" after the gold was ingested.

The first great alchemists were Wei Bo-yang (fl. 120–150 C.E.) and Ge Hong (fl. 300 C.E.). The case of Ge Hong is worth noting here, since he was subsequently adopted by some Taoists as a seminal figure in their tradition.

Ge Hong was from an aristocratic family that fled political disturbances in the north; he would have been an outsider in the southwestern Taoist community of the Way of the Celestial Masters. He and his associates aligned themselves with the aristocratic alchemical tradition (alchemical experimentation was extraordinarily expensive) and against Sect Taoism. Ge Hong was aware of the Celestial Masters and adopted a highly critical attitude toward the sect. He indicted Zhang Heng (the Tai-ping leader) as a common rebel. His Taoism was quite distinct from the Sect Taoism of Zhang Daoling and the Celestial Masters.

Ge Hong was the author of a work entitled *Pao-pu-zi (The Master Who Embraces Simplicity),* one of the first alchemical treatises. The *Pao-pu-zi* describes moral purification, the use of charms and incantations for protection from danger, and ingestion of various medicines and elixirs for the preservation of one's life.

Among the early sects, it appears that the *Shang-qing* ("Highest Purity") School was the first to practice immortality cultivation through both meditation and external alchemy. Tao Hong-jing (456–536 C.E.), redactor of the Mao-shan revelations, was especially interested in the cultivation of immortality, and he was an expert on herbal pharmacology, editing a book of plants that survives to this day. He described two kinds of immortal: "superior" and "second class." A superior immortal "ascends in broad daylight," that is, while still living. A second-class immortal transcends the world through "liberation of the corpse": the adept "appears to die" and is buried, but later when his or her coffin is examined, it is discovered to contain a sword, or staff, or pair of sandals in place of the body. Tao insisted that the world of the spirits and immortals and that of humankind were separated by "only a thin line," so that beings move from one realm to the other with great frequency.

Practices associated with this branch of Taoism include the following:

1. Macrobiotics: herbs, fungi, medicinal plants. The alchemists were vegetarians, limiting their diet to particular plants and herbs. One of the most significant factors in the macrobiotic diet was actually seeking out and collecting the materials, as the plants had to be natural—that is, growing in the wild—and not cultivated. This is in keeping with the classical Taoist emphasis on naturalness and spontaneity (*zi-ran*). Many of these plants grew in treacherous terrain: cliff-faces, mountain valleys, river banks, and forests. It's no wonder that Ge Hong's *Pao-pu-zi* includes charms and incantations for protection against wild animals. The figure of the solitary herb-gatherer on a mountain peak is typical of Taoist-inspired landscape painting.

2. The "arts of transmutation." Literally, *alchemy* refers to the mixing and refining of rare or precious metals. The most common ingredient in the alchemical furnace was cinnabar (mercury sulfate). The cinnabar, naturally red in color, was refined by a process that extracted pure mercury, which was formed into pills. The pills were ingested with water or wine. Other minerals subjected to alchemical transmutation included lead, mica, realgar, alum, lake salt, sandstone, soapstone, and talc, among others, which are now difficult to identify. It is now known that the accumulation of lead, mercury, and other minerals in the body, even in small quantities, is toxic. Mercury poisoning, for example, is known to produce rashes, a crawling sensation on the skin, fevers, hallucinations, and madness—symptoms assumed by the early Taoist alchemists to be evidence of their efficacy. Death, which must have been inevitable with such a diet, was interpreted to be "apparent" or "feigned," with the adept's "purified body" actually ascending into the mountains to join the "accomplished ones," the immortals. Nevertheless, it was probably the growing realization among Taoists that accidental death was the most likely consequence of external alchemy that led to its gradual replacement by internal alchemy.

3. Cutting off cereals to starve the Three Corpses or Three Worms. Taoists believed that there were cancerous forces at work within the body that contributed to the decay of the mortal organs and flesh. These demonic figures relied on a diet of cereals or grains. Therefore, unlike most people, Taoists refused to eat rice. This practice had tremendous significance, as grain (particularly rice and wheat) was the staple of the traditional Chinese diet. Moreover, the

cultivation of grain represented the settled, even sedentary, agricultural life-style of the common people—as opposed to the wandering, itinerant life-style of the Taoist adept. As far as the state was concerned, a diet of grains was highly encouraged, as the traditional taxation system depended upon a fixed proportion of the harvest for the imperial granaries. The state commanded one-ninth of the people's harvest. Typically, villages cooperated in a "well-field" system (named after the Chinese character for well, shaped like a tic-tac-toe board), with the central parcel being farmed communally for tax purposes. The Taoists, by avoiding grain and subsisting on a macrobiotic and mineral diet, opted out of this system, and thus, out of any financial obligation to the state.

4. Preservation of corpses. The Alchemical Taoists perfected the science of preserving corpses, which were described as the "immortal bodies" of the deceased. Embalming agents included fruit, spices, and chemicals, while the bodily orifices were closed using gold and jade. These, in combination with the mineral diet produced by the arts of transmutation, were in fact quite effective. The body was embalmed from within during life, and then externally embalmed after death. Indeed, when the corpses (or, from the Taoist perspective, "immortal bodies") of the adepts were exhumed, even decades or centuries later, they were found to be astoundingly well preserved.

5. Sacrifices to deities for the express purpose of extending life. The protective spirits of alchemical practice included the Three Pure Ones, star gods, and the immortals themselves. They were worshipped as "spirits of life." These gods were distinguished from the folk deities of the common people, the "spirits of the dead," and received "pure offerings" of incense and wine rather than the "bloody offerings" of popular religion (cooked meat and rice).

6. Other physical activities. Exercises associated with the alchemical diet included the "circulation of breath," massage or acupressure, and yogic calisthenics. These practices survived the extinction of external alchemy and became the core practices of internal alchemy.

Although it is true that external alchemy was replaced by internal alchemy by the Song Dynasty (960–1279 C.E.), its legacy was far-reaching. Traditional Chinese medicine owes a great debt to the early Taoists, with its emphasis upon dietary prescriptions (including rare medicinal herbs), techniques of "firing" and "cooking" (most Chinese medicine is prepared by slow cooking or thickening, to produce a broth or paste), acupressure and acupuncture, moxibustion (burning an herbal mixture on specific parts of the body), meditation on the breath, and exercise. All of these methods are still widely practiced in China. Today, Chinese traditional medicine is spreading to the West. How many of its practitioners are aware that they are following the way of early Taoism?

Chinese family visiting ancestral tomb. Courtesy of the author.

Internal Alchemy

Internal alchemy employs the language of external alchemy but actually refers to processes occurring within the body. Some of the techniques associated with internal alchemy include:

- "circulation of breath"
- "embryonic breathing"
- "interior vision"
- "returning the essence"
- "mixing the breaths"
- "massage and gymnastics"

What all of these practices have in common is the objective of *preserving vital energy (qi)* by means of perpetual recirculation within the body. The *qi* is never "exhausted" (which leads to death) and, through meditation and exercise, any *qi* that is lost in the course of everyday life is constantly replenished. The goal, then, is for the body to become a self-contained system. The external means of traditional alchemy, which relies upon the production and ingestion of foreign substances, are no longer needed.

For example, "returning the essence" and "mixing the breaths" refer to Taoist sexual techniques aimed at creating and "storing" sexual energy within the body. The idea is to stimulate the body sexually, but not to lose or dissipate that energy in orgasm. In this rite, there is a marked emphasis on *control* and *restraint.* All passion is absent.

The principles of internal alchemy are based upon a common Chinese conception of the human body, psyche, and souls. The origins of this conception are ancient *yin-yang* cosmology, but it was developed fully by both Taoist and Confucian thinkers in the Song Dynasty and later. It remains the common understanding of the human being to this day.

Chinese cosmological treatises describe two souls, or aspects of the soul, within a living person. They are called *hun* and *po*. The *hun* soul is animated by *yang*, the *po* soul by *yin*. The Song Dynasty Neo-Confucian scholar Zhu Xi (twelfth century C.E.) summarizes this conception as follows:

> Consciousness and movement are due to *yang*, while physical form and body are due to *yin*. The clear breath (*qi*) belongs to the heavenly aspect of the soul (*hun*) and the body is governed by the earthly aspect of the soul (*po*).
>
> A person is born as a result of integration of essence and material force. One possesses this material force only in a certain amount, which in time necessarily becomes exhausted. This is what is meant by physicians when they say that *yin* or *yang* no longer rises or falls. When exhaustion takes place, the heavenly aspect of the soul (*hun*) and the clear breath (*qi*) return to Heaven, and the earthly aspect of the soul (*po*) and the body return to the Earth, and the person dies. When a person is about to die, the warm material force leaves the body and rises. This is called the *hun* rising. The lower part of the body gradually becomes cold. This is called the *po* falling. Thus as there is life, there is necessarily death, and as there is beginning, there must be an end.

As long as *hun* and *po* are within the body, there is life. But as soon as they separate, and the *hun* soul leaves the body, there is death. In the classical sources, after death, the *hun* soul flies around the heavens, as a god or immortal, while the *po* soul stays with the body and returns to the earth. In an ancient funerary ritual of "calling the *hun* soul," the bereaved family would assemble on a rooftop or other high place, and call out the name of the deceased, in hopes that the *hun* soul would return to reanimate the body and restore the dead to life. After death, it was assumed that the *po* soul gradually decayed and disappeared, just as the body decays within the earth. Thus, graveside rites on death-day anniversaries and the springtime Tomb Festival (or Pure Brightness Festival) were traditionally discontinued when there was no living memory of the ancestor, and this is still true today. The *po* of an unvenerated ancestor (in a tomb or gravesite that is neglected) becomes a "hungry ghost," striking at random against the living. The *hun* soul lives indefinitely and is traditionally thought to reside in an ancestral tablet set on a shrine and worshipped in the home. There may be several tablets for the same ancestor (kept, for example, by brothers in their homes), but only one contains the soul: it is normally in the tablet held by the eldest son. Daily offerings are made to this tablet. Today, this represents the most common form of religious practice throughout East Asia.

Although *hun* and *po* describe two aspects of the spiritual body, there are in fact three *hun* souls and seven *po* souls.

The three *hun* souls (with name, location, and function) are:

1. "breath" (*qi*): head, intellect
2. "spirit" (*shen*): heart, will
3. "essence" (*jing*): solar plexus, intuition

The seven *po* souls (located in and interacting with the five organs: heart, spleen, liver, lungs, kidneys) are:

1. joy
2. anger
3. pleasure
4. sorrow
5. like
6. dislike
7. desire

The *hun* souls, manifesting *yang* energy, are active, creative, and rational. They circulate up and down the spinal column. The "essence," associated physically with the sexual organs, is the source of "conception"—the conception of new life (pregnancy) and the conception of rational creativity ("conceptualizing"). This energy flows up the spine to the breath within the cranium and is expressed as thought. Finally, this energy is expressed in the spirit as will, that is, by putting ideas into action. Circulation is essential. People who have blocked *hun* energy are slow-witted or unable to put thought into action.

The *po* souls represent *yin* energy, because they are receptive or reactive. Emotions, too, are receptive or reactive: emotions are responses to external stimuli or to thought and action, the activities of the *hun* souls. Unlike the Buddhists, who reject all emotions as harmful to spiritual development, or Western ethicists, who tend to label some emotions as positive and others as negative, Chinese Taoism affirms the importance of all emotions, as long as they are balanced. Proper balance among the *po* souls is important for good physical and psychological health in the same way that balance among the *hun* souls ensures the proper circulation of energy in the body. For example, when certain emotions dominate, there is an imbalance among the *po* souls, and illness ensues (whether physiological or psychological).

Ideally, balance is maintained not only *within* the *hun (yang)* and *po (yin)* souls, but also *between* the two. One whose *hun* souls are dominant is aggressive and overly rational. This is typically a problem for men, who (according to classical Chinese medicine) are *yang*-oriented. One whose *po* souls are dominant is passive and overly emotional. This can be a problem for women, who are *yin*-oriented. Taoist-inspired medicine studies the physical manifestations of imbalance and prescribes remedies that address both physical and psychological well-being.

The goal in Taoist internal alchemy is to maintain a balance within the body between *yang* forces and *yin* forces, and to recirculate *qi* energy. Taoism seeks a balance of *yang* and *yin*, of activity and quiescence, of masculinity and femininity. (This is seen in Sect Taoism, with the equal representation of men and women among the libationers in the sectarian hierarchy.) This balance creates harmony within the body, and both preserves and replenishes the *qi*. Notice that Taoism makes no distinction between the physical aspects, the psychological aspects, and the spiritual aspects of human beings: all are composed of *qi,* and all are essential for the health and longevity of the individual practitioner.

This second branch of Taoism, Esoteric Taoism, remains strong today. It is practiced by Taoist priests, by ordinary Chinese in their daily exercises and their attitudes toward good physical and psychic health, and, increasingly, by Westerners, who have seen in Taoist harmonizing and self-sufficiency a creative model for their own spirituality.

Priestly Taoism

What is the relationship between Taoism and popular religion, the unorganized and diffuse local community cults of gods, ghosts, and ancestors? Taoism has adopted two strategies in dealing with these cults: *repudiation* and *incorporation*. Although at first the Taoist tradition was eager to separate itself from the religion of the common people, and to become what one scholar has called "China's indigenous higher religion," gradually it assimilated the religious beliefs and practices of popular religion and made them its own. Today, Priestly Taoism and Chinese popular religion are largely indistinguishable.

Popular religion refers to the religion of the people; it is the common or shared religion of village and countryside, city and county, rich and poor, merchant and peasant, gentry and commoner, young and old. In China, popular religion consists principally of offerings made to spirits of the dead—first and foremost, spirits of the family dead (ancestors), but also spirits of notable or worthy persons, who are enshrined in community temples. The most powerful spirits of the dead are spirits whose identity while living is no longer known. Beginning as "ghosts" (the unvenerated dead), some of these spirits are elevated to the status of "gods"—often due to miraculous occurrences associated with their graves. They, too, are enshrined in local community temples and are the recipients of regular offerings of food (meat, rice, and wine) and incense. They are also honored in temple festivals and neighborhood processions, as they are invoked to bring protection and blessings to the people of the community. These religious traditions are very old in China and are still practiced today.

The early Taoists expressed great ambivalence toward the widespread religious beliefs and practices of the common people. They approached popular religion in two ways, repudiation or incorporation.

Repudiation

Ge Hong and Tao Hong-jing were vehement in their attacks on "excessive worship," "heterodox pneuma," "popular divinities," and "demon religion." Taoism represented to them a new revelation, superior to the "bloody sacrifices" of the popular cults. Taoism was a religious revolution inasmuch as it attempted to abolish many of the chief characteristics of Chinese popular religion: worship of the deified spirits of the dead, animal sacrifices, and cash offerings to priests.

Whereas the divinities of folk religion are by and large deified humans, Taoist divinities are "pure spirits" and cosmic forces, located within the universe and within the priest's body. Astral and celestial in origin, they are personifications of abstract qualities or forces. For the Taoists, gods, ghosts, and ancestors—the key figures in the religion of the culture—are relatively unimportant. The correct spiritual focus is simply the Dao.

Priesthood is nonexistent in folk religion. Taoist priests, by contrast, are subjected to a long and arduous process of selection and training. They are ritual masters who have memorized rites of many hours' or even several days' duration. They are expert in the arts of dance, drawing, and calligraphy. They have mastered the literary tradition (in Classical Chinese), and are conversant with the ritual and cosmological texts of the Taoist Canon. They are expected to lead a morally faultless life and to practice austerities (dietary restrictions, sexual abstinence, and so on) at crucial times of their training and ritual practice. Finally, they are dedicated to a strict regimen of alchemical practice, including meditation and physical exercise. None of these expectations are present in the history of popular religion prior to the emergence of Taoism.

Incorporation

Eventually, Taoism assimilated the local cults, by subsuming the popular deities in a cosmic system. Though this strategy emerged at a somewhat later period in Taoist history, it should be noted that the mystical and shamanistic strains at the core of Taoism had popular, folk origins—thus, Taoism and popular religion were intertwined from the beginning.

In Priestly Taoism, the gods of the common people are made to serve subordinate positions in an integrated celestial hierarchy. Today, Taoist priests participate in the consecration and enthronement of gods and goddesses and intercede with them on behalf of the community. In regard to ghosts and demons as well, the Taoist ritual master—by virtue of his knowledge of the "divine registers," his mastery of charms and incantations, and his ability to internalize god-power and astral-power—is an effective exorcist. The idea is not so much that Taoism opposes and replaces popular cults as that it transcends and reinterprets them in light of Taoist cosmology.

In Taiwan and southern China, where Taoism is still quite active, three types of religious specialists operate in village and neighborhood temples.

Dao-shi, Masters of the Dao, "Black Heads" (for the formal hats they wear). The high priests of religious Taoism are formally ordained in consecration ceremonies after years of preparatory instruction and discipline. Taoist priests perform solemn, restrained purification and offering rites *within* the temple, concealed from the uninitiated masses in the temple courtyard. Taoist priests are trained in the mystical arts of Alchemical Taoism, as well as the ritual instructions of the Taoist Canon. They perform rites of purification for the community and oversee privately sponsored funerals, primarily through the mastery of talismanic calligraphy as well as minutely choreographed movements and dances.

Fa-shi, Masters of the Law, "Red Heads." *Fa-shi* are more visible to spectators and the common people, performing rites of exorcism *outside* the temple. Exorcists are skilled in marionette theater, drama, and acrobatics, which are part of public Taoist rites. In addition, the Red-Headed priests are the masters of the uneducated spirit mediums who communicate directly with the "lower spirits" of popular religion. One of the most exciting spectacles in Priestly Taoism is the initiation ceremonies of the Red-Headed priests, which involve the ascent of Nail-Sword Ladders and other dramatic rites.

Ji-tong, Spirit mediums. Mediums are passive vehicles of the spirits, controlled by gods, ghosts, and ancestors, and manipulated by the Red-Headed priests. Spirit mediums have no special training, as they cannot choose their vocation—they are chosen by the spirits to communicate with the living. Often, mediums are marginal persons from the lower, working classes, looked down upon by the ritual masters. Nevertheless, their tradition is extremely ancient, even predating Taoism itself. Spirit mediums are typically engaged by families seeking contact with the dead.

Of the three branches of Taoism identified in this chapter—Sect Taoism, Esoteric Taoism, Priestly Taoism—it is Priestly Taoism that survives to the present day as the most visible form of Taoism in China. To be sure, the cosmological vision and institutional forms of Sect Taoism, as well as the individual practices of Esoteric Taoism, are now part of the liturgical life of Taoist priests. Today, priests identify themselves with lineages that were once institutionalized Taoist sects. They engage in esoteric practices of meditation and exercise in preparation for their ritual performances, as well as for their own personal benefit. But it is Priestly Taoism that is most readily encountered in Chinese communities in the modern world.

Chapter 5 will discuss in more detail the modern-day forms and remaining beliefs and practices of Priestly Taoism.

FURTHER READINGS

On the development of the Confucian tradition, John Berthrong's *Transformations of the Confucian Way* is recommended, as well as the articles collected by Irene Eber in *Confucianism: The Dynamics of Tradition.*

For Mencius, the standard translation, and still the best, is by D. C. Lau. For the Third Sage of Confucianism, Xun-zi, the thoroughly annotated, multivolume translation by John Knoblock is recommended. For the "anthropocosmic vision" of Tu Wei-ming and the Third Epoch of Confucianism, see his *Confucian Thought: Selfhood as Creative Transformation.*

The study of religious Taoism is still a relatively new field, and there are not many books dedicated to the specific branches of Taoism examined here. For translations of early scriptures of Sect Taoism, see Stephen Bokenkamp's *Early Daoist Scriptures*. For a broad sampling of specific techniques of Esoteric Taoism, all of the articles collected by Livia Kohn in *Taoist Meditation and Longevity Techniques* are enjoyable. Finally, for insight into Priestly Taoism, there is no better resource than a book written by a Dutch scholar who was himself ordained as a *Dao-shi*. That is Kristofer Schipper, and the book is *The Taoist Body*.

Berthrong, John. *Transformations of the Confucian Way*. Boulder, CO: Westview, 1998.

Bokenkamp, Stephen R. *Early Daoist Scriptures*. Berkeley: University of California Press, 1997.

Eber, Irene. *Confucianism: The Dynamics of Tradition*. New York: Macmillan, 1986.

Knoblock, John. *Xun-zi: A Translation and Study of the Complete Works*. 3 vols. Stanford, CA: Stanford University Press, 1988–94.

Kohn, Livia, ed. in cooperation with Yoshinobu Sakade. *Taoist Meditation and Longevity Techniques*. Ann Arbor: Center for Chinese Studies, University of Michigan, 1989.

Lau, D. C., trans. *Mencius*. New York: Penguin, 1970.

Schipper, Kristofer. *The Taoist Body*. Translated from the French by Karen C. Duval. Berkeley: University of California Press, 1993.

Tu Wei-ming. *Confucian Thought: Selfhood as Creative Transformation*. Albany: State University of New York Press, 1985.

4

PRACTICE WORLDWIDE

CONFUCIANISM AND TAOISM AS WORLD RELIGIONS

Confucianism and Taoism are not exclusively Chinese. As early as China's Han Dynasty, Confucian influence was felt in Korea, which adapted Confucian bureaucratic structures and a Grand Academy modeled upon the Grand Academy of China. Intellectuals of the late Koryo (918–1392 C.E.) and Choson (1392–1910 C.E.) Dynasties were well versed in Chinese Neo-Confucianism and founded their own schools modeled upon Neo-Confucian thought. By the eighteenth century, Korea was almost thoroughly Confucianized, top to bottom: at the level of the family, Confucian norms of patrilineal succession had replaced the ancient Korean practice of equal inheritance, and Confucian family rituals were practiced universally. Though Korea was heavily Christianized in the twentieth century (today, 40 to 50 percent of South Koreans are Christian, according to government statistics), Confucian values and domestic rituals are upheld. All of the major Taoist sects also developed branch lines in Korea, and though Sect Taoism has largely died out in Korea as it has in China, many young urban professionals are drawn to Taoist principles and teachings, and Priestly Taoism still functions at the level of local, popular religion.

In Japan, Confucian influence at court was felt as early as the reign of Prince Shotoku (573–621 C.E.), whose Constitution quotes directly from *The Analects* and emphasizes social harmony based upon hierarchical social relations. Though Buddhism and Shinto dominated Japanese religion in its formative period from the Nara (710–784 C.E.) to the end of the Muromachi Period (1336–1573 C.E.), by the late imperial period Confucian norms and values were widely disseminated, and Tokugawa (1600–1868 C.E.) Neo-Confucianism is vital to the history of Confucian intellectual thought. In modern times, Japanese social ethics are thoroughly Confucian, and the Confucian emphasis on family, on educational attainment, and on social harmony and hierarchy are as much valued by Japanese as they are by Chinese. The influence of Taoism in Japan is less direct, but still significant—many scholars believe that the iconoclastic creativity of Japanese Zen Buddhism was inspired by Chinese Taoism.

Confucianism and Taoism are also becoming world religions, rapidly gaining popularity in Europe and the United States. In the case of Confucianism, this is a very recent development and centers on a group of university professors and public intellectuals who have begun to identify themselves explicitly as Confucians, even though they may or may not be ethnically Chinese. This movement—sometimes called Boston Confucianism because most of its members are professors from Harvard University and Boston University—has embraced Confucianism as a world religion or world philosophy. They regard Confucianism and its values as positive resources for both individual and global transformation and have made a personal commitment to realizing those values in themselves and in their communities. Euro-American Confucians are not of one voice on questions of religious transcendence (is there a place for God in Confucianism? is transcendence possible?), but they have committed themselves to the Confucian values of *propriety* and *benevolence,* and to Neo-Confucian practices of self-cultivation such as "quiet sitting" and the recognition of "Principle" in all beings. The history of Confucianism as a world religion is very brief and its course has not yet been set, but it is clear that Confucianism has emerged as a religious and philosophical alternative among the major traditions of the world for all persons, regardless of ethnic origins or national identity. In this sense, Confucianism is entering a new and exciting phase of its development.

The same can be said of Taoism. In the twentieth and twenty-first centuries, Europeans and Americans have become increasingly aware of some of the failings of both Judeo-Christian and Western Enlightenment values. For its critics, the Westernization of institutions and values on a global scale has had a number of negative consequences:

- violence arising from ethnic and political conflict;
- urbanization and its attendant ills (from crime to unsightly cityscapes);

- ecological degradation and the worldwide decrease in forested or virgin land;
- medical technologies that preserve life, but often at great material and spiritual cost;
- greed and avariciousness, expressed both personally and nationally;
- sexual ethics that are often distorted on the one hand by demeaning images and attitudes or, on the other hand, by religiously motivated prudishness; and
- lifestyles focused on personal achievement in highly artificial environments, with little opportunity for physical exercise, creative expression, or communion with nature.

Many who have observed these ills have seen in Taoism an alternative religious orientation, offering tools for understanding and self-cultivation as a counterbalance to Western values. With its emphasis on naturalism, holistic development of the physical and emotional aspects of human identity, political and ecological harmony, healthy sexuality, noninvasive medicine, and the "feminine values" of nurturing and caring, Taoism has emerged as a viable religious practice for people all over the world. A number of Taoist masters (usually, but not exclusively, of Chinese ancestry) now live in the West and have adapted Taoist alchemy, physical and psychological exercises, and related practices to Western lifestyles and goals. Although Confucianism and Taoism are only loosely based institutionally in the West, many individuals see them as viable religious alternatives for their personal lives and have joined with like-minded persons in informal groups for study, ritual practice, and support. In the future, it is likely that Confucianism and Taoism will be included among the major religions of the West as well as the East.

RELIGION IN CONTEMPORARY CHINA

The practice of religion in China in the modern era has been weakened by a series of cataclysmic events that have shaken the very foundations of Chinese culture. China's tumultuous modern history began with a crisis of cultural identity, a crisis that in some respects is still ongoing. Following a military uprising bordering on civil war (the Taiping Rebellion, 1851–1864 C.E.) and the forcible opening of trade to the West (a drug trade in opium supported by the British and American governments), many Chinese intel-

lectuals in the late Qing Dynasty (1644–1911 c.e.) blamed Confucian tra-
ditionalism, "bookishness," and self-restraint for China's failure to compete
economically and militarily with the West. This led to a wholesale rejection
of China's Confucian past by late nineteenth- and early twentieth-century
students and intellectuals and, most notably, by the Communist revolu-
tionaries who eventually succeeded in gaining power and establishing the
People's Republic of China of today. "Down with Confucianism [and the
backwardness for which Confucianism was blamed]!" "Smash the Confucian Shop!" "Eliminate the Four Olds [old habits, old ideas, old culture, and
old customs]!" "Root out unscientific superstition [veneration of gods and
ancestors, shamanism, temple construction, and divination]!" These were
the rallying cries from the May Fourth Movement of 1919 to the Cultural
Revolution of the 1970s.

Chinese intellectuals of the New Culture and May Fourth Movements
(in the late Qing and early Republican period) criticized Confucianism as
the product of a feudal age. Chen Duxiu, a founder of the Communist Party,
saw Confucianism as China's great oppressive force. He rebelled against
Confucian constraints in favor of independence and personal choice. Chen
sympathized in particular with sons, younger brothers, daughters, and
wives, who have suffered under the tyrannical institutions of the Confucian
family and state. A leading feminist of the same period, He Zhen, stated
that Confucianism "promotes male selfishness" and "deprives women of
their natural rights"; Confucianism justifies "polygamy [for men] and chas-
tity [for women] ... driving women to their deaths with empty talk of virtue
... [and] condemning women to the hells."

After the victory of Communist forces and the establishment of the
People's Republic of China in 1949, the Chinese government continued its
attacks on Confucianism and all things "old." Confucius himself was reviled
as a feudal "slave-holder," and Confucian values were condemned as oppressive and class-based. The Mencian ordering of "people who labor with
their minds" above "people who labor with their strength" was reversed, as
intellectuals were "sent down to the countryside" to learn from the peasants the values of hard work and physical self-sacrifice. For most of the past
century, the nation's intellectual and political leaders have blamed Confucianism for everything that was wrong with "feudal" China.

Against this tide of cultural self-loathing is a modern tradition of Confucian resurgence. Since the 1980s, the central government has begun a
reluctant resuscitation of Confucius and traditional Chinese culture, spon-

soring academic conferences and even, at least rhetorically, taking public pride in Confucianism as the basis of Chinese civilization. But this follows a much longer effort by a small number of Chinese intellectuals—at home and abroad—to preserve the tradition, and to adapt Confucianism to changing conditions within China and the world.

Even during the most virulent government attacks on Chinese tradition, a few intellectuals argued that Confucianism represents what is best of China's cultural past and the hope of China's cultural identity in the future. Late Qing Dynasty reformers tried to protect Confucianism from a dying imperial system. Their efforts failed, and many were exiled or put to death. Still, their example inspired a second generation of modern Chinese intellectuals, who fled China in the 1930s and 1940s, creating a new wave of Confucianism in Taiwan, Hong Kong, and expatriate intellectual communities abroad. They in turn taught the present generation of scholars and teachers who are committed to the restoration of Confucian learning and Confucian self-cultivation.

Just as the Song and Ming Dynasty Neo-Confucians represented a revival of Confucianism one thousand years after the Han (when Confucianism enjoyed its greatest visibility), modern-day New Confucianism represents a second Confucian revival, nearly eight hundred years after Zhu Xi.

Epochs of Confucian Intellectual History

First Epoch	Classical Period (Confucius, Mencius, Xun-zi)
Second Epoch	Song and Ming Neo-Confucianism (Zhu Xi, Wang Yang-ming)
Third Epoch	New Confucianism of the Modern Era

Three Generations of New Confucianism in Modern China and Abroad

First Generation	Liang Qichao (1873–1929)
	Kang Youwei (1858–1927)
Second Generation	Liang Shuming (1893–1988)
	Xiong Shili (1885–1968)
	Feng Youlan (1895–1990)
	Tang Jünyi (1909–1978)
	Mou Zongsan (1909–1995)
Third Generation	Li Zehou (1930–)

Yü Yingshi (1930–   )
Liu Shuxian (1934–   )
Cheng Zhongying (1935–   )
Tu Weiming (1940–   )

New Confucianism stands firmly within the tradition of Confucian spirituality elaborated by Mencius and the Neo-Confucians Zhu Xi and Wang Yang-ming. Contemporary Confucian intellectuals emphasize personal commitment and moral/religious self-cultivation. Though socially engaged, they tend not to be political—that is, they are reluctant to "politicize" Confucianism and do not advocate a state-sponsored Confucian regime. In fact, most of the New Confucians have argued for a Confucianism that is prophetic and social-critical, a "Confucian conscience" for the nation.

Just as Song and Ming Neo-Confucianism benefited from Buddhist and Taoist insights and practices, modern New Confucianism has developed very consciously in dialogue with the West. The New Confucians of the last one hundred fifty years are all conversant in Western philosophy (most have traveled and studied in the West), and many have incorporated Western theoretical and moral principles in their work. At the same time, they see a special place for Confucianism in and of itself, as an equal partner in the pluralistic arena of comparative religion and philosophy in the modern age.

The New Confucians are well aware that the Confucian tradition has at times in its history lapsed into extremes of oppression and inflexibility. At its worst, the Confucian tradition has—as Chinese anti-Confucian intellectuals charged in the late nineteenth and early twentieth centuries—severely limited individual initiative, political liberalization, and economic progress. At its worst, Confucianism has hardened social inequalities, including the oppression of daughters, wives, and mothers; tyranny and despotism within the family and the state; and a stifling sense of fatalism for the lowest classes of Chinese society. To be viable participants in a worldwide religious dialogue, New Confucians realize that they must address the negative side of the tradition, and must create a modern Confucianism that embraces political freedom, gender equality, nonauthoritarian leadership, individual and social human rights, and global awareness. Tu Wei-ming, perhaps the most articulate of the third-generation New Confucians, has defined this enterprise as an "anthropocosmic vision," casting the self as a "center of relationships" fully invested in family and community. At the same time, Tu describes a personal transformation that is religiously "ultimate," even "transcendent." It requires a profound personal commitment, which involves the individual deeply and attentively in the creative arts (poetry, art, and music); in study; in interpersonal relationships and civic participation; and in environmental and ecological preservation.

LASTING INFLUENCE OF CONFUCIANISM IN MODERN EAST ASIA

Socially and politically, modern East Asia retains many of the core values of the Confucian tradition. The predominantly Confucian countries—China, Japan, Korea, and Vietnam (as well as Taiwan, Hong Kong, and Singapore)—have affirmed the institutions of the family and community, and emphasized the ideals of educational attainment, filial piety, and social grace, despite almost two centuries of Westernization and modernization. This section examines eight traditional Confucian values and their modern-day legacy.

> Traditional Confucian norm: the civil service examination system, establishing government position through examination—inaugurated in the Han, lasting through the Qing.

> Modern-day residue: the emphasis on education in East Asian culture.

A formal examination system at the prefectural, county, provincial, and national levels was the primary means of political and social advancement for nearly two thousand years of Chinese history. Laddered examinations based upon Confucian learning were also adapted by Korea and Japan. This system ensured a government bureaucracy of highly educated, accom-

Table 4.1
Confucian Values in Modern China

Traditional Confucian Practice/Value	Modern-day Form
1. the examination system	1. education as principal means of advancement
2. dynastic stability	2. political authoritarianism
3. li as public ritual	3. li as politeness and decorum
4. emphasis on community	4. civic values
5. emphasis on family	5. family values
6. filial piety	6. ancestor veneration
7. Tian as object of veneration	7. human-centered spirituality
8. Spring and Autumn Sacrifice	8. Teacher's Day

plished scholars—in line with Confucius's own principles of egalitarianism and of status based upon merit rather than wealth.

The system did not work perfectly. The examinations were theoretically open to all, but it was primarily families of some means who were able to afford the tutelage, private schooling, and leisure time necessary for success in the rigorous course of examinations that took candidates from village to county seat to provincial and national capitals. The examinations themselves were narrow, impractical, constraining, and bookish—even those who succeeded in passing the civil service examinations at the highest levels found them stifling and irrelevant to the needs of political administration. Moreover, successful candidates were given administrative positions far from their home provinces, to avoid favoritism and to prevent the accumulation of local power; in their personal diaries, these Confucian elites often lamented their lonely lives.

Still, the examination system instilled a firm belief in social attainment based upon study and measurable success. The emphasis upon education in modern East Asia is one of the most abiding cultural values of the Confucian tradition. Literacy rates in China, despite its economic status as a third-world nation, are among the world's highest, and the record of achievement at the highest levels is the envy of many countries. Children in China, Korea, Japan, and Vietnam demonstrate a Confucian work ethic that is astoundingly rigorous. Most go to tutors or private "cram schools" at the end of the regular school day, and do homework late into the night. These values are maintained by East Asian immigrants in the West, as evidenced by the high rate of success on standardized tests and in college admissions—even among students whose first language is Chinese, Korean, Japanese, or Vietnamese. Teachers, who are highly respected, are honored for their work. As a cultural value and institutional priority, education is Confucianism's most obvious legacy, and the Confucian remnant that has been least affected by the winds of change.

> Traditional Confucian norm: a political doctrine of "enlightened authoritarianism," which supported the imperial system (of emperor, court, governors, and magistrates) for some 2000 years.
>
> Modern-day residue: reluctance to adopt democratic institutions; uncritical acceptance of political authority; conservatism in politics and economics.

Confucianism provided the institutional means and the cultural values to support centuries of imperial rule. The Five Permanent Relationships included the ruler-subject relationship, and the Confucian tradition developed qualities of leadership that sustained powerful governments. Though in theory the classical Confucian tradition advocated "righteous rebellion" if the ruler was deemed unjust, this was rarely put into practice, and imperial governments from the Han to the Qing made use of Confucianism to build up and maintain their power. The civil service examination ensured that the best minds were put in service to the state, and Chinese political philosophy has always been thoroughly conservative.

Today, despite the overthrow of the imperial system in China and its diminishment in Japan, the East Asian political ethos remains authoritarian and averse to change. Political leaders are trusted, respected, even idealized, to represent the best interests of the nation, and most East Asians are fiercely loyal to the state and to the governments that represent them. Although Communism is frequently cited as the cause of political authoritarianism in China and Vietnam, the power of East Asian governments owes as much to Political Confucianism as the dominant ideology of East Asian heritage. Present-day authoritarian governments from Beijing to Singapore have appealed to the Confucian tradition as the basis for their conservation of power.

> Traditional Confucian norm: ritual (*li*) as the standard of social interaction, with an emphasis on politeness, reserve, and decorum.

> Modern-day residue: hospitality, social grace, emphasis on social identity.

The traditional Confucian vision sees the self as a "center of relationships," internalizing societal norms of etiquette and cooperation. Relationships are constitutive of individual identity. As a result, the maintenance of harmonious family and social relationships is a deeply held personal commitment.

As seen in Chapter 2, Confucius extended the traditional meaning of *li* (narrowly defined as "rites" or "ceremonies") to a normative pattern for everyday life. *Li* refers to the proper patterns of behavior for all social encounters, in a living human context. The individual-in-community regards his or her personal relationships as essential to individual and social well-being, adopting a "ceremonial" attitude toward all persons.

What is meant by "ceremonial living"? The idea of *li* as "ritual," "etiquette," or "decorum" is a good definition, but it does not capture the importance of *li* to the Confucian tradition. Here are some examples of modern-day behaviors that Confucians would describe as "acting in accordance with *li*":

- looking others in the eyes when speaking with them;
- identifying oneself when making a phone call;
- greeting people one meets;
- introducing people who do not know one another;
- avoiding gossip;
- saying "May I help you?" to lost strangers;
- saying "How are you?" on the street/sidewalk/halls;
- saying "Excuse me";
- following through on promises;
- addressing elders respectfully;
- inviting acquaintances to social events; and
- helping friends in need.

Perhaps these are thought of as rules for everyday life. Individually, they may not seem important—certainly not "religious" in the Western sense of the term—but from a Confucian point of view, they are extremely important. They are important because they both *symbolize* and *create* a more ideal society. They are symbolic of values that Confucians hold dear: a harmonious, well-ordered society in which the young respect their elders, friends are loyal, and strangers are considerate of one another. These small gestures, when repeated over and over and practiced consistently, help to create and sustain a civilized society.

The *li* of everyday life are so highly regarded in the East Asian cultural region that they are taken to be obvious. They are fundamental, so much so that they are not labeled as "Chinese" or even "Confucian," but simply "human" and "right." In the details of social life, in the lessons taught to children and the patterns followed by adults, modern-day East Asians are unselfconsciously Confucian, as they have been for two millennia. The patterns of *li* are the social code or behavioral idiom of East Asian society.

> Traditional Confucian norm: emphasis on the community over the individual.

> Modern-day residue: self-sacrifice for the benefit of others; rejection of Western individualism, privacy, and self-interest; ethic of conformity.

In contemporary China, Confucianism is employed as an ideology that supports the rights of the community (including the rights of the state) against individual self-interest. In contrast to the anti-Confucian stance of the Chinese Communist Party through most of its history, the new regime, shaped by Deng Xiaoping and carried forth by his protégé Jiang Zemin, has embraced Confucianism as an indigenous defense against the hegemonic influence of the West, and in particular, against the accusations of human rights abuses voiced by Western governments. This is not simply a Communist argument: the current leadership of the People's Republic of China is following the footsteps of Taiwan's Chiang Kai-shek and Singapore's Lee Kwan-yu in defining Confucianism as "benevolent authoritarianism." The use of Confucianism as an apology for states' rights over individual freedom is the ironic byproduct of the drive to modernization, which affirms Western techniques but rejects Western "spiritual pollution."

These values, advocated cynically by authoritarian governments as a buttress to their suppression of individual rights, are still viewed positively at the grassroots level. Many Chinese and Japanese see American-style individualism as extreme and socially divisive, even as harmful to individuals themselves. Individualism in East Asia is associated with isolation, loneliness, and outsider status. For contemporary East Asians, a person's social identity is far more important than his or her sense of privacy or individuality.

There can be no doubt that Confucian communitarian values have created an East Asian "ethic of conformity"—an ethic frequently observed by sociologists studying Japan in particular. But this characterization is highly Western: from a Chinese or Japanese point of view, Confucian communitarianism provides individuals with a strong sense of meaning and purpose in their lives.

> Traditional Confucian norm: emphasis on the family over either the individual or the community.

> Modern-day residue: filial piety, active participation of parents in children's affairs, support of parents in old age, strong extended family identity.

In the early years of the Republic of China, the great reformer Sun Yat-sen (Song Zhongshan) complained that the Chinese people were like a "tray of shifting sand." By this, Sun did not mean that China suffered from excessive individualism, but rather that the power of "familism" in Chinese Confucian culture—the unwavering allegiance to one's family or clan—was undermining the ideals of public service and the strengthening of the nation. Despite the efforts of the early reformers and, in the present day, the Chinese Communist Party, loyalty to family remains paramount, and all other interests—from individual self-interest to a broader-based civic or national identity—are subsumed under the ties of family.

The centrality of the family is China's most abiding cultural value. From the home radiate moral values, spiritual beings, and ritual action. The primary moral tie is the tie between parents and children, and moral consciousness begins with training in the Confucian virtues, especially filial piety.

Among family relationships, the vertical/generative always takes precedence over the horizontal/affiliative. Thus, the parent-child relationship is emphasized over the husband-wife relationship, the latter patterned after but always secondary to the former. This is reflected historically in the private writings of the scholar-official class (the Confucian intellectuals), who wrote of their mothers without fail and at length, but rarely if ever, of their wives. And it remains true today, where parent-child relationships are given much greater attention than marital relationships. Up until the twentieth century, East Asian marriages were arranged by parents. Although this is no longer the case, parents still play a significant role in the choice of marriage partners by their children, and divorce brings shame to the family as a whole, not just the husband and wife. Divorce rates in China and Japan, while on the rise, are only about one-tenth those of Europe and the United States.

Of the Five Permanent Relationships of classical Confucianism, three are related to the family: parent-child, husband-wife, and sibling-sibling. These ties are stronger than ever. As people have become disillusioned with the grand promises of Communism as well as the alienating isolation of Western individualism, the family has remained the principal source of personal value in every country in the East Asian region.

> Traditional Confucian norm: extension of filial piety to the dead as well as the living.

> Modern-day residue: persistence of ancestor veneration as the predominant form of religious practice in East Asia.

The religion of China (including the Chinese-dominant states of Taiwan, Hong Kong, and Singapore), Korea, Japan, and Vietnam is, first and foremost, family religion. Throughout East Asia, the most revered of all spiritual beings are the family ancestors. Families make offerings of incense, rice, meat, and fruit every morning at the family altar and on anniversary days at the family gravesite. The cult of the ancestors makes the home the most central "sacred space." Periodic rites at local shrines and temples are equally for the benefit of family: its health, harmony, and preservation.

Traditional Confucian norm: the Spring and Autumn Sacrifice to Heaven, advocated by Confucius and practiced without interruption from 740 to 1927 c.e.

Modern-day residue: annual festival for Confucius held on Teacher's Day.

Despite his own emphasis on ritual, the Confucian rites have all but disappeared in modern China. Religious rituals at the level of the village or neighborhood community are not specifically Confucian: they are the rites of Priestly Taoism and will be described in Chapter 5. State sponsorship of religious ritual, traditionally associated with political or imperial Confucianism, is nonexistent in contemporary East Asia—condemned by the People's Republic of China as "feudal superstition" and constitutionally banned in postwar Japan. It can be said that the separation of church and state is complete in modern East Asia. As much as Confucius himself upheld the ideal of the ruler as religious and moral exemplar, religion is no longer encouraged by the state (and is in fact actively discouraged in Communist China).

This is not to say that state-sponsored ceremonies have disappeared altogether. The civil religion of China, Korea, Japan, and Vietnam is highly ceremonial, and public gatherings such as school assemblies, graduations, inaugurations, and other commemorative events are promoted by state and local governments and are generally well attended. People enjoy and appreciate public ceremonies, and the kind of cynicism and disinterest so often seen in the West is almost completely absent in East Asian contexts. Public ceremonial is highly valued in the East Asian cultural region.

Among these state-sponsored events is an annual festival for Confucius held on Teacher's Day in late September. On this day, a grand ceremony honoring Confucius is held. The most elaborate Teacher's Day celebrations are performed in Seoul, Korea, and Taipei, Taiwan. The ceremony features the use of traditional instruments by dancers and musicians in classical dress. The rites are based upon *The Book of Rites,* dating to the Han Dynasty. Attendees are generally confined to government officials, foreign dignitaries, and tourists. The Teacher's Day celebrations have none of the public importance that the rites favored by Confucius once enjoyed.

TAOISM AND THE MODERN WORLD

Is Taoism still a viable religious option in the modern world? After fifty years of Communist rule in Mainland China, Sect Taoism has largely ceased to exist. Though several Taoist monasteries of the "Complete Reality" (*Quan-*

zhen) tradition have been restored as tourist attractions—most notably the White Cloud Temple in Beijing, which attracts thousands of foreign and domestic tourists—few monks live or practice there, and Taoism is now confined primarily to the Esoteric and Priestly streams. However, despite the fact that Taoism has very little institutional identity today, it remains vital to contemporary Chinese religious life. On a social level, Priestly Taoism is still practiced, especially in rural villages and in Chinese communities in Taiwan, Hong Kong, and Southeast Asia, as part of the diffused religion of traditional China: beliefs and practices surrounding human interaction with gods, ghosts, and ancestors. Taoist priests are still subjected to years of apprenticeship and rigorous training and have mastered the arts of Esoteric Taoism. They are well educated in the history of Taoism, alchemical practices, the preparation of talismans and amulets, and the conduct of religious ritual. The Taoist priesthood is a vital resource for the preservation of traditional Chinese medicine, religion, and culture. A detailed discussion of modern-day Priestly Taoism appears in Chapter 5.

On a personal level, Taoist values remain strong, including the belief in individual "ease" and freedom against social constraint, as a check on everyday duties and responsibilities; the practice of exercise and traditional medicine, which are still favored over Western pharmaceuticals; and the appreciation of nature and natural impulses. Young people in China who may be disenchanted with the political manipulation of Confucianism by authoritarian governments, or who have become less sanguine about the promise of modernity represented by the West, find in traditional Taoist practices a viable, home-grown solution to personal, societal, and global conflict. Increasingly as well, Europeans and Americans have been drawn to Taoist literature and to practices associated with Esoteric Taoism, from gymnastics exercises (Shadow Boxing and Qigong) to herbal medicine and a more naturalistic view of religion and personal cultivation.

Taoist practices and values still upheld in the modern world include the following:

- Modern and contemporary Chinese art is significantly influenced by Taoist naturalism, as it has been throughout Chinese art history.
- The longevity practices of Esoteric Taoism are evident in Chinese cooking (a diet rich in leafy green vegetables, tubular vegetables such as fungi and mushrooms, vitamins, herbs, and spices).
- Chinese maintain a holistic conception of personal identity, and see a balanced life as crucial for physical and psychological health: work is balanced with rest and relaxation, sedentary activity with physical activity.

- Physical activity, while strongly valued, is not competitive or sports-oriented, as it is in the West; Taoist-inspired physical exercises are aerobic, yogic, and meditative.
- Nature is idealized. Though modern China is plagued with pollution problems associated with rapid economic growth, the *idea* of nature is highly valued, as expressed in the cultivation of plants, pet ownership (traditionally songbirds and singing insects, but now including dogs and cats), hiking, nature photography, and family outings.
- Although family and profession are prioritized, in keeping with a more Confucian orientation toward life, Taoist ideals of self-expression, freedom from constraint, and recreation are highly valued—Chinese like to have fun and regularly indulge in parties, including consumption of alcohol, singing, and composing poetry.
- Sexuality, while constrained by Confucian family and marital obligations, is considered natural and healthy.
- In the siting of homes and graves, Chinese refer to the principles of geomancy (*feng-shui*), though they may or may not make use of the services of a *feng-shui* master.
- Temple construction and temple-based activities such as festivals, pilgrimage tours, and community rites enjoy more public support than they have in a century of social and political transformation; typically, they involve the participation of Taoist priests, mediums, and shamans. These will be described in greater detail in Chapter 5.

CONFUCIANISM, TAOISM, AND RELIGIOUS DIVERSITY

How have Chinese resolved the obvious conflicts between Confucianism and Taoism? How is it that these two seemingly opposite value systems have been able to exist harmoniously for most of their two thousand years of existence?

Partly, this is a function of an inconsistency in the English language: there is a single word for the religions of India, *Hinduism,* but no such word for the religions of China. The word *Hinduism* masks a remarkable diversity of religious beliefs and practices. In fact, some scholars have argued that Hinduism as a single, coherent religion does not exist except as a figment of the Western colonial imagination. China scholars believe that Chinese religions are much more closely attuned than the religions of India, and they have even proposed the term "Chinese Religion" (rather than "Chinese religions") to describe Chinese religious life and culture.

On the face of it, Confucianism and Taoism would appear to be quite distinct—even contradicting one another in their core values and prescriptions. In Chapter 2, on the classical texts and teachings of Confucianism and Taoism, they were seen as two traditions, which often defined themselves explicitly in contrast to one another. Most Western interpreters of Confucianism and Taoism rely exclusively on these classical sources for their understanding of Chinese religion, thus solidifying the impression that they are opposed and distinct. Looking at the whole of Chinese culture, however, gives a more accurate perception: although Confucianism and Taoism have at times engaged in polemical conflict, they are in fact aspects of a single tradition rather than two separate traditions.

What is the single tradition that serves as the foundation for both Confucianism and Taoism? The conceptual underpinning of both traditions is *yin-yang cosmology*, the view that the universe is composed of opposing but complementary forces in perpetual evolution. *Yin-yang* cosmology was introduced in Chapter 2. This section will examine how this system forms the unifying structure of Chinese religion in its two aspects.

Chinese cosmology identifies two forces or potentialities acting within the cosmos, in nature, and within living beings. The more prominent of these forces is *yang*, the potentiality of movement, action, and resurgence. The less prominent is *yin*, the potentiality of quiescence, passivity, and regression. The universe as a whole is activated by the interactions of these forces.

The *yin-yang* diagram, called the "Diagram of the Great Ultimate" (*tai-ji tu*) in Chinese, shows the complementary dualism of *yin* and *yang* forces. Though rarely in perfect equilibrium, the cosmos "tends toward" balance, moving in oscillation from the dominance of *yang* to the dominance of *yin* and back again. Note that even at the height of *yang*, there is the kernel of *yin*; and at the height of *yin*, the kernel of *yang*. That is to say, all things in the universe, as well as the universe as a whole, develop and express themselves through the interactions of *yin* and *yang*, sometimes displaying one or the other in manifest form, but containing the equal and opposite force in latent form.

Yin-yang cosmology has shaped the Chinese view not only of the universe, but also of their own social and religious history. Dynasties are seen to rise (*yang*) and fall (*yin*) in cyclical fashion, in accordance with the ebb and flow of the universe as a whole. And the major religious traditions indigenous to China, Confucianism and Taoism, are also seen as complementary expressions of *yin-yang* forces: Confucianism as the expression of *yang* (rational, aggressive, and active) and Taoism as the expression of *yin* (intuitive, passive, and quiescent). From the perspective of *yin-yang* cosmology, these expressions are complementary, not conflicting, and are in fact the manifestations of a single life force, called in Chinese *qi* ("spirit" or "breath"). To put it in religious terms, Confucianism and Taoism are the opposing but complementary expressions of the "spirit" of Chinese culture.

Chinese Approaches to Religious Diversity

In light of Chinese cosmology, are Confucianism and Taoism two religions, or are they opposing alternatives within a single religious tradition? From a Chinese cultural perspective, Confucianism and Taoism are opposing but *complementary* aspects of the unifying *Dao* or "Path" of religious cultivation. Most Chinese are, to one extent or another, both Confucian *and* Taoist, and very few are exclusively one *or* the other. Describing Confucianism and Taoism as the two religions indigenous to China, and further identifying their branches, distorts the actual practice of religion in China.

Generally speaking, the metaphor of root and branches is not well suited to religion in China. The idea of branches suggests rigid distinctions and separation. The Chinese have rarely allied themselves with a single religion or sect, but have tended to see all religions—in particular, Confucianism, Taoism, and Buddhism—as manifestations of a single "Way" or *Dao*. Despite their differences, Confucianism and Taoism are seen to be complementary, and religious self-cultivation in China typically combines elements of both. Even within the Confucian and Taoist traditions themselves, the subtraditions that were labeled in Chapter 3 as Religious Confucianism, Political Confucianism, Sect Taoism, Esoteric Taoism, and Priestly Taoism do not command an exclusivistic allegiance or membership. They are more like varieties or streams of Confucianism and Taoism than branches. As streams of Chinese religion, Confucianism, Taoism, and their subtraditions are dynamic, fluid, intersecting, and intermingling—aspects of a singular Chinese religion.

Confucianism and Taoism are not the only major religions of China. They are two of three that Chinese refer to as the "Three Teachings." The third, Buddhism, originated in India and was first introduced to China in the Later Han Dynasty (25 to 220 c.e.). In general, Chinese Buddhism is as important to the story of Chinese religion as Confucianism and Taoism, though it did not originate in China and has had fewer active adherents than the two native or indigenous traditions.

When religions exist in close geographical proximity, a number of options are available to the culture. They might be described as follows:

Exclusivism: The religious exclusivist insists that one's own tradition is the "right" or "orthodox" way, while other religions are "heterodox" or "superstitious." Exclusivism states that there is only one true religion.

Inclusivism: The religious inclusivist (or "universalist") believes that there is only one truth (often expressed as monotheism, the belief in one God), but that the truth/God is "known by many names." The inclusivist sees no significant difference between one religion and another.

Relativism: A relativist recognizes that there are many standards of truth, beauty, and goodness, but sees no way of resolving the differences. According to this view, all religions are "true" in their own way to their own adherents, and there is little need for interaction between them.

Syncretism: The religious syncretist "takes what is best" from various traditions to form a creative unity out of the diversity. Syncretistic religions tend to be highly individualistic, or attract a small following (often identified as "cults" or "sects" by more mainstream believers).

Complementary Pluralism: The religious pluralist recognizes real differences between religions, but sees t\hose differences as complementary. The world is a "mosaic" of religious and cultural traditions existing, ideally, in a harmonious relationship.

In China, the most common strategies for dealing with religious diversity have been the fourth and fifth options listed above, *syncretism* and *complementary pluralism*. The introduction of Buddhism to China was a case of religious syncretism on a grand scale. In the period from the end of the Han to the end of the Tang Dynasty (220–906 C.E.), Buddhism was thoroughly made Chinese and incorporated both Confucian and Taoist elements. Buddhism in China was more family-oriented than the reclusive monastic traditions of India—a feature of East Asian Buddhism that clearly demonstrates Confucian influence. In response to Taoism, Chinese Buddhism was dominated by the Chan school of intuitive meditation (known in the West by its Japanese pronunciation, "Zen") that resembled Taoist meditation. China's preference for religious syncretism made Chinese Buddhism distinct from Indian Buddhism because it drew heavily upon native Confucian and Taoist elements.

Throughout Chinese history, there has been the emergence of innumerable syncretistic religious movements, often short-lived and confined to relatively restricted geographical areas, but appearing so often and so widely that syncretism has clearly been a favored strategy for dealing with religious diversity.

For example, the Ming religious leader Lin Zhao-en (1517–1598 C.E.) integrated Chan Buddhist meditation upon "emptiness," Taoist "inner alchemy," and Confucian "seriousness" in a religious practice of self-improvement that he called *san jiao he yi*, the "Unity of the Three Traditions." His creative combination of Confucianism, Taoism, and Buddhism led to the emergence of a new, syncretistic religion. A modern-day sectarian group, the "Way of Unity" (*Yi-guan dao*), expands this doctrine to include five religions: Confucianism, Taoism, Buddhism, Christianity, and Islam.

Chinese describe religious syncretism as the teaching of "three in one," and throughout history many Chinese have seen Confucianism, Taoism, and Buddhism as different elaborations of a single "Way." At many stages, their adaptation and mutual borrowing has been so extensive that it is difficult to find any clear lines of demarcation, with Buddhist monks quoting Confucian classics, or Confucian scholars becoming Taoist recluses. Today, a Chinese religious temple in an urban alleyway or country lane will have images and objects from all three traditions. Even Chinese find it difficult to distinguish among them.

Carried to an extreme, syncretism erases all differences and affirms a single, albeit eclectic, system of values and practices. Although this strategy has appeared often in Chinese history, still Confucianism, Taoism, and Buddhism have persisted as identifiable traditions, and syncretism has not been the only strategy for dealing with religious diversity in Chinese society.

In rare instances, an attitude of *exclusivism* has temporarily prevailed. In an oft-quoted memorial to the Tang Dynasty emperor, the Confucian Han Yü (768–824 C.E.) condemned Taoism and Buddhism, accusing both of antisocial behavior, idleness, and free-loading. This memorial contributed to a nationwide suppression of Buddhism and Taoism, forcing their monks and priests back into lay life and confiscating their temples and lands. This proved to be a major turning point in the institutional histories of both Buddhism and Taoism.

For the most part, however, China has embraced *complementary pluralism* as a primary religious, ethical, and aesthetic value—seeing the three religions in harmony rather than discord. Differences are recognized and acknowledged, but the teachings and practices of one tradition are complementary to the teachings and practices of another. Thus, one might be

Confucian in some elements of one's life, or at certain stages of life, and Buddhist or Taoist in other elements and stages. Admittedly, conflicts exist, but the diversity of religious beliefs and practices reflects the fact that life itself is sometimes "untidy"—sometimes active, at other times more sedentary; sometimes socially engaged, at other times more reclusive; sometimes oriented toward this world and its concerns, at other times directed toward realities external to the world of everyday experience.

Over the course of Chinese history, Confucianism, Taoism, and Buddhism influenced and shaped one another, sometimes as rivals, sometimes as allies. In general, the pluralistic orientation has been the dominant view and practice at every level of society, from the uneducated peasantry to officials, ministers, and emperors. The Chinese attitude toward religion has been to combine what is best, and to see differences as complementary rather than conflicting. Moreover, most Chinese would see themselves as being adherents of all three traditions. One saying expresses the harmonizing of the three in this way: "With respect to my family and community, I am Confucian; with respect to nature and my physical and spiritual identity, I am Taoist; with respect to death and what comes after death, I am Buddhist."

As the three traditions are not mutually exclusive, their total membership includes most Chinese. Scholars estimate that 93 to 97 percent of Chinese are adherents of all three traditions, though it should be understood that none requires initiation, payment of dues or tithes, or regular attendance in the way that church membership does in the West. Rather, Confucianism, Taoism, and Buddhism have been part of the civil religion or common religious system of Chinese society for the past two millennia and are sustained by the everyday beliefs and practices of Chinese from all walks of life.

How have the Chinese so successfully integrated the three religions and been able to adopt a nonexclusivistic attitude toward religious differences? The cosmogonic myth was discussed briefly in Chapter 2 and will be examined here again. Here is a translation of the actual Chinese text from the Han Dynasty treatise, the *Huai nan zi:*

> Before heaven and earth had taken form all was vague and amorphous. Therefore it was called the Great Beginning. The Great Beginning produced emptiness and emptiness produced the universe. The universe produced material-force which had limits. That which was clear and light drifted up to become heaven, while that which was heavy and turbid solidified to become

earth. It was very easy for the pure, fine material to come together but extremely difficult for the heavy, turbid material to solidify. Therefore heaven was completed first and earth assumed shape after. The combined essences of heaven and earth became the yin and yang, the concentrated essences of yin and yang became the four seasons, and the scattered essences of the four seasons became the myriad creatures of the world. After a long time the hot force of the accumulated yang produced fire and the essence of the fire force became the sun; the cold force of the accumulated yin became water and the essence of the water force became the moon. The essence of the excess force of the sun and moon became the stars and planets. Heaven received the sun, moon and stars, while earth received water and soil. (de Bary 1960, 192–93)

If the story of creation found in Chinese religion is contrasted with that of the Abrahamic traditions (Judaism, Christianity, and Islam), as told in the Book of Genesis, some significant differences become apparent. There are four significant characteristics of *yin-yang* cosmology—non-anthropomorphism, organic model, complement dualism, and non-anthropocentrism—all quite different from the Genesis account.

Non-anthropomorphism

Anthropomorphism is the ascription of *human form* to religious authority (God as a father or "wise old man"). The *Dao* is never anthropomorphized in Chinese religion. It is an abstract force or principle, without personal (human) characteristics. In the Genesis account, the agent of creation is not an abstract "Way," but God. God is a personified or anthropomorphic being (*anthropomorphic* means literally "having the form or characteristics of humans"). This is not to say that God is a person, but that God manifests human characteristics: God walks, speaks, delights, mourns, shows anger and kindness, and so on. The *Dao* is not portrayed in this way.

Organic model

The Chinese narrative describes an organic progression, both in the cosmogonic myth of creation and in the theory of the Five Phases. In an organic progression, an element or force ("A") gives rise to another ("B"), which in turn gives rise to yet another ("C"), and so on indefinitely. This is why creation is never complete or final. Chinese culture is continually evolving as well, and both Taoism and Confucianism are transforming and evolving in response to changing cultural conditions.

According to the Book of Genesis of the Hebrew Bible, the Judeo-Christian God created the world in six days. These acts are portrayed in Genesis as separate, even independent events. They do not follow a natural order. For example, Genesis reports that light is created on the first day and vegetation on the third, but the sun is not created until the fourth day—a progression that is not organic or naturalistic. From the perspective of the history of religions, Judaism, Christianity, and Islam find their basic meaning in the "original" teachings, and their respective canons (or scriptures: Hebrew Bible, New Testament, and Qur'an) are "closed canons"—perfect and complete, without the possibility of addition or change. Chinese religion, by contrast, is evolutionary and open-ended.

Complement Dualism

One scholar has described Chinese yin-yang cosmology as "complement dualism," in contrast to the "conflict dualism" of the West (Smith 1998). *Yin* and *yang* are opposites, to be sure, but they represent "complementary opposition" rather than "opposition in conflict." Ultimately, the opposing forces are mutually necessary. By contrast, God's acts in Western religions create a preferential ordering or hierarchy of value that defines the traditional Western view of the world. Interestingly, God's acts of creation are not "out of nothing." Even prior to the first act, God looks out upon a seemingly preexistent, watery mass—a sea—not unlike the initial condition described in the Chinese creation narrative. Rather than creating "something from nothing," God's creative activity is a process of *separation*, of distinguishing one thing from another. A series of binary oppositions are asserted, and God states His preference for one side or the other in each dualistic conflict.

For example, on the first day, "God separated the light from the darkness" (Genesis 1:4). His preference was clear: "God saw that the light was good."

The second day of creation was also an act of separation: a firmament separating the waters of the sky from the waters of the earth. On the third day, God separated seed-bearing plants from fruit-bearing plants (Genesis 1:12); on the fourth day, light from darkness once more (Genesis 1:14) as well as the light of the day (the sun) from the light of the night (the moon) (Genesis 1:16). On the fifth day, God distinguished between creatures of the air and creatures of the sea, and on the sixth and final day of creation, God distinguished between creatures of the land and humans. In a subsequent development of the story, there is, of course, a further separation, the separation of male and female in Adam and Eve.

The fact that God's acts of creation are actually acts of separation is significant for the subsequent development of the Western religions, all of which emphasize a dualistic orientation toward reality and morality. There is "spirit" and "matter," "good" and "evil," "mind" and "body," "saved" and "unsaved," "sacred" and "profane"—with a clear preference for the first term in each opposing pair. Western religions conceive of opposition as "either/or," whereas Chinese religion conceives of opposition as "both/and."

Non-anthropocentrism

Anthropocentrism is the idea that human beings are the most important beings in the universe, the center of worth and value. In the Chinese cosmogonic myths, humans are noticeably absent. The story of creation makes no mention of humans at all. In the Genesis account, by contrast, humans are the culmination of God's acts of separation/creation. They are charged with "dominion over the fish of the sea and over the birds of the air and over every living thing that moves upon the earth" (Genesis 1:28). The rest of the Biblical canon is concerned with the relationship between God and humankind, clearly placing humans at the center of the story. In Chinese religion (especially Taoism), humans are not the only beings worthy of attention or value.

Confucianism and Taoism from the Perspective of Yin-Yang Cosmology

The *yin-yang* cosmological system is at the heart and foundation of both Confucianism and Taoism. As opposed as Confucianism and Taoism have been in some periods of their history, they have both assumed this system as a common cultural and philosophical heritage. At this fundamental level, there is no disagreement, and *yin-yang* cosmology plays a central role in both traditions.

This is important for two reasons: first, Chinese religion should be seen as a single system having two aspects or native (indigenous) elaborations, rather than an arena of conflict between two (or three, if Buddhism is added) religions. Second, the interaction of Taoism and Confucianism has always been idealized as a complementary relationship, like the relation-

Table 4.2
Contrasts between Chinese and Western Cosmogonic Myths

Huan nan zi and Other Sources	Genesis
non-anthropomorphism	anthropomorphism
organistic model	mechanistic model
complement dualism	conflict dualism
non-anthropocentrism	anthropocentrism

ship between *yin* and *yang*. The healthy individual is neither (exclusively) *yin* or *yang*, nor is he or she exclusively Taoist or Confucian. In fact, just as life cannot exist without both *yin* and *yang*, it is difficult to conceive of Chinese culture in the absence of either Taoism or Confucianism.

This understanding of the cosmos intersects and overlaps with Confucianism and Taoism in a way that makes Chinese Religion a single whole. Just as *yin* and *yang* are both necessary for the creation and continuing evolution of the cosmos, so too Confucianism and Taoism are necessary for the cultural vitality of Chinese civilization. And just as *yin* and *yang* energies are mutually complementary, "giving rise" to one another in a cyclic pattern of eternal change, so too Confucianism and Taoism are complementary and mutually enhancing as systems of belief and practice, rather than conflicting or mutually exclusive. The one cannot exist without the other, and the healthy, balanced society or individual will maintain both Confucian and Taoist orientations. Chinese cosmology supports the co-existence, even the mutual compatibility, of seemingly opposite tendencies, and serves as the foundation for the *syncretism* or *complementary pluralism* that has typified China's response to its religious diversity.

Classical Confucianism and Classical Taoism are compared here with a series of oppositions:

Confucianism	**Taoism**
Heaven (*Tian*)	Nature (*Dao*)
ceremony	simplicity
action	non-action
society	individual
male	female
adulthood	infancy and old age
moral perfection	spiritual tranquility
"build"	"nourish"
"establish"	"return"

being	non-being
education	self-transformation
hierarchy	unity
named	nameless
North	South
knowledge	intuition
the ancients	prehistory

Though it is tempting to look at these values and images dualistically, from a Chinese point of view—based upon the goal of harmonizing complementary opposites—both are necessary for the full flowering of the person and the culture. This is why Chinese see themselves as "both/and" when it comes to Confucianism and Taoism rather than "either/or."

Because Chinese culture is grounded in this cosmological understanding, Chinese value balance, harmony, and the reconciliation of opposites. Confucianism and Taoism are not so much in conflict as they balance one another in harmonious interaction. This is not to say that there have not been periods in Chinese history where conflict was expressed, but the gen-

Table 4.3
Confucianism and Taoism as Complementary Traditions

	Confucian Values and Behaviors	Taoist Values and Behaviors
Cosmological Vision	the veneration of ancestors	the sense that reality extends beyond the observable realm and includes spiritual power
Self-cultivation	education in history and culture (poetry, music, painting, and calligraphy)	the practice of meditation and physical exercises that emphasize the unity of an individual's psychological, emotional, physical, and spiritual identity
Harmony as an Ideal	the cultivation of harmonious, hierarchical relations in one's family and social life	the belief in harmony between persons, the natural world, and the cosmos
Social and Personal Welfare	the grounding of moral teachings and ethical principles in a religious or cosmic reality	the belief that internal and external harmony has practical benefits, from social welfare to individual health and longevity

eral perspective is that both Confucianism and Taoism have been necessary for the healthy growth and evolution of Chinese civilization as a whole.

A list of the general characteristics of Confucianism and Taoism shows their complementary nature. See Table 4.3. Clearly, there is nothing inherently contradictory in these values and practices. Although the potential for conflict exists, Chinese have tended to see them as complementary rather than conflicting. Consequently, most Chinese are *both* Confucian *and* Taoist rather than *either* one *or* the other and actively integrate both perspectives into their daily lives and thought.

FURTHER READINGS

For an illustration of the syncretistic approach to religious diversity in Chinese history, Judith Berling wrote a book on the Ming Dynasty religious leader Lin Zhao-en entitled *The Syncretic Religion of Lin Chao-en.* She has written a marvelous book on Chinese religious pluralism and her personal encounters with Chinese religion, *A Pilgrim in Chinese Culture: Negotiating Religious Diversity.* The idea that Chinese religious diversity masks a hidden unity is discussed by Robert P. Weller in his *Unities and Diversities in Chinese Religion,* a sociological study of Chinese religion, especially at the popular level.

The growing popularity of Taoism in the West is evident in the astounding number of popular self-help books appearing in North American and European bookstores teaching Taoist insights and exercises. A good discussion of this phenomenon can be found in J.J. Clarke's *The Tao of the West: Western Transformations of Taoist Thought.* For Western interest in Confucianism as a living practice, see Robert Neville's book, *Boston Confucianism: Portable Tradition in the Late-Modern World.*

Berling, Judith. *A Pilgrim in Chinese Culture: Negotiating Religious Diversity.* Maryknoll, NY: Orbis, 1997.

Berling, Judith. *The Syncretic Religion of Lin Chao-en.* New York: Columbia University Press, 1980.

Clarke, J.J. *The Tao of the West: Western Transformations of Taoist Thought.* New York: Routledge, 2000.

de Bary, William Theodore et al., eds., *Sources of the Chinese Tradition,* vol. 1 (New York: Columbia University Press, 1960), pp. 192–93.

Neville, Robert Cummings. *Boston Confucianism: Portable Tradition in the Late-Modern World.* Albany: State University of New York Press, 2000.

Smith, Wilfred Cantwell. *Patterns of Faith around the World.* Oxford: Oneworld Publications, 1998.

Weller, Robert P. *Unities and Diversities in Chinese Religion.* Seattle: University of Washington Press, 1987.

5

RITUALS AND HOLIDAYS

Religious practice is the heart of Chinese religion and can even be said to supersede religious belief. Chinese throughout history have been unfailing in the conduct of ancestor veneration, formal religious ceremony (as well as the *li* of everyday life), and the observance of seasonal holidays—even in the absence of sect membership, conscious religious belief, or a specific religious identity.

China enjoyed a remarkable cultural unity over two thousand years of imperial history. This was thanks to its written language: the use of pictographic characters that can be read independently of their pronunciation. As a result, the Chinese were able to transmit ideas and values, not to mention the bureaucratic institutions and laws of the imperial state, across vast spaces and times. The same can be said of China's religious traditions: grounded in their own textual canons, the scriptures of Chinese religion were transmitted and preserved across many generations. Finally, as discussed in Chapter 4, China's cultural unity was also based upon *yin-yang* cosmology, a system that unifies apparent opposites (including Confucianism and Taoism) as a single whole.

CHINESE RELIGION: A SOCIOLOGICAL OVERVIEW

The religious life of a people is grounded in their social and political situation. *Sociology* is the study of social structure and the impact of the social situation of individuals, families, and communities upon their beliefs and cultural expression. Social situation includes income and education levels, political standing, marital status, family structure, occupation, regional identity, and so on. It is not necessary to argue that one's social situation *determines* one's beliefs and values or to reduce religion to social class, but it is helpful to see religious expression embedded in the social networks in which individuals, families, and communities live. The social dimension of religion is only one of many elements, but it is the arena in which religious belief is expressed through action. So, before looking at specific rituals and holidays of Chinese religion, a review of the social structure of traditional China is appropriate.

The social structure of traditional China was complex and diversified. It was never a simple division of haves and have-nots, of the politically power-ful and the politically powerless, or of the literate and the illiterate. Rather, China in imperial times was divided into a multiplicity of social groups and classes. In terms of wealth, status, and level of education, these groups inter-sected and overlapped in complex ways, but in general, Chinese society can be viewed as a web of relationships with several layers of status and power. For example, despite a centuries-old ideal that the government bureaucracy would be made up of meritorious Confucian scholars, individuals high on a scale of literacy were not always high on the scale of bureaucratic power, and it was common in traditional China for accomplished scholars to fail in the imperial examinations and turn to other pursuits—writing, medicine, mercantilism, and so on. Religious professionals such as Buddhist monks and Taoist priests included individuals of great intellectual accomplishment who may also have failed to secure a government career. The scale of edu-cational attainment was not always parallel with the scale of political status. However, education was always a more accurate barometer of social status than wealth; the Chinese do not define class in terms of wealth at all, and it was common in traditional times for a person of considerable wealth, such as a merchant, to have a lesser class status than a poor teacher or literatus.

Social Groups of Imperial China (Shang to Qing Dynasties)

1. The Emperor
2. Officials
3. Scholar gentry class
4. Peasants and farmers
5. Artisans, merchants of the middle class
6. Itinerant laborers and social outcasts

Though six distinct social groups can be identified, the traditional class system was divided into two: "those who work with their minds" and "those who work with their strength." This was expressed initially by the Second Sage of Confucianism, Mencius: "Some labor with their minds; others labor with their strength. Those who labor with their minds govern others; those who labor with their strength are governed by others. Those who are governed by others support them; those who govern others are supported by them. This is a principle universally recognized."

At the top of the social ladder, the emperor was politically powerful but not always among the cultural elite. Although some emperors were accomplished literati, others had peasant roots and enjoyed humble pursuits. The Chinese emperors generally held great power, and their sponsorship of religious institutions often had a profound effect on the intellectual and bureaucratic strength of Confucian, Taoist, and Buddhist traditions. At the level of villages and families, however, religious life was totally unaffected by the sectarian leanings of the imperial household.

The discussion that follows will look briefly at the religious practices of six social groups. As these groups overlap in many cases, they are not meant to represent distinct units of Chinese society.

Social Status and the Practice of Religion in Traditional China

The Emperor

- Public rituals: great sacrifices
- Sponsorship of religious institutions, temple construction, and canonical texts
- Private religious cultivation

For much of Chinese history, the most detailed records of ritual performance appear in the imperial dynastic histories, which contain a section on *li* ("rites and ceremonies") describing the court rituals of the imperial house. Great sacrifices, which were overseen by the emperor, included burnt offerings of oxen and sheep, the performance of music and dance, offerings of jade and silk, offerings of wine, and prayers of blessing and thanksgiving to *Shang Di*, the "Lord on High."

It can be said that the imperial court was steeped in religious ritual, and the emperor was a "great priest" of a ceremonial national religion. Natural calamities were seen as reflections of divine justice. Often, general amnesties were awarded at times of eclipse, earthquake, fires, drought, comets, or floods. The emperor himself was addressed as *Tian-zi*, "Son of Heaven," recipient of "Heaven's Mandate" to rule. Dynastic stability was highly valued, but even in times of dynastic succession or the overthrow of one imperial family by another (a remarkably rare occurrence in the two thousand five hundred years of recorded dynastic history), religious justification was sought. To this end, the conquering royal family might adopt a sectarian form of Confucianism, Taoism, or Buddhism as a buttress to their imperial claim, contrasting their sectarian allegiance with the state cult of the prior dynasty. Often as a political ploy, if not because of personal religious conviction, emperors approved vast expenditures from the imperial treasury for temple construction, artistic patronage, and the publication of canonical texts. For example, the edition of the Taoist Canon that survives today was sponsored by Ming Emperor Ying Zong of the Zhengtong Reign Period (1436–1449 C.E.) and is called in Chinese the *Zhengtong Daozang* ("Taoist Canon of the Ming Dynasty").

Privately, the emperor was fully a member of China's popular culture. Though confined for most of his life to the imperial palace, he was educated not only by tutors in the Confucian classics or Buddhist scriptures, but also by his mother, maids, wife, and concubines, who brought him tales of the gods of the common people and of ghosts and spirits. The emperor engaged in many of the religious practices described in this book, including the ingestion of Taoist elixirs, the worship of spiritual beings, Confucian Quiet Sitting, and Buddhist meditation, as well as the rites of the imperial cult.

Officials

- The examination system
- Official appointments
- Leadership in state-sponsored cults

China's bureaucratic government structure was based upon an imperial examination system. Zhu Xi's annotated editions of the Confucian Four Books (*The Analects* of Confucius, *The Book of Mencius, The Great Learning,* and *The Doctrine of the Mean*) were made the official texts of the civil service examinations in 1313 C.E. As a result, China's official class was dedicated to Confucian learning, and there were many instances in Chinese history when officials reprimanded the emperor for dabbling in unorthodox religious beliefs and practices. At this level—the level of highly educated political leaders and bureaucrats—the divisions among the Three Religions were most clear. This class was the least likely to see the three religions as one. Because Western travelers and scholars of the last few centuries learned about Chinese culture from the official class, they too saw Chinese religion as sectarian and compartmentalized, a view that only recently has been understood for what it truly was: a peculiar, exclusivistic view confined to a very small segment of the population.

The official class has always favored the norms and practices of Political Confucianism, tolerating religion as a means of social control but largely critical of excessive worship and heterodox cults. This sense of distrust, and of psychological distance from the common people, was intensified by the fact that government appointments were made far from home—to prevent the accumulation of local power. Religious participation of the official class was rare, serving the interests of the imperial state—disseminating the Sacred Edicts, enfeoffing local gods with honorary titles (which in effect made them subservient to the emperor and imperial authority), honoring "chaste women and filial sons" with banquets and gifts of silk and coins, and conducting ceremonies in honor of "bureaucratic deities" (such as *Cheng huang*, the "God of Walls and Moats," and *Tu di gong*, the "God of the Earth Mound"—divine bureaucratic functionaries responsible for moral accounting and criminal punishment, as opposed to the charismatic healing gods of the people).

Scholar Gentry Class

- Leadership in community religion
- Clan worship and ancestral temples

The scholar gentry class consisted of degree-holders (men who had passed some level of the civil service examinations) who had not, for various reasons, attained government positions. At times in Chinese history, this class was surprisingly large, surpassing many times over the number of successful degree-holders who had become government officials. (By the Qing Dynasty, fewer than 5 percent of degree-holders held government office.) Often frustrated by their lack of success, this class was most likely to claim leadership in local religious associations, to found syncretistic religious sects, to reject government service as Taoist recluses or Buddhist monks, and to express themselves in poetry, essay, and philosophical writings. This was especially true in the Ming Dynasty, an extraordinarily creative period in the history of Chinese syncretistic religion ("Three-in-One Thought"): studies estimate that the number of nonofficial scholars rose from thirty thousand in 1400 C.E. to six hundred thousand in 1600 C.E., a remarkable number of frustrated scholars, seeking creative outlets for their intellectual abilities.

In terms of everyday life, the scholar gentry class organized schools, temple committees, and clan or lineage (extended family) associations. They taught the Taoist and Confucian Classics, composed popular novels (often with religious themes), and served as conduits of local opinion as well as unofficial recorders of local custom. And because they were able to read and write, they are the most exciting resource for the history of Chinese religion from the ground up. They became the Taoist priests, conducting rituals of purification and exorcism in the village square; the Confucian scholars, doubling as *feng-shui* masters and fortune-tellers; the Buddhist monks, performing funeral rites for the people. Frustrated as political officials, they were the religious officials of Chinese public ceremonies.

Peasants and Farmers

- Productive of the material needs of all classes, and therefore the highest of the mean classes
- Material conditions of poverty and hardship
- Primary ritual expression: marriage rites, rites of passage, funeral rites, daily offerings to ancestors
- Domestication of Confucian values: filial piety, brotherly harmony, submission of wives to husbands

Among the classes that constitute "those who labor with their strength"—that is, the common people of traditional China—the class of farmers has been most honored. Every Confucian teacher and every Taoist sage has spoken in almost glowing terms of the industriousness, purity, and simplicity of the peasant. This belies the terrible hardship faced by millions of ordinary people over centuries of history, struggling to produce enough food for their children, enough income for the state taxes, and enough "excess sufficiency" for any hope of economic advancement. Given these conditions, it is not surprising that the popular religion of China is highly materialistic—focusing upon the material conditions of existence: food, health, and security.

The religion of the peasantry is domestic: it is concerned with family survival and prosperity. Its ritual expression is the cult of the ancestors, taking the form of daily offerings within the home as well as periodic offerings at the grave. Its ceremonies are marriages and personal rites of passage: from childhood to adulthood, and from old age to honored ancestor.

China has been remarkably successful in unifying its moral and cultural values, top to bottom and bottom to top. Popular literacy was widespread in the late imperial period, and even farmers who could not read or write enjoyed other kinds of exposure to culture: in village plays and temple-sponsored operatic performances, public readings of official edicts by the official class as well as public readings of popular novels by the scholar gentry class, and the sermons of Buddhist monks. Confucian values in particular were embraced by the common people and still stand at the moral center of Chinese popular religion today. Never exclusively Confucian, Taoist, or Buddhist, the religion of the common people was eclectic or syncretic, but rarely unorthodox from a conventional, Confucian point of view.

Artisans, Merchants of the Middle Class

- Centrality of the ancestral cult, clans and lineages
- Leadership in temple-based community religion

For the merchant class, religion was often a means of mobility, both physical and social. Because China has traditionally practiced equal-shares inheritance (with family wealth split evenly among every son), the only possibility of accumulating wealth was at the level of the clan or extended family. The merchant class had an interest in maintaining genealogies and setting aside funds for the purchase of common property and the construction of ancestral shrines serving the entire clan. Remnants of these great families are now few and far between but can still be found in southern China and Hong Kong.

The greatest contribution of the mercantile class to the religious life of China has been in the construction of temples. The Chinese landscape is dotted with thousands of temples and shrines, dedicated to culture heroes, such as the Confucian sages, and to the gods and goddesses of Chinese folk religion. Chinese temples can be humble and plain, or grand and ornate, and even today they reflect the traditional architectural style of imperial times. With their vermilion columns, tile roofs, and upturned eaves, their statuary and painted friezes, local temples are reminders of China's religious and architectural heritage. The construction and maintenance of these temples is funded by the merchant class, and the list of donors is given a prominent position in the temple, often inscribed in stone. Because Chinese popular religion has no priesthood, the temples are managed by committees of local business leaders, headed by a "Master of the Incense Burner" elected by the community.

Religious activities associated with the temples will be described further below, but neighborhood and village temples are also sites of mercantile and civic events. Traditionally, the temple courtyards were used for produce markets, with the peasants bringing their wares to sell on periodic market days. Even today, small-scale merchants set up kiosks outside the temple gates. The temples also sponsor community events, from film showings to political meetings; they are informal gathering places of retirees, who arrive early in the morning for shadow boxing and ballroom dancing, and wile away the morning hours playing *go* or chess, exchanging gossip, and discussing politics. On weekends, the temples are full of worshippers, and the incense burner at the main entrance is roiling with the smoke of hundreds of joss sticks. Outside, the local merchants have goods and snacks for sale.

The merchant class since the Song Dynasty was extraordinarily mobile, seeking new markets for their products. This led to a kind of religious mobility as well, as merchant families from one locality would carry their gods (in the form of wooden or bronze statues, transported by sedan chair) from their home villages to distant places. Other families would follow, and the local deity cult would serve as a native-place association for traveling merchants as well as a convenient site for neighborhood markets and temple fairs. To a significant extent, temple-based religion became more important to the merchant class than the ancestral cult. Even today, the leadership of village temple associations and the principal sponsors of temple festivals are local merchants, even if their own ancestors are from another town or region.

Taiwan, which is made up almost entirely of immigrants from the Chinese Mainland (the first migration was in the seventeenth century, the second in the twentieth century), has not only a robust merchant class, but also a strong emphasis on community, temple-based religion over the family, home-based religion of the ancestral cult. As a principal repository of traditional Chinese culture and religion, Taiwan is a laboratory for the study of Chinese popular religion at the level of temple organization, deity cults, and periodic festivals.

Itinerant Laborers and Social Outcasts

- Itinerant laborers: urban laborers, coolies, canal boatmen
- Social outcasts: beggars, slaves, prostitutes, criminals
- Relative unimportance of ancestor veneration
- Guild organizations and sectarian religion, with patron deities

This social class represents China's "floating population"—uneducated, often unattached workers, and shadowy figures at the peripheries of traditional Chinese society. For such persons, neither family nor community is a source of identity, and so the religious practices of ancestor veneration or temple worship are inaccessible to them. They form their own social groups, including beggar guilds, criminal gangs, prostitutes' mutual protection societies, and so on. These guilds often have patron deities who address the peculiar wants and needs of their devotees.

For example, the boatmen who worked the Grand Canal in the Ming and Qing Dynasties were the principal members of a syncretistic religious sect called the "Way of Non-Action." The sect had its own scriptures, written in a hybrid classical-vernacular style, and worshipped a goddess called the "Eternal Venerable Mother." The goddess promised a marvelous transformation of the world, after which all of her many children would return to her side. This sect, and others like it, suffered severe government persecution but managed to survive to the present day.

On a regular basis, these marginal persons visit temples and consult with spirit mediums, much as ordinary folk do. But their temple activities are typically late at night, and the shamans who serve them have contact with gods and spirits who are especially attentive to their needs. In these religious expressions, social outcasts enjoy a sense of belonging and security that they cannot find in ordinary society.

GODS, GHOSTS, AND ANCESTORS

The Chinese built upon early cosmological conceptions of *yin* and *yang* to describe the nature-spirit continuum. The *yang* world is the world of light: spirits of life (humans and deities). The *yin* world is the world of shade: spirits of death (ghosts and ancestors). Just as *yin* and *yang* are in constant interaction and mutual penetration, the world of humans and the world of the ancestors are not actually two worlds at all, but two interacting and mutually penetrating realms of existence.

Anthropologists speculate that the characteristic East Asian mix of gods, ghosts, and ancestors reflects the order of society in traditional times. The world of the spirits, in other words, is a mirror image of the world of the living.

- Ancestors are equivalent to parents and grandparents.
- Ghosts resemble bandits and beggars.
- Gods resemble officials of the state.

People treat their *ancestors* with the same care and attention they treat their living parents and grandparents, view *ghosts* with the same fear and loathing they view bandits and beggars, and treat *gods* with the same respect and obeisance they treat officials of the state (emperors, ministers, and magistrates).

Ancestor Veneration

Though China is becoming more and more modern, and its agricultural economy is evolving steadily into an industrial economy, the rituals and values of its agricultural past are still upheld. Among religious rituals, ancestor worship remains the most widespread practice among Chinese of all social classes. When an honored grandmother or grandfather dies, arrangements are made at the local Buddhist temple for a funeral service. At the same time, a fortune teller is consulted to determine the most auspicious day for burial and the location and orientation of the grave. The best locations are on hillsides, facing south (the sunny side of the hill, as China is in the Northern Hemisphere), with views of water, mountains, and valleys. After burial, regular offerings are made to the ancestral spirits, both at the gravesite and in the home.

In Chinese religion, the spirit world is on a continuum with the world of the living. This is clearest in the case of ancestors, the spirits of the family dead. If there is any religious practice that has remained constant and virtually unchanged from antiquity to the present, it is rituals surrounding the veneration of ancestors. Ancestor worship is the core of daily religious practice for virtually every family from China to Korea to Japan to Vietnam. Most East Asian households have an ancestral tablet or shrine before which food offerings have been placed and incense is burned. In a relationship of pure reciprocity, ancestors requite the respect and sustenance offered by the living through blessings and aid for their descendents.

Care of ancestors begins with a proper burial. The rites of burial are the first demonstration of the continuing filial piety of the living descendents. Following the encoffining of the body, which must take place on an auspicious day (chosen by a professional diviner), a Taoist priest is called to perform a rite of exorcism. This is needed because the family and surrounding households have been polluted by the presence of death, drawing homeless ghosts to celebrate the death and pilfer the family's offerings. Funeral rites are conducted by Buddhist monks.

The burial itself requires the aid of a different kind of specialist: a *geomancer* or *feng-shui* master. Using a special compass, and an intuitive sensitivity picked up over years of training and experience, the *feng-shui* master attempts to choose a comfortable and potent abode for the dead. He studies the intercourse of mountains and water, the undulations of the land, the presence of auspicious "dragon" and "tiger" formations (peaks and valleys), and the configurations of the stars and planets above, then selects the site that will bring the greatest blessings—both to the dead and to his or her descendents. Quoting the *Yellow Emperor's Siting Classic*, "If a site is peaceful, a family will have generations of good fortune. If not, the family will decline."

During the nineteenth century, Westerners working in China as missionaries, investors, and engineers attacked *feng-shui* as "an abyss of insane vagaries," "a perverse application of physical and meteorological knowledge," "a mere chaos of childish absurdities and refined mysticism," "a ridiculous caricature of science," and "the biggest of all bugbears." They were frustrated by local resistance to the construction of railroads, mines, telegraph lines, and Western-style churches. The Chinese, familiar with *feng-shui* principles, believed that such modern constructions would disrupt the *feng-shui* of the land.

But *feng-shui* is not mere superstition. It is the basis for early Chinese geology, geography, astronomy, and architecture. More fundamentally, *feng-shui* is an extension of the Chinese appreciation of nature as a living, complementary force, and of the delicate interaction between natural forms and human constructions. Chinese and Japanese architecture—both ancient and modern—has earned international acclaim as a product of this traditional sensitivity.

Ancestor worship is not the only form of contact between the living and the dead. Gifted persons called *shamans* or *spirit mediums* are able to receive the spirits of the dead within their bodies, or to send their own souls on spirit journeys to distant places and into the spirit world. Spirit mediums tend to be poor, living on the outskirts of neighborhoods and villages. They practice out of their homes or, late at night, in community temples. They are most often consulted by families to establish contact with their ancestors, for the purpose of resolving a dispute within the household. Spirit mediums can be male or female, and they include young adolescents; older women are considered to be especially skillful in contacting the recently deceased.

Ghosts

Ghosts are the spirits of the unvenerated dead. That is, they are the spirits of persons who have been neglected in death: they may have died in times of war or famine, or they may have had no descendents to make the regular offerings that sustain them in the spirit world. Because they do not receive offerings, they are "hungry." They are also resentful and envious of the love and care that ancestors receive. For this reason, they cause havoc among the living and were traditionally held responsible for illnesses, family quarrels, financial misfortune, and other unlucky events.

Types of Ghosts

Marauding Ghosts

1. Those who go about their business; do not interact with people
2. Those who make mischief; frighten, and harm people
3. Those seeking aid or fellowship from humans (often animals spirits like fox-maidens, dragon-princes, or snake-princesses)
4. Those who are agents of Heaven or hell on official business (to exact retribution for evil deeds)

Ghosts with Unfinished Business

1. Those who have died before their time (accident, murder); seeking vengeance or "soul-exchange" with the living; they may exact revenge on the perpetrator or lash out at anyone near the place of death
2. Those not properly buried or cared for (the most common form of hungry ghost)

Without a proper burial and the daily offerings of food and incense, a dead spirit will become a "homeless" ghost. Ancestors and ghosts are both spirits of the dead, the distinction being that ancestors are revered and nurtured by the living, while ghosts are "wronged, neglected, or abused."

- ancestors = spirits of the family dead
- ghosts = spirits of the unworshipped dead

In both cases, humans and spirits exist in a relationship marked by *reciprocity.* For their care, ancestors reward the family with blessings, harmony, and well-being; it is the responsibility of the living to perpetuate their memory through worship and offerings. For their neglect, ghosts cause illness, infertility, failure, bad luck, disease, and death; they must be propitiated.

Gods

Whereas ghosts and ancestors are by definition the spirits of the dead, gods are of various kinds. In the popular religion of village shrines and temples, the great majority of Chinese gods are also spirits of the dead, but these spirits have been elevated in the spiritual hierarchy because of some good they have done for the community—either because of heroic deeds performed while living or because of miraculous events associated with their bones or tombs after death. In fact, the distinctions among gods, ghosts, and ancestors are sometimes hard to find; many gods were first feared as ghosts before being transformed into gods, by virtue of some fortunate event surrounding their remains.

Types of Gods

Nature deities: rivers, mountains, trees, stones
Astral deities: Big and Small Dipper, North Star, other constellations (generally associated with the Taoist priestly tradition)
Deified persons:

1. Ghost-gods (usually associated with miraculous occurrences at a grave or bone site)
2. Heavenly bureaucrats
3. Sages and worthy persons

Transcendent deities (these include deities outside the traditional Chinese pantheon, including Buddhas and Bodhisattvas, and the Western God)
Non-anthropomorphic "Heaven" (*Tian*)

One example of a deified person who began her spiritual career as a ghost (the "unvenerated dead," without descendents to provide for her ancestral cult) is the goddess Mazu, known in Hong Kong and other Cantonese-speaking communities as *Tin-hau,* the "Empress of Heaven." Mazu is perhaps the most popular deity in Hong Kong, on the island of Taiwan, and in the coastal provinces of Mainland China, as she is widely venerated in fishing and seafaring communities. Her name means "Venerable Mother," and in addition to the title "Empress of Heaven," she is also known as the "Imperial Concubine" and the "Holy Mother of Heaven on High." She is the goddess of fishermen, but her spiritual efficacy extends to all persons, especially families, women, and children.

According to legend, Mazu was the deified daughter of a fisherman, born on the twenty-third day of the third lunar month of the first year of the Song Dynasty (960 C.E.). As a young girl, Mazu was able to send her spirit across the waters and to rescue sailors in distress. Exhausted by her virtuous deeds, she died at the age of twenty-seven, unmarried

Goddess Mazu. Courtesy of the author.

and childless. Today she is still worshipped as a protector of seafarers, but Mazu is much more: though a childless young woman herself, she is worshipped as a kind mother, treating her devotees as if they were her own children.

One story of her life can be found in a temple broadsheet, distributed by a large-scale Mazu Temple in southern Taiwan. Here is a translation:

> More than a thousand years ago, on Meizhou Island, Fujian Province, there lived a young girl named Silent Miss Lin (Lin Mo-niang).
>
> When Lin Mo-niang was born, a sweet smell was dispersed all over the island. Everyone who lives on Meizhou Island is a fisherman, accustomed to the odor of fish. So everyone believed that this newborn baby would grow up to be an extraordinary person.
>
> After Lin Mo-niang was born, she neither cried nor laughed. She slept for a month without making a sound. Because of this her mother gave her the name *Mo,* which means "silent." Silent Lin was very bright as a young girl. She could put her two hands together, as if she was in prayer. When she was five years old, she could read all of the *Scripture of Avalokitesvara* [a Buddhist scripture].
>
> One day after she had grown up, Lin's mother went into her room and found Silent Lin lying on her bed with her eyes closed, waving her arms in a gesture of warning and beckoning. Alarmed, her mother awakened her, but she remembered nothing of her dream. Two days later a fleet of fishing boats returned to Meizhou Island. The fishermen told of a storm at sea and a miraculous occurrence: just when their boat was about to sink beneath the waves, they saw Lin Mo-niang come walking across the water. She grasped the tow-line, and pulled the boat out of danger.
>
> The story spread almost instantly across Meizhou Island. If, when out at sea, the fishermen met with winds and waves, they turned to Lin Mo-niang and cried for help. Immediately she would come walking towards them across the water.
>
> Still an unmarried childless young woman, Lin died at the age of twenty-seven. The morning of her death, people saw her sitting properly, her two hands together in an attitude of prayer. Again the sweet smell was dispersed, exactly like the circumstances of her birth.
>
> After Miss Lin died, her soul appeared as before on the sea, saving ships that met with danger. Later, in order to revere her, the people referred to her as *Mazu:* "Grandmother Matriarch" or "Great Holy Mother."

Mazu has been worshipped in Taiwan and along the southeast coast of China for one thousand years.

Some gods have a briefer history. One case involved the worship of a young woman who died at the age of nineteen in Lintou, Taiwan. With no husband or children to worship her, she should have become a ghost, but a miraculous healing associated with her grave transformed her into a goddess, known simply as the "Virgin of Lintou." In two months' time, she became known throughout Taiwan for her healing ability. But suddenly, disaster struck: an accident claiming twenty lives on the bus route to her temple during a typhoon and flood. Due to the disaster, the people abandoned the goddess and her worship ceased. As quickly as it had come into existence, the cult disappeared.

Chinese gods are worshipped with offerings of food and heavenly currency. But the most important offering is the burning of incense, and the great brazier at the entrance to every temple is its spiritual focus, the point of contact between Heaven and Earth. When a new temple is built, ashes from the incense burner are transferred from one temple to the other to confer spiritual power upon the new location. This is carried out in a public incense-cutting ceremony, which celebrates the dedication of the new temple. The ceremony is performed by Taoist priests.

Temples have ancestral relations with one another. They have "mothers" and "grandmothers." When a new Mazu temple is built, for example, petition is made to an established temple to "share its incense" in an incense-cutting ceremony. In addition, the new Mazu statue is placed beside the old one for a period of time to share in its spiritual power, before being carried by sedan chair in a grand procession to the new temple. Then, once a year, the younger Mazu "goes home to her mother" to pay respects and renew her power.

The most famous of these annual pilgrimages is from Dajia to Beigang, on the island of Taiwan, a 250-kilometer round trip. Up to six thousand people make the eight-day journey every year, most of them on foot, and upward of thirty thousand converge on Beigang for the return of the Dajia Mazu to her mother's side. The procession is patterned on an imperial inspection tour: it is led by a scout on horseback, and the image of Mazu is guarded by two ten-foot-tall generals, named *Qian-li yan* ("Eyes That See a Thousand Miles") and *Shun-feng er* ("Ears That Hear What Comes on the Wind"). She is followed by pilgrims dressed in the costumes of flag-bearers and foot soldiers.

The key ritual once she arrives in Beigang is the incense-cutting rite. Smoldering ashes from the Beigang incense burner are placed in a small Dajia urn, to be carried back to Dajia: a reenactment of the founding rite of the temple. Once back in Dajia, these embers are used to relight the fires of the Dajia Mazu Temple incense burner, by the chief official of the annual pilgrimage, whose title is *lu-zhu,* "Master of the Incense Burner."

The rite of incense-cutting originated in the Song Dynasty (960—1280 C.E.), and developed as a result of growing interregional trade throughout the empire. Sojourning merchants would establish temples to their home-deities, carrying the images with them in sedan-chair processions that often covered many hundreds of miles. The images were spiritualized in an incense-cutting ceremony back home, then carried by sedan chair to be installed as the patron deity of the merchant community. Powerful at home and on the journey, they continued to embody religious power for the new settlers. And just as the immigrants felt the pull of family ties and nostalgia for their native place, returning periodically to rejuvenate their spirits, so too the religious images of the cult were taken on regular pilgrimages back to the founding temple and their mother-image, to restore their spiritual power.

Temple festivals and fairs were also tied to trade. In traditional China, a honeycomb network of regional markets provided the setting for trade between farmers and merchants. Usually, the markets were located on temple grounds. Held in three- or ten-day cycles, market days provided occasions not only for trade, but also for religious worship and popular entertainment. Local opera, plays, and puppet shows were performed. The stage was always set up facing the entrance to the temple, so that the god could enjoy the performance. The stories enacted were taken from religious mythology.

Today, most Chinese shop in stores and supermarkets, but temple fairs are still the setting for community rituals and popular entertainment. At the fair, one can buy snacks and handicrafts, and patronize fortune-tellers, traditional doctors, and magicians.

In addition to the temple fairs, the gods conduct periodic inspection tours of the community. Their images are carried on sedan chairs along a route that encircles the village or neighborhood. This secures the peace and prosperity of the gods' jurisdiction. The times and places of these tours are determined by the gods themselves, through local temple divination. They follow a circuit of all the participating temples in the area, exchanging tributary gifts along the way, accompanied by guards, musicians, dancers, spirit mediums, and Taoist priests—conferring blessings as they go. In this sense, the gods mimic the emperor and magistrates of imperial times, securing the allegiance of local populations and ritually marking the boundaries of their political power. This is why the images are seated on thrones and dressed in emperor's clothes.

Temple organization in China is still based largely on merchants and their networks. Community temples adopt many of the formal characteristics of professional associations, including rules of incorporation and record-keeping. Temple leadership is based significantly upon wealth and status in the community. Financial contributions to temple construction and maintenance are a symbol of honor and prestige. Worship of gods is often economically motivated as well. Offerings are made in search of wealth and prosperity, or for specific advice (learned by divination) on financial investments. Some gods are patron deities of occupational groups, including fishermen, craftsmen, shopkeepers, cab drivers, and even teachers and students.

Extensive participation of the state has been integral to the development of temples and deity cults in China. In imperial times, the emperor as well as provincial governors and local magistrates sponsored temple construction, approved the canonization of the gods and the deification of exemplary citizens and erected commemorative plaques and steles. Most Confucian officials were ostensibly religious skeptics, but they believed that religion reinforced morality and provided hope and encouragement for the people. This is still largely true today: even in the People's Republic of China, which has condemned "superstition" and "wasteful expenditures," government officials typically attend temple fairs and support the construction or restoration of local shrines.

THE CHINESE RELIGIOUS YEAR

Throughout the world, holidays mark seasonal changes, reenact the origins of life, and reinforce the harmony of human relationships and the synchronicity of human, natural, and religious aspects of existence. The Chinese ritual calendar celebrates life and its renewal. The principal religious holidays resonate with the ebb and flow of *yin* and *yang* forces.

Ideally, *yin* and *yang* should be maintained in equal measure: an excess of either *yin* or *yang* is potentially hazardous to nature and humankind. Humans, through rites and festivals, participate in the balancing of these complementary forces. The major religious holidays occur at the "height of *yang*" (when *yang* is at its highest point, and *yin* is eclipsed), at the "height of *yin*" (when *yin* is at its highest point, and *yang* is eclipsed), and at the two points of equilibrium.

Spring Festival

First day of the first lunar month. *Yang* rising. Festival of renewal of the earth (the Chinese New Year or "Spring Festival"), balanced by offering to ancestors (*yin* spirits of the dead).

As early as the seventh century B.C.E., the ancient Chinese celebrated various festivals associated with the New Year. These included the La Festival, held at the Winter Solstice, when offerings were made to ancestors, the sages, and cultural heroes of antiquity; the Nuo Festival ("Great Exorcism") for the expulsion of diseases and evil forces; and a "Parade of Dragons and Fishes" held on the Lunar New Year. Today, elements of these ancient rites are evident in Chinese New Year celebrations.

Chinese New Year, called *chun-jie* ("Spring Festival"), takes place on the first new moon of the lunar year, in February or March of the solar calendar. Preparatory to the New Year, families clean house, pay off debts, purchase new clothes, and send off the Kitchen God (a household deity) to report to the Jade Emperor on the behavior of the children during the past year. On New Year's Eve, a great meal is prepared. Sacrifices are made to the family ancestors, and at midnight the children bow respectfully to their elders and are rewarded with red envelopes containing candy and cash. On New Year's Day, families call on one another and go out for restaurant meals or enjoy lion dances in the streets of their neighborhoods and towns, traditionally a means for expelling evil forces and ensuring prosperity and good health in the community.

Pure Brightness Festival

April (one hundred days after the Winter Solstice). Festival in remembrance of the family dead.

This is the only solar festival on the Chinese ritual calendar. It is called either "Pure Brightness Festival" or the "Festival of the Tombs." On this occasion family members visit the graves of their ancestors for the annual cleaning of the tombs. Chinese graveyards are crowded with families cutting back weeds and cleaning up the gravesite, burning incense and paper money, and eating a mid-morning picnic, ritually shared with the dead.

Double Five Festival

Fifth day of the fifth lunar month. Height of *yang*. "Dragon Boat Festival."

This festival, called "Double Five" or "Double *Yang*," is one of the most ancient holidays in the Chinese calendar. It falls in the middle of the summer (June or July on the solar calendar), when the forces of *yang* (heat and drought) are at their greatest and most dangerous extreme. This festival features water play (water is *yin*), particularly the Dragon Boat Races of

Dragon boat at the Double Five Festival in
Hong Kong. Courtesy of the author.

southern China and Hong Kong. In the Han Dynasty, the holiday was called
"Cold Food Festival." On that day, cooking fires were prohibited, for fear of
exacerbating the dangerous excess of yang in Heaven and Earth. Today, it is
an occasion for fun and recreation—no one works on Double Five.

Ghost Festival

Fifteenth day of the seventh lunar month. Balance of *yin* and *yang*.
"Ghost Festival," during the ascending of *yin,* remembering the "unfamiliar
dead" (ghosts).

The Ghost Festival is celebrated on the full moon of the seventh lunar
month, in late summer or early fall. It is just prior to the autumn equi-
nox, which inaugurates six months of *"yin* ascending"—the season of with-
drawal, dormancy, and death. On this day only, offerings are made to the
unvenerated souls of the dead—those who died violently, prematurely, or
without descendents. The food offerings given to ghosts differ from the
food offerings given to ancestors in three respects. First, the rice, meat,
eggs, and vegetables of the offering table are set outside the house—the

ghosts are encouraged to partake, but they are not welcome in the home (like beggars, to whom they are often compared). Second, the offerings are raw and uncooked. Finally, they are discarded at the end of the day, not consumed by the family within the household, as are the offerings to ancestors. The Ghost Festival falls in the seventh lunar month, the "Ghost Month," when temple doors are closed and shamans retire, for fear of possession by unwelcome spirits.

Festival of Offering

Fifteenth day of the eleventh lunar month. Height of *yin*. Festival of rebirth of *yang*, dedicated to the gods (pure *yang* spirits).

This day marks the dead of winter (it falls in December or January) and the lowest point in the *yang* cycle. From this point forward, the order of growth and diminution is reversed, with *"yin* falling" and *"yang* rising." In traditional times, there were no executions for six months from this date, in observance of the seasons of growth and maturation.

The *jiao* festival is a community festival in honor of the gods (pure *yang* spirits, in contrast to the *yin* spirits of ancestors and ghosts). It is sponsored by neighborhood and village temples, and officiated by the high priests of Taoism. Inside the temple, the Red-Headed Priests perform rites closed to the public, preparing charms and amulets for the protection of the community from *yin* forces that, in excess, are inclined toward evil and death. Outside the temple, the people of the community welcome the gods with

Temple worshippers at the Jiao festival. Courtesy of the author.

circuit processions around the village, operatic performances and puppet plays, and banquets lasting through the day and into the night.

GENDER AND CHINESE RELIGION

Over the course of Chinese history, religion has contributed to both the subjugation and the liberation of women. According to the Five Permanent Relationships, women are distinctly inferior to men and are bound first and foremost to the "three obediences": obedience to the father in childhood, obedience to the husband in adulthood, and obedience to the son in old age. A woman's primary duty to her husband and his family in traditional times was to bear a son, so that the family name and the ancestral cult would be carried on.

Because of their status, and the fact that daughters were married out of their natal families, the birth of a girl was considered less than fortunate. With China's one-child policy of the past twenty years, this prejudice can still be found today. Especially in rural China, the birth of a son is the only blessed event for a family struggling to sustain a living and to maintain an ancestral line.

For the vast majority of Asian women, life has been defined in the context of family and the home. Their principal religious activities are generally confined to

- household rituals, including daily offerings to family ancestors at a miniature shrine in the home
- worship at village shrines and temples
- pilgrimage to religious sites
- preparation of food for calendrical and community festivals
- participation in weddings and funerals
- worship of female deities who are efficacious in childbirth and protection of infants
- consultation with shamans to resolve family quarrels

There is some evidence that Chinese women in ancient times enjoyed more power outside the home and played a significant role in public religious rituals. As early as the Zhou Dynasty (1122–255 B.C.E.), spirit mediums called *wu* —a word related etymologically to dancing—were employed by the court as exorcists, diviners, and magicians. They waved spears, bundles of reeds and peach branches, danced, and chanted incantations. The *wu* were priestesses whose power derived from possession by gods or spirits. The spirit mediums were consulted for communication with gods and ancestors.

Today, some three thousand years later, female spirit mediums can still be found in significant number. In Korea and Japan, they tend to be young women who are ritually married to gods of mountains and streams; in China, especially Taiwan and Canton Provinces, they are usually older women referred to as "old ladies who speak to spirits." Some women became shamans after the deaths of their own children. The spirits of these children are among their helpers.

With the establishment of Confucian values as the standard of orthodoxy by the Han Dynasty (200 B.C.E.), women's roles were clearly defined in relation to men. The ecstatic shamanism of earlier times was actively discouraged—in fact, punishable by death. In Confucian Asia for centuries, women have been regarded as inferior and subservient to men. Only married women with male children are fully accepted in the fabric of Asian social and religious life. These women offer incense and food to their husbands' ancestors, and themselves become ancestors worshipped by their descendents. Marriage and childbirth, then, are traditionally the key defining events of life for the great majority of Asian women.

Marriage rituals, like rituals of burial and ancestor worship, reinforce family ties and obligations. Traditionally, the marriage standard was for a young man to marry a virgin bride, who was brought from her natal home to the paternal house to participate in the daily affairs and ancestral cult of her husband's family. Anthropologists call this patrilocal marriage.

The traditional marriage rite follows six steps:

1. Inquiries are made in the girl's family by a go-between sent by a family seeking a bride.
2. Genealogical records are provided by both families.
3. The girl's horoscope is matched with the horoscope of the boy.
4. The betrothal is secured by the transfer of gifts from the boy's family to the girl's family.
5. The date of the wedding is fixed by astrological divination, using *The Book of Changes* or some other divination source.
6. The bride is moved by sedan chair to the husband's household.

Chinese weddings are public, family affairs. Most young people accept the fact that the wedding celebration is basically for their parents, representing a tie between families, not just two individuals. Wedding-day rituals are based on respect for ancestors and parents and continuation of the family line; the bride and groom worship at the ancestral tablet, bow before the groom's parents and grandparents, and eat foods and wear clothing and jewelry symbolizing family prosperity and the birth of children.

Although it was typical for the bride to come to live with the groom's family, certain deviations existed in traditional times. Sometimes the groom came to live with the bride's family, and the children of the union had the bride's family name and worshipped the bride's paternal ancestors (especially if the bride's parents had no sons).

Until the twentieth century, agreements were made by the two sets of parents for the betrothal and marriage, with little participation of the prospective bride and groom. The young man was viewed as an ideal groom if he was successful in the examinations and government service, backed by family status and wealth, conscientious and filial toward his parents. The young girl (traditionally between thirteen and twenty years of age) was regarded as an ideal bride if she was obedient, modest, cultured, and attractive. Today, young men and women choose their own spouses and typically live on their own. Chinese women are now encouraged to gain an education and most young women are interested in pursuing a career.

Nevertheless, the remnants of traditional Confucian values remain strong, and double standards persist: a man should be steady, serious, and career-minded; a woman should be modest, pretty, and family-oriented. Sexual infidelity is tolerable for men, intolerable for women. Divorce is not common, and it is especially hard on women, who are blamed as a matter of course. The children are almost always left with the husband and his family, and divorced women find it difficult to remarry. The family ethic of stability and personal sacrifice continues to be the norm, and the responsibility for harmony within the family falls heaviest on the wife.

On the other hand, religion in China has also offered alternatives beyond the confines of everyday existence in the family. Religious expression outside the home has been a real choice for generations of Chinese women, as Buddhist nuns, Taoist immortality adepts, or as participants in religious sects and cults. In the case of Taoism, the classical texts favored all things *yin*, including femininity and feminine imagery. For example, the *Dao de jing* states:

> The Spirit of the Valley is eternal; it is called "the mysterious female." The gateway of the mysterious female is called the root of Heaven and Earth. Though constantly flowing, it seems always to be present. Though used, it is never used up.

Can you carry the soul and embrace the One without letting go?
Can you concentrate your *qi* and attain the weakness of an infant?
Can you adopt the role of the female when the gates of Heaven open and
close?
Can you abandon all knowing even as your intelligence penetrates the universe?
To give birth and to rear, to give birth but not to possess, to act but not to
depend on the outcome, to lead but not to command: this is called "mysterious power."

I alone am different from other people, and value being fed by the Mother.

Understand the male but keep to the role of the female, and you will be the
river of the world. As the river of the world, you will not lose your constant
energy, and return to infancy.

In the history of Sect Taoism, women enjoyed positions of power alongside
men, and gender balance was sought among the "libationers" who headed
the sectarian bureaucracy. In the Esoteric stream of Taoism, women as well
as men practiced alchemical self-cultivation, with the goal of long life and
immortality. For both men and women, the goal was to create within the
body a "re-circulating system," where the vital energy (*qi*) of the physical
and spiritual body is regenerated endlessly. The metaphor of pregnancy
and birth was frequently invoked, such that both men and women were
said to generate a spiritual "embryo" of eternal life. In this tradition, feminine traits and the female body are portrayed positively as models for religious cultivation.

The modern era is seeing Chinese women writers and intellectuals beginning an evaluation of China's cultural and religious traditions in terms
of women's rights, obligations, and expectations.

FURTHER READINGS

On the sociological study of Chinese religion, the classic work by C. K.
Yang, *Religion in Chinese Society,* is still unsurpassable. For a more recent
work, read Robert Weller's *Unities and Diversities in Chinese Religion.* For
the role of the emperor in religious rites and patronage, a classic study is
John Shryock's *The Origin and Development of the State Cult of Confucius*—a book on imperial religious practice generally, despite its more narrow title. Actual records of religious rites conducted by the official class
are found in *A Complete Book Concerning Happiness and Benevolence: A*

Manual for Local Magistrates in Seventeenth-Century China, composed by Huang Liu-hong in 1694, but recently edited and translated by Djang Chu.

There are many excellent historical and anthropological studies of Chinese popular religion. For an overview of the religion of the peasantry, see Lloyd Eastman's *Family, Field, and Ancestors*. For the ancestral cult and its ties to the merchant class and the accumulation of family wealth, Hugh D. R. Baker's anthropological study of *Chinese Family and Kinship* in Canton, Hong Kong, and the New Territories is illustrative. A brief, highly readable introduction to folk religion at the village level can be found in David Jordan's *Gods, Ghosts, and Ancestors*. There is as yet no good book on the experience of women in Chinese religious life, though specific studies are now emerging.

Baker, Hugh D. R. *Chinese Family and Kinship*. London: Macmillan, 1979.

Djang, Chu, trans. *A Complete Book Concerning Happiness and Benevolence: A Manual for Local Magistrates in Seventeenth-Century China by Huang Liu-hung*. Tucson: University of Arizona Press, 1984.

Eastman, Lloyd. *Family, Field, and Ancestors: Constancy and Change in China's Social and Economic History, 1550–1949*. New York: Oxford University Press, 1988.

Jordan, David K. *Gods, Ghosts, and Ancestors: The Folk Religion in a Taiwanese Village*. Berkeley: University of California Press, 1972.

Shryock, John. *The Origin and Development of the State Cult of Confucius*. New York: Century, 1932. Reprint, New York: Paragon, 1966.

Weller, Robert P. *Unities and Diversities in Chinese Religion*. Seattle: University of Washington Press, 1987.

Yang, C. K. *Religion in Chinese Society*. Berkeley: University of California Press, 1961. Reprint, Waveland Press, 1991.

6

MAJOR FIGURES

MAJOR FIGURES OF THE CONFUCIAN TRADITION

Kong-fu-zi (Confucius) (551–479 B.C.E.)

The inspiring founder of the Confucian tradition is known in Chinese as the First Sage, or Grand Master of the Kong family.

When Confucius was born at the end of the Spring and Autumn Period, the empire was divided into a number of competing feudal principalities. The time in which he lived was characterized by social and political turmoil on a huge scale. Large states invaded and overpowered their smaller, weaker neighbors. Feudatory nobles resorted to lies and assassination to maintain their desperate grip on power. Interstate alliances were made and broken based not on principle but on military expediency. As the states dedicated their resources to war and security, they ignored agriculture and public works, resulting in mass migrations of entire populations in search of food.

Confucius traveled from one state to another, offering council to dukes and kings in the hope of restoring the religious and political ideals of an earlier, more peaceful era. But his moral and religious standards were too high, and he was a political failure. He was never given a position of authority, ignored or rebuffed in his travels, and even pursued by assassins from the state of Qi as a gadfly unwilling to flatter warlords whose only objective was conquest.

There is no reliable biography of Confucius—Confucian biographies of the First Sage invent or exaggerate his accomplishments, and most were composed some centuries after the Master's death. But his character can be grasped in some of the recorded conversations and sayings of *The Analects*, composed by his immediate disciples and their followers.

- Confucius composed a very brief autobiography: "When I was fifteen years old, I became serious about my studies. When I was thirty, I was established in my career. When I was forty, I was no longer uncertain about right and wrong. When I was fifty, I understood the will of Heaven (*Tian-ming*). At sixty, my ear was attuned to the truth, and at seventy, I could do whatever my heart desired without overstepping the bounds of decorum."
- If his mat was not straight, Confucius would not sit on it.
- In a conversation with hermits, he mocked their "flocking" with birds and beasts. "The world has a certain *Dao*," he said. "Who am I to change it?"
- A stable was destroyed in a fire. Confucius asked: "Was anyone hurt?" He did not inquire about the horses.
- He would deny himself anything—wealth, comfort, even food—in order to serve his fellow human beings. Confucius said: "I can find happiness even in eating course food, drinking plain water, and sleeping with my arm as my pillow. To be wealthy and honored without righteousness is like a floating cloud to me."
- He loved books, especially books of poetry and history. According to tradition, Confucius edited the great classics of Chinese literature.
- Confucius loved music and dance. Once, after hearing a performance of ancient music, he was "unaware of the taste of food" for three months.
- He loved friends and conversation. The very first chapter of *The Analects* quotes Confucius as saying, "Isn't it a joy when friends come from far away?"
- He felt that he could learn from anyone. "Wherever three men are walking, I can find my teacher among them."
- Confucius said: "In every village of ten households, there is undoubtedly someone who is as conscientious and trustworthy as I am, but no one who loves learning as much as I do."
- Though an elitist, he believed that culture, learning, and status should accessible to anyone, regardless of birth or wealth. Confucius said: "Where there is teaching, there should be no discrimination according to class."
- Though much of his advice is directed to lords and kings, he believed that any young man, from any walk of life, could become a great ruler, and he educated his own students as future leaders of the nation. Anyone, he said, could become a *jun-zi*, a virtuous leader who rules others by moral example.

Meng-zi (Mencius) (371–289 B.C.E.)

Mencius is the Second Sage of the Confucian tradition, living approximately two hundred years after Confucius. He was a contemporary of the Taoist sage Zhuang-zi.

There is a famous legend about Mencius as a child. Mencius was fatherless from a young age. According to legend, Mencius and his mother first lived near a gravesite, and the young boy enjoyed playing among the tombs. Alarmed by this, his mother moved house to an urban center. Here, too, the environment was not ideal, and Mencius was exposed to gamblers, criminals, and idle ne'er-do-wells. Once more, his mother moved. Finally, mother and son settled near a school-temple, where the boy pretended to be an officiant at a great sacrifice. The mother's willingness to find the best environment for her child is seen to be a model of Confucian parenting, and Chinese cite this legend to this day with the expression "*Meng mu san qian* ('Meng-zi's mother moved three times')." An incident in *The Book of Mencius* recalls this experience.

> During his travels from Fan to Qi, Mencius came upon the son of the King of Qi, and sighed, "The effect of one's home on one's character is like the effect of one's food on one's body. But the more important of the two is the home. Isn't it true that we are all sons? The King's son's palace, horses, and clothes are not all that different from everyone else's. What makes him different is his home. How much more is this true if we can look at the whole world as our home!"

Mencius was a self-conscious Confucian, and he contrasted Confucian teachings with the teachings of Mo-zi, who proposed a radical doctrine of social equality called "universal love," and with the teachings of other competing schools of the Warring States Period: the "Tillers" (hermits), the "Hedonists," and the "Relativists." Mencius does appear to have had some success in gaining official position, but he lacked the charisma of the First Sage and did not enjoy a noteworthy career. He was certainly a great essayist, and the *Meng-zi* book is an excellent primer of classical Chinese. He wrote about Confucian morality and abstract theories of human nature in a way that was descriptive and accessible. Today, all Chinese recall Meng-zi's stories of the "foolish farmer of Song," the "child about to fall into a well," the "mountain forest denuded by axes," and so on—all moral tales expounding Meng-zi's deep conviction of the innate goodness of human beings.

Xun-zi (c. 300–215 B.C.E.)

Xun-zi is the Third Sage of the Confucian tradition, an advocate of formal ritual and rule by law, and a skeptic with regard to basic human nature.

Xun-zi, "Master Xun" (traditionally romanized Hsün-tzu or Sun-tzu), was born Xun Qing (Ch'ing) in the last years of the Warring States Period of the Zhou Dynasty, and near the end of his life, he saw the unification of the empire under the First Emperor of the Qin. Among the last of the "hundred philosophers" who established the intellectual heritage of China, Xun Qing studied in his thirties and forties with the great thinkers of his day at the renowned Jixia Academy. He served as an advisor to a king and prime minister of the state of Qi as well as two kings of Qin, later serving as a county magistrate in the state of Chu (where he eventually retired) and a senior minister in the state of Zhao. These experiences shaped his writings, which took the form of philosophical argumentation and political persuasion, and addressed issues of character, morality, statecraft, and social organization.

Xun-zi idolized Confucius, but he was highly critical of the Confucian schools of his day. He met a number of these Confucians (known as *Ru*, "scholars" or "ritualists") at the Jixia Academy and directed many of his strongest polemical arguments against "heterodox *Ru*." The most significant were the followers of Mencius, and some of Xun-zi's most spirited writing is in refutation of the Mencian interpretation of human nature. The other group that most concerned Xun-zi consisted of the followers of Mo-zi, who subscribed to the doctrines of social egalitarianism, frugality, religious literalism, and universal love. These doctrines were, for Xun-zi, not only naive with regard to human nature and the natural world, but also threatening to the stability of the state. In addition, Xun-zi was exposed during his tenure at the Jixia Academy to works of the Taoists, Hedonists, Logicians, and Legalists. Consequently, Xun-zi's writings are an excellent source for the intellectual life of the final years of the Zhou—the so-called Six Schools of pre-Qin philosophy.

Xun-zi never enjoyed the esteem of his greatest intellectual rivals, Mencius and Mo-zi. He died with the knowledge that the new empire was loathe to implement his traditional models of ceremony and social organization, adopting instead the harsh measures of the Legalist school. His own disciples Han-fei-zi and Li Si abandoned his teachings in favor of Legalism, and the *Ru* school was fractured and unable to influence the policies of the Qin emperor.

With the revival and elaboration of Confucian thought in the Han, Xun-zi's interpretation of ritual became normative, and whole passages of his works were copied into *The Book of Rites* (*Li Ji*). His demystification of the idea of Heaven was also accepted by Han Confucians, who rejected the belief in gods and ghosts and the ethical interpretation of natural portents. The view that religion has no spiritual efficacy but functions as a positive agent of social control and moral persuasion has been the predominant view of Confucian officialdom throughout Chinese history; it can be traced in the first instance to Xun-zi.

As for the issue of human nature, the Mencian view generally has been preferred, and Mencius has enjoyed a much higher status in history. Zhu Xi, prime architect of the Neo-Confucian revival in the Song Dynasty, es-chewed Xun-zi, and he was largely ignored until modern times. But even before the Song, there was only one commentary written on the *Xun-zi*, compared to nine on the *Mencius*. Nonetheless, the debate between Men-cius and Xun-zi defined an ongoing dialectic in the history of Chinese thought, and Xun-zi's view appears as a subtext in every significant moral treatise.

Zhu Xi (1130–1200 c.e.)

Zhu Xi is the most famous Confucian after Confucius himself. He was the architect of a Confucian revival in the Song Dynasty (fifteen hundred years after Confucius), known as Neo-Confucianism.

As the son of a district magistrate, Zhu Xi was exposed to Confucian studies at a young age. After a rebellious phase of Buddhist and Taoist stud-ies, he reconverted to Confucianism. Often in adulthood, he spoke of the "foolishness" of his youth, and the "nonsense" of Taoist and Zen Buddhist teachings. He was the author of twenty books and commentaries—includ-ing annotated versions of the Four Books and Five Classics that eventually became the basis for the imperial examinations. Zhu Xi's career alternated between periods of government service (as a judge and county-level official) and scholarship. Disapproving of military campaigns undertaken by the Song imperial court, Zhu lived quietly as a district superintendent in Fujian, the province of his birth, and refused to participate actively in state affairs.

Zhu Xi was a consummate scholar-gentleman, and his legacy is his edi-torial work, which revived the Confucian tradition as a rival to Taoism and Buddhism in the Song Dynasty. Philosophically, he is best known for his idea of "Principle" (*li*) and the "investigation of things" that illuminates the underlying moral nature of the universe. In practice—and despite his anti-Buddhist polemics—Zhu adopted Zen meditation for the purpose of reflection on science, history, and art, which he called "Quiet Sitting." He was also the author of a guidebook on "family values," governing every aspect of personal and domestic life.

His disciples must have hung on every word uttered by their master, as they produced a gargantuan record of his sayings. His son-in-law wrote a lengthy biography as well, which still survives today. These, in addition to Zhu Xi's own books and diary, give as a very complete sense of the man and his career.

"When I was five or six, I was curious about what the sky was and what lay beyond it." By the age of twelve, Zhu had already studied *The Analects, The Book of Mencius, The Great Learning,* and *The Doctrine of the Mean* (the Confucian Four Books). By the age of fourteen or fifteen, he had discovered *ge-wu* ("the investigation of things"). At this time, his father died, and after two years of mourning, Zhu Xi studied with Buddhist monks and Taoist masters from the age of sixteen to twenty. Though he later rejected their teachings as "nonsense" and "chicanery," he frequently quoted from Buddhist sutras and Taoist texts in his mature years, and his idea of Principle often seems to resemble the "emptiness" or "vacuity" of Buddhism and Taoism. Though his subsequent life saw tremendous accomplishments (he lived to the age of seventy), he often said that he never had more profound thoughts, more creative energy, or more intellectual ability than he did at the age of twenty.

Wang Yang-ming (1472–1529 c.e.)

Wang Yang-ming (born Wang Shou-ren), who came from a family of accomplished scholars and officials, was encouraged at a young age to sit for the civil service examinations and to serve in public office. Since 1313 c.e., the standard for the examinations had been the Confucian Four Books and Five Classics as annotated by the Song Neo-Confucian scholar Zhu Xi. The intellectual life of the Ming was dominated by Zhu Xi's "School of Principle" (*li-xue*) and the Neo-Confucian educational program. Wang Yang-ming felt especially constrained by this state-sanctioned orthodoxy, but he could never escape his intellectual indebtedness to it. His personal struggles with both government service and its intellectual basis were defining issues in his life, and his self-questioning, critical spirit had as much of an impact on his times as his mature philosophical thought. Wang is credited with being the guiding light of the "School of Mind" (*xin-xue*) or

"Ideationist School" of Ming Neo-Confucianism, characterized by a thorough and severe self-scrutiny. Wang's father once said of him that he was "ardent" or "untamed," a quality of character that defined the Yang-ming School for several generations.

Three events typified Wang's struggles. In 1492 C.E., at the age of twenty, Wang set out to put Zhu Xi's teachings into practice, through an intense, seven-day meditation in a bamboo grove. Zhu Xi had written that an intuitive grasp of "Principle" (*li*)—the intelligible order and metaphysical basis for all things—could be found through the disciplined concentration on "external things and affairs." This understanding was fundamental to a true understanding of the self, which, in its basic nature, is indistinguishable from Principle. Wang's efforts to master Zhu Xi's instructions precipitated a psychological crisis that resulted in a series of poor performances in the imperial examinations.

The second crisis came in 1502 C.E., after Wang had finally succeeded in the examinations and attained high office in the capital. Exhausted from overwork and overcome by the competitive strains of advancement in the imperial system, he resigned, and, for two years, abandoned the Confucian program altogether, experimenting with Taoist and Buddhist forms of self-cultivation in a rural retreat. The outcome of this self-imposed exile was a newfound commitment to Confucianism, growing out of an affirmation of "natural feelings" (feelings of attachment to home and family, in particular) that the Taoists and Buddhists both rejected. It was at this point that Wang began to call himself "Yang-ming," after the grotto in which he had experienced his enlightenment, and to gather disciples.

The third defining event in Wang's life came after a government-imposed exile from 1506 to 1508 C.E., when he served as a district magistrate in an aboriginal community in southwest China. This experience was an enlightenment to the fundamental goodness and purity of the mind as the source of virtue and the basis of knowledge. Perfect virtue, Wang discovered, is within oneself, not in external things or situations. These principles are the core of Wang's discourse in the *Chuan-xi lu* (*"Instructions for Practical Living"*), composed after his retirement from public service.

Tu Wei-ming (b. 1940 C.E.)

Tu Wei-ming was born in Kunming (southwestern China) and educated in Taiwan, but he has made his home in the United States since the age of twenty-one, earning a Ph.D. from Harvard University in 1968 C.E. Following teaching stints at Princeton University and the University of California at Berkeley, Tu has served on the faculty of Harvard University since 1981 C.E.

Tu Wei-ming's scholarship focused on Mencius and Wang Yang-ming, but he is now best known as a creative student and practitioner of Confucianism as a living tradition in the modern world. He is representative of the Third Epoch of New Confucianism, which he describes as "philosophical anthropology" or "religious philosophy." Heroic in his efforts to create a reenergized Confucian China, Tu is at the same time one of the most outspoken critics of China's Confucian past and its tendencies to excess. In this sense, Tu's voice is truly prophetic.

Moreover, Tu is the primary interpreter of contemporary Confucianism to the West. He writes in both Chinese and in English, and he travels broadly in China and the West, where he lectures on Confucianism as a vital tradition and as a great religion among all of the great religions of the world.

Tu Wei-ming's interpretation of Confucianism is informed by a profound knowledge of Western religion and philosophy, and he has commented profoundly on Western individualism and Enlightenment thought. He understands the Confucian self in very different terms from the Western conception of identity, describing the self as a "center of relationships" and self-transformation as "a deliberate communal act." Although this is a profoundly humanistic vision (Tu has said that "the idea of a theistic God is totally absent from the symbolic resources of the Confucian tradition"), Tu insists that it is also a so-called religious vision, a process of deeply felt, even "ultimate" self-realization.

MAJOR FIGURES OF THE TAOIST TRADITION

Lao-zi (dates unknown)

Though Lao-zi was said to be the author of the *Dao de jing* and the purported founder of Taoism, there is no historical evidence that he actually existed, or that the *Dao de jing* was composed by a single hand. It is very likely that the *Dao de jing* itself was a relatively late compilation of poems and aphorisms that had existed for several centuries. The oldest copy of the *Dao de jing* that has been discovered thus far was found in the tomb of a Han nobleman buried in 168 B.C.E. Surely the book was put together before then, and some of its sayings date to antiquity, but its explicit mention of Confucian values such as *li* ("propriety") and *yi* ("righteousness") means that it could not have predated Confucius and the early *Ru* school.

What about Lao-zi himself? He is not mentioned in *The Analects* of Confucius, nor is he mentioned in either the *Mencius* or the *Zhuangzi*. His first biography does not appear until 100 B.C.E., in the *Shi Ji* (Historical Memoirs), by the "Grand Historian," Si-ma Qian. According to that highly fanciful account, Lao-zi's real name was *Li Er* or *Li Dan* ("Long-Eared Li"). "Long ears" were a symbol of longevity, and indeed, Si-ma Qian reports that Lao-zi lived to be nearly two hundred years old. The name *Lao-zi* itself is a play on words. All of the great thinkers of the Six Schools were honored with the title *zi*, meaning "Master." *Meng-zi* means "Master Meng," *Zhuang-zi*, "Master Zhuang," *Xun-zi*, "Master Xun," and so on. The name *Kong-fu-zi*, meaning "Grand Master Kong," is the basis for the Anglicization to "Confucius." In other words, *Meng, Zhuang, Xun*, and *Kong* are all surnames, and the second character is an honorific title. The word *Lao*, however, is not a surname, so the translation of *Lao-zi* as "Master Lao" is not possible. Instead, the name is a play on words: *Lao* means "Old" or "Venerable," and, in this instance, *zi* means "Infant" or "Boy"—thus, "Old Boy" or "Venerable Infant"—not so much a name as the title of a mythical being who captures both wisdom and youthful abandon.

Si-ma Qian's biography of Lao-zi is as fanciful as his name. It tells, for example, of an encounter between Lao-zi and Master Confucius himself. Lao-zi reprimands Confucius; he suggests that Confucius is "funny-looking," hypocritical, ambitious, and arrogant. Far from being offended, Confucius is amazed and describes Lao-zi as a dragon that cannot be caught; he is "beyond my knowledge," says Confucius.

This account also tells of Lao-zi's displeasure with the world, and his retirement to the western desert, riding an ox. The Keeper of the Pass, named Yin Xi, implored him to leave something behind, that others might benefit from his wisdom. Lao-zi, reports the *Shi Ji*, "composed a book in two parts and five thousand characters," then departed for the West and was never seen again.

In later centuries, tales of Lao-zi's mysterious power were embellished further. The Celestial Masters worshipped a god whom they called "Unsurpassed Lord Lao." Another Han Dynasty Taoist sect composed a scripture, entitled the "Record of the Transformations of Lao-zi," which described Lao-zi as a divine personification of the Dao itself. Various sectarian groups predicted that Lao-zi would appear once more in the world, with the surname *Li* (as reported in Si-ma Qian's *History*), and that Li would be a divine ruler, bringing about a total transformation of the empire. The Tang Dynasty royal family took the name *Li* and claimed to be the manifestation of this prophecy.

Zhuang-zi (368–289 B.C.E.)

Zhuang-zi ("Master Zhuang") is the honorary name of the Zhou Dynasty recluse Zhuang Zhou, who is recorded by Si-ma Qian in the *Historical Memoirs* as having lived during the reigns of King Hui of Liang (370–319 B.C.E.) and King Xuan of Qi (319–301 B.C.E.). His flippancy and disregard for social convention suggests that he was a follower of Yang Zhu, a famous recluse of the time—Mencius wrote of Yang Zhu that he "would not sacrifice even a single hair from his calf for the sake of the empire." The story is told of Zhuang-zi that once, while fishing by the Pu River, he was approached by a minister from the state of Chu to give advice to the king. Zhuang-zi asked if the rumor was true that the King of Chu was in possession of a magnificent, jewel-encrusted tortoise.

> "Indeed," said the minister.
> "Do you think that this tortoise would rather be honored as a preserved shell, or alive, dragging its tail in the mud?"
> "It would rather be alive, dragging its tail in the mud."
> "Leave me alone, then," said Zhuang-zi. "I'll drag my tail in the mud!"

On another occasion, Zhuang-zi compared public service to fattening an ox as an offering to the royal ancestors. He preferred, he said, to be a water buffalo swimming in a muddy canal than an ox being prepared for slaughter. Zhuang-zi's heroes, as seen in Chapter 2, were madmen, cripples, gnarled trees, and other "useless" figures. He was disdainful of Confucian mores and values, and made no apology for his own antisocial behaviors.

One of Zhuang-zi's favorite targets was a companion named Hui Shi, a member of the School of the Logicians, another of the Six Schools of the

Spring and Autumn Period. Zhuang-zi's persistent attacks on language and logic are directed against rationality and discursive knowledge as the only so-called proper forms of knowledge. One day, gazing from a bridge into the Hao River, Zhuang-zi sighed,

> "How happy! The floating and wandering of minnows!"
>
> "You are not a fish," said the logician. "How would you know that they are happy?"
>
> "You are not me," replied Zhuang-zi. "So how would you know that I do not know the happiness of fish?"
>
> "OK. I'm not you, so I don't know what you do not know. But neither are you a fish. So you cannot know that they are happy."
>
> "You asked me how I knew they were happy, so you already knew that I knew. I knew it standing here above the Hao River."

Zhuang-zi "knows the happiness of fish" intuitively. It is beyond logic, and he mocks Hui Shi's logical mind to make his point. Zhuang-zi admired the creative, empathic mind, not the mind of logic and reason.

Though never explicit in the seven Inner Chapters of the *Book of Zhuang-zi*, there are also suggestions of mystical consciousness in the images and metaphors that Zhuang-zi employs to describe the "Perfect One" or sage. Zhuang-zi talks about shamanistic flights through the heavens and marvelous beings who "can enter fire without being burned and enter water without getting wet." He speaks often of dreams and magical transformations and has no fear of death, which he sees as just one more "transmutation" among the many other transmutations of the natural world. Later Taoists believed that Zhuang-zi had attained immortal status—his indifference toward death was in fact a victory over death.

Zhuang-zi is known today primarily as an inspiration of China's tradition of the hermit—emphasizing poetic expression, love of drink, and lack of concern for the social ladder of success and accomplishment.

Zhang Dao-ling (d. between 157 and 178 c.e.)

Zhang Dao-ling, founder of the "Way of the Celestial Masters" (*Tian-shi Dao*) or the "Way of the Five Bushels of Rice" (*Wu dou mi Dao*), is the first of the so-called sectarian Taoists. His movement can be described as the beginnings of Taoism as a true religion, with a priesthood, a community of followers, institutional organization, and a corpus of scriptures.

Zhang was himself a master of immortality cultivation, and he composed texts on diet and hygiene, now lost. Most important for the history of Taoism, he received a series of revelations in 142 C.E. from *Tai-shang Lao-jun,* "Lord Lao Most High," who identified himself as "Celestial Master" and passed this title down to Zhang Dao-ling as his disciple. As part of these revelations from the deified Lao-zi, Zhang was directed to give up the "bloody sacrifices" of the popular religion (which venerates gods, ghosts, and ancestors—the spirits of the dead) and instead to make "pure offerings" of vegetables and wine to the immortals and astral deities who had never been touched by death. He established a theocratic state, divided into twenty-four parishes, each governed by male-female pair called "libationers" or "wine-pourers." Sect followers were tithed five pecks of rice, from which the sect got its name.

The Way of the Five Bushels of Rice enjoyed some bureaucratic success in the distant southwest (present-day Sichuan Province), and both Zhang Dao-ling's son, Zhang Heng (dates unknown), and his grandson, Zhang Lü (fl. 190–220 C.E.), inherited the leadership of the organization as "Celestial Masters." Zhang Lü participated in rebellion against the Han imperial state. Zhang Lü ceded administrative power to the rebel leader Cao Cao, who was eventually successful in his overthrow of the Han Empire. From this point on, the Way of the Celestial Masters was more priestly and liturgical than administrative or political, and while it did participate in political campaigns at some stages of its later history, it largely abandoned its theocratic aspirations after the Han.

Zhang Dao-ling's sect still exists, and the current Celestial Master, who lives in Taiwan, is said to be a direct descendent of the founder.

Ge Hong (fl. c. 300 C.E.)

Ge Hong is known as the first of the great "alchemists" and can be considered a founding figure in the Esoteric stream of religious Taoism. Like Zhang Dao-ling, he was a critic of the popular religious veneration of gods, ghosts, and ancestors, and the "excessive expenditures," healing rites, and shamanistic practices of village religion. He advocated personal physical-spiritual cultivation and the attainment of immortality within one's lifetime. As much as he influenced the subsequent development of Taoism, however, in the time in which he lived, Ge Hong was anything but a Taoist. He thought of Zhang Lü (Zhang Dao-ling's grandson) as a common rebel.

He identified more with Confucian intellectuals than with Taoist sectarians, and he was a member of the southern aristocracy. Nevertheless, he is a key figure in the history of Taoism, based upon two books, the *Shen-xian zhuan (Biographies of Gods and Immortals)* and the *Bao-pu-zi (Master Who Embraces the Uncarved Block)*.

The *Bao-pu-zi* contains all of the practices associated with the full development of Esoteric Taoism: the alchemical transformation of base materials into gold, physical exercises, deep breathing, a diet of herbs and minerals, and practices aimed at the production and retention of sexual fluids and sexual energy. In addition, Ge Hong's books include liturgical instructions that were especially effective in warding off dangerous animals and evil spirits—rites that were very useful to the so-called wandering Taoists of the Alchemical tradition. He describes sacred dances, secret prayers, magical "shouts" and invocations, and forms of calligraphy for the production of charms and amulets. All of these liturgical methods were adopted, in various forms, by the Priestly stream of Religious Taoism in later centuries.

As in the case of Zhang Dao-ling, Ge Hong's family played a crucial role in the subsequent history of Taoism. His uncle, Ge Xuan, was the recipient of the Ling-bao revelations, and his nephew, Ge Chao-fu, was the redactor of those revelations. The Ling-bao corpus consists of ritual manuals that make up the great majority of the Taoist Canon. Moreover, the Ge family was related by marriage to the family of Xu Hui (flourished 341–370 C.E.), who had received the Shang-qing revelations in the Bucklebent Hills of Mao Shan. Those revelations were set in writing by Tao Hong-jing (456–536 C.E.), and constitute the second most voluminous portion of the Taoist Canon. Family connections are at the heart of the early history of Esoteric Taoism.

Zhang San-feng (fl. 1216–1424 C.E.)

When it comes to Taoism, there is no clear distinction between history and mythology; often mythical figures, such as Lao-zi, are given dates of birth and death, hometowns, and bureaucratic titles and are said to have met with known historical persons at specific times and places. Zhang San-feng, one of many such figures from the history of Taoism, can serve as a representative example.

Zhang San-feng is a semihistorical figure whose biography is well known to Taoists from the Ming Dynasty to the present day. Enjoying a lifespan of some two hundred years, Zhang San-feng was one of the best-known of all the Taoist immortals, but he is unique in the historically precise details that appear in his biographies.

In the Ming and Qing Dynasties, various emperors sponsored the publication of massive encyclopedic collections. These collections included studies of nature or astronomy, imperial dynastic histories, local histories, dictionaries, almanacs, and biographies of eminent figures. Among the biographies are hundreds of idolized accounts describing "saints and immortals." The saints and immortals are described as accomplished masters of esoteric arts. They are wanderers with no fixed abode. They defy traditional social norms. They are often seen in rags or covered with dust or dirt, and they have few possessions. They collect herbs, minerals, and magical recipes for supernatural powers and long life. They are capable of shapeshifting, instantaneous travel, and flight, and their lifespans extend over dynasties, to two and three hundred years.

Zhang San-feng was one such figure. Still famous today, he is credited with inventing Chinese Shadow Boxing. He was sometimes called "Crazy Zhang" or "Filthy Zhang." He is portrayed in art as a ragged figure with a spiked beard, leaning on a staff, covered in dirt. He was a collector of rare herbs and minerals, and he was a master of immortality cultivation—even the dirt on his skin, rubbed into pellets, served as "long life pills" for those fortunate enough to meet him. The biographies report a number of miraculous events associated with Zhang San-feng. In one tale, he flies off on a crane's back; in another, he squeezes into a gourd; he appears in different places at the same time; he walks on water, freezes fire, cures illnesses, and boxes one hundred robbers. Surprisingly, given his slovenly appearance, Zhang San-feng was also associated with Taoist sexual alchemy and was canonized after his death as a God of Wealth.

Two emperors sent out emissaries in search of Zhang San-feng, culminating in a thirteen-year search ordered by Ming Yong-le Emperor Cheng-zu (reigned 1403–1425 C.E.). Though many sightings were reported, Zhang was never found. Nevertheless, in 1459 C.E., Emperor Ying-zong canonized Zhang as "The Perfect One (*zhen-ren*) Penetrating the Abyss and Unveiling Transmutation." Zhang San-feng manifests the highest goals of Esoteric Taoism: mastery of nature (including the physical body), spiritual cultivation, the rejection of social convention, aid to those in need, physical healing, and the attainment of long life and immortality.

Kristofer Schipper (b. 1940 c.e.)

Kristofer Schipper may represent the future of Taoism as a world religion: a Westerner expert in Taoism both as a scholar and as a practitioner. An ordained Taoist priest, Kristofer Schipper is Directeur d'Études at the *École Pratique des Hautes Études*, Sorbonne, Paris, and Professor Emeritus of Chinese History at Leiden University, the Netherlands. As a young man, Schipper majored in Oriental Art, but turned in 1958 c.e. to the study of Chinese religions. Moving from academic study in Paris to fieldwork in Taiwan, Schipper apprenticed himself to a Taoist master in 1964 c.e., and was ordained as a Taoist Master (a *dao-shi*) in 1968 c.e.—the only Westerner ever to have done so. His ordination master was the sixty-third Celestial Master, Zhang En-pu, in direct descent from Zhang Dao-ling.

Schipper is an expert not only in Taoist ritual—including the complex calligraphic arts of Taoist charms and amulets, as well as the priestly rites of Taoist funerals, consecrations, blessings, and ceremonies—but also in Taiwanese marionette theater, a traditional art form closely tied to Taoist storytelling and shamanism. His book on Taoism, *Le Corps Taoiste* (translated into English as *The Taoist Body*, 1993 c.e.) is the best introduction to Taoism as a priestly tradition, drawing significantly on his own apprenticeship in liturgical Taoism in his youth.

Schipper is representative of a distinctively modern trend in the spread of Chinese religions throughout the world. He, and other Western students who have followed in his footsteps, are in many respects more active than Chinese intellectuals in preserving the riches of Chinese religious history. Many younger scholars of Chinese religion in Europe and the United States now see the importance of direct observation and experience in the study of religion. At the same time, a number of young Chinese scholars in both Taiwan and the People's Republic of China are rediscovering the Taoist tradition, and are making great efforts to uncover its past and to ensure its future.

FURTHER READINGS

A readable biography of Confucius is by Kaizuka. The best new translation of *The Analects* is by Ames and Rosemont. There is still only one truly superior translation of *The Book of Mencius,* and it includes biographical information from many sources. That is *Mencius: Translated with an Intro-*

duction by D.C. Lau. For Xun-zi's biography and a translation, see Homer Dubs's *Hsuntzu: The Moulder of Ancient Confucianism.* A more modern and more scholarly translation was done by John Knoblock. The great modern scholar of Zhu Xi is Wing-tsit Chan. See his biography of Zhu Xi (in *Chu Hsi and Neo-Confucianism*) and his translation of Zhu Xi's *Reflection on Things at Hand.* The best biographies of Wang Yang-ming are by Tu Wei-ming and Julia Ching. Tu Wei-ming has published a number of books on the history of Confucianism as well as the practice of Confucianism in the modern world. For the first, see his *Neo-Confucian Thought in Action: Wang Yang-ming's Youth (1472–1509).* For Confucianism as a living religious tradition, Tu's *Confucian Thought: Selfhood as Creative Transformation* is recommended.

Biographical data on Lao-zi can be found in D. C. Lau's translation of the *Dao de jing.* Biographical data on Zhuang-zi can be found in A. C. Graham's translation of *The Book of Zhuang-zi.* Biographical notes and a partial translation of the *Bao pu zi* of Ge Hong can be found in James Ware's *Alchemy, Medicine, Religion in the China of A.D. 320.* Kristofer Schipper's work is primarily in French; *Le Corps Taoiste* has been translated into English as *The Taoist Body.*

Ames, Roger, and Henry Rosemont, Jr., trans. *The Analects of Confucius: A Philosophical Translation.* New York: Ballantine, 1999.

Chan, Wing-tsit, ed. *Chu Hsi and Neo-Confucianism.* Honolulu: University of Hawaii Press, 1986.

Chan, Wing-tsit, trans. *Reflections on Things at Hand: The Neo-Confucian Anthology Compiled by Chu Hsi and Lü Tsu-ch'ien.* New York: Columbia University Press, 1967.

Ching, Julia. *To Acquire Wisdom: The Way of Wang Yang-ming (1492–1529).* New York: Columbia University Press, 1976.

Dubs, Homer H. *Hsuntzu: The Moulder of Ancient Confucianism.* London: Arthur. Probsthain, 1927.

Graham, A. C., trans. *Chuang-tzu: The Seven Inner Chapters and Other Writings from the Book Chuang-tzu.* Boston: Allen & Unwin, 1981.

Kaizuka, Shigeki. *Confucius.* Translated from the Japanese by Geoffrey Bownas. New York: Macmillan, 1956.

Knoblock, John. *Xun-zi: A Translation and Study of the Complete Works.* 3 vols. Stanford, CA: Stanford University Press: 1988–94.

Lau, D. C., trans. *Lao Tzu: Tao Te Ching.* New York: Penguin, 1963.

Lau, D. C., trans. *Mencius.* New York: Penguin, 1970.

Schipper, Kristofer. *The Taoist Body.* Translated from the French by Karen C.
    Duval. Berkeley: University of California Press, 1993.

Tu, Wei-ming. *Confucian Thought: Selfhood as Creative Transformation.* Al-
    bany: State University of New York Press, 1985.

Tu, Wei-ming. *Neo-Confucian Thought in Action: Wang Yang-ming's Youth
    (1472–1509).* Berkeley: University of California Press, 1976.

Ware, James, trans. *Alchemy, Medicine, Religion in the China of A.D. 320: The
    Nei p'ien of Ko Hung (Pao-p'u tzu).* New York: Dover, 1966.

GLOSSARY

Dao (**Way**): Sometimes romanized "Tao," the guiding principle of existence. Confucians interpret the Dao as the "Way of Right Action" (an ethical path); Taoists interpret the Dao as the "Way of Naturalness" (a cosmic path).

Dao de jing (**Classic of the Power of the Way**): Also known in Chinese as the "Five Thousand Character Classic" or the "Book of Lao-zi," the mystical text attributed to the legendary figure Lao-zi ("Old Infant"). The *Dao de jing* was composed during the Warring States Period (480–220 C.E.) by a community of Laoists who reacted against Confucian social norms.

dao-shi (**Taoist Master**): A Taoist priest. *Dao-shi* perform purification and offerings in community temples. They are expert practitioners of calligraphy, painting, and complex rituals. Today, Taoist priests practice their ancient rites in village temples in Taiwan, Singapore, and southern China.

fa-shi (**Ritual Master**): A Taoist priest, lower in status than the Taoist Master (*dao-shi*). Ritual Masters perform exorcisms and healing rituals in the courtyard in front of a village temple. They are skilled in puppetry (marionette theater), acrobatics, and dramatic performances.

feng-shui (**geomancy, lit. "wind and water"**): The orientation and placement of habitations of the dead (cemeteries and graves) and the living (villages, homes, and furnishings). *Feng-shui* is practiced by a *Feng-shui* Master on behalf of a family or community, most commonly in choosing a location for a gravesite that will bring comfort to the dead and good fortune to their descendents. *Feng-shui* is an example of Chinese reverence for nature and broader ecological awareness. It has contributed to the underlying principles of Chinese art and architecture as well as the practice of ancestor veneration.

hun-dun (chaos): The original condition of the universe. *Hun-dun* describes an undifferentiated mass of energy and potentiality from which the "breath of life" (see *qi*) arises.

hun and po (souls): The multiple souls of the body in traditional Chinese religion. Both Taoist and Confucian texts describe three active (*yang*) souls called *hun*, and seven receptive (*yin*) souls called *po*. The *hun* souls are associated with intellectual thought and willful action, and the *po* souls are associated with the emotions. Like *yin* and *yang*, the *hun* and *po* souls should be balanced to ensure physical, psychological, and spiritual well-being.

ji-tong (spirit medium): A *ji-tong* performs in the temple courtyard and is possessed by one of the gods of Chinese popular religion or by an ancestor. Spirit mediums are sometimes hired by families experiencing difficulties and seeking counsel from their deceased parents and grandparents.

jün-zi (gentleman): The "cultivated person" of the Confucian tradition. A *jün-zi* is both well educated and virtuous; his mastery of literature and the arts, the rites, and history makes him morally upright. The ideal Confucian society is one that is ruled and administered by gentlemen of character and learning.

li (rites, propriety): One of two principal religious expressions of the Confucian tradition (see *ren*). *Li* refers to proper patterns of interaction, in a living, human context. Confucius, who admired the harmony and grandeur of the traditional rites, established the rites as a model for a "ceremonial" attitude toward life. Confucianism extends the meaning of *li* to include politeness, etiquette, decorum, and tact.

Lun-yü (*The Analects*, lit. "Conversations and Sayings"): A collection of the sayings of Confucius as gathered by his students. *The Analects*, which includes some 496 conversations in twenty chapters, was composed within two generations of Confucius's life.

qi (breath): The basic energy of the universe, sometimes translated as "pneuma" or "vitality" in addition to its basic meaning of "breath" or "vapor." *Qi*, which is both material and spiritual, is described in Confucian cosmology as the underlying substance and energy of all things. In contemporary practices of *qi-gong*, shadow boxing, and other martial arts, emphasis is placed upon the harnessing and circulation of *qi*-energy.

ren (**benevolence, co-humanity**): One of two principal religious expressions of the Confucian tradition (see *li*), often translated as "kindness" or "love." *Ren*, the inner emotion that should accompany the performance of *li*, is the distinguishing quality of a *jün-zi*. A person of *ren* "feels joy at the good luck of others, and misery at their misfortune."

Ru (**Confucian, lit. "scholar"**): The closest Chinese equivalent to the religion or school called "Confucianism." The *Ru* scholars were known in ancient times for their love of learning, their practice of traditional rites, and their eccentric dress (the clothes of the early Zhou Dynasty). The *Ru* had expert knowledge of the Five Books: *The Book of Changes, The Book of History, The Book of Songs, The Book of Rites,* and *The Spring and Autumn Annals*.

shi (**advisor**): Wandering advisors of the Zhou Dynasty. The best known was Confucius, the First Sage.

Tian (**Heaven**): The High God or Principle of Order in the Confucian tradition. Although some Confucians personalized *Tian* as a Creator God and arbiter of justice, others saw *Tian* as simply the natural order or a general standard of goodness. Among Song Dynasty Neo-Confucians, *Tian-li* (the Principle of Heaven) described both the moral and the physical structure of the universe.

Tian-shi Dao (**Way of the Celestial Masters**): The earliest of the Taoist Sects. Founded in the later Han Dynasty by Zhang Dao-ling, the *Tian-shi Dao* was the prototype of a number of Taoist sectarian movements throughout Chinese history. The present Celestial Master is said to be a direct descendent of Zhang Dao-ling.

wu (**shaman**): A shaman or spirit medium. The *wu* date to a very early period of Chinese history, when they were primarily women, indicating women's high political and religious status in the pre-Qin era. Taoist shamans were able to send their souls on "spirit journeys" to the realms of immortals or of the dead.

wu-wei (**non-action**): Non-purposive or non-manipulative action, non-interference, taking no artificial action, allowing things or events to follow their natural course. This is a key concept of the *Dao de jing*, attributed to Lao-zi. The *Dao de jing* advocates simplicity and plainness, non-aggression, and yielding. By applying "non-action" in this way, "there is nothing that cannot be done."

wu-yong (**uselessness**): A key concept of the *Book of Zhuangzi,* the eremitic Taoists sought to be "useless" in practical terms. In this way, they could preserve and extend their lives. Uselessness also suggests a different way of looking at "lowly" things: what is "useless" in a conventional sense may be very "useful" from a religious or creative perspective.

yin and yang **(passive and active energy):** The principles of "passivity" and "activity" that underlie all things in the universe. Ideally, yin and yang are balanced and harmonized, without an overemphasis either on femininity, yielding, and quiescence (associated with *yin*) or on masculinity, aggression, and activity (associated with *yang*).

zhen-ren (**sage, lit. "Perfected One"**): The wise person of the *Book of Zhuangzi.* The *zhen-ren* is unaffected by pleasure or pain, by excess or want, by fame or infamy. There are suggestions that the *zhen-ren* had supernormal powers, and the zhen-ren is a model for adepts of the Taoist immortality cult.

zi-ran (**nature, spontaneity**): "Non-intentional self-evolution." *Zi-ran* is key concept of the *Dao de jing* and a model for persons, who are urged to act spontaneously, to avoid artificial action, and to harmonize with the natural world. It represents the ecological consciousness of the Taoist tradition.

SELECTED BIBLIOGRAPHY

Ames, Roger, and Henry Rosemont, Jr., trans. *The Analects of Confucius: A Philosophical Translation.* New York: Ballantine, 1999.

Baker, Hugh D. R. *Chinese Family and Kinship.* London: Macmillan, 1979.

Berling, Judith. *A Pilgrim in Chinese Culture: Negotiating Religious Diversity.* Maryknoll, NY: Orbis, 1997.

Berling, Judith. *The Syncretic Religion of Lin Chao-en.* New York: Columbia University Press, 1980.

Berthrong, John. *Transformations of the Confucian Way.* Boulder, CO: Westview, 1998.

Bokenkamp, Stephen R. *Early Daoist Scriptures.* Berkeley: University of California Press, 1997.

Chan, Wing-tsit. *A Source Book in Chinese Philosophy.* Princeton: Princeton University Press, 1963.

Chan, Wing-tsit, ed. *Chu Hsi and Neo-Confucianism.* Honolulu: University of Hawaii Press, 1986.

Chan, Wing-tsit, trans. *Instructions for Practical Living and Other Neo-Confucian Writings by Wang Yang-ming.* New York: Columbia University Press, 1963.

Chan, Wing-tsit, trans. *Reflections on Things at Hand: The Neo-Confucian Anthology Compiled by Chu Hsi and Lü Tsu-ch'ien.* New York: Columbia University Press, 1967.

Chang, Chung-li. *The Chinese Gentry: Studies on Their Role in Nineteenth-Century Chinese Society.* Seattle: University of Washington Press, 1955.

Chang, Raymond, and Margaret S. Chang. *Speaking of Chinese.* New York: Norton, 1978.

Ching, Julia. *To Acquire Wisdom: The Way of Wang Yang-ming (1492–1529).* New York: Columbia University Press, 1976.

Clarke, J.J. *The Tao of the West: Western Transformations of Taoist Thought.* New York: Routledge, 2000.

Dubs, Homer H. *Hsuntzu: The Moulder of Ancient Confucianism.* London: Arthur Probsthain, 1927.

Eastman, Lloyd. *Family, Field, and Ancestors: Constancy and Change in China's Social and Economic History, 1550–1949.* New York: Oxford University Press, 1988.

Eber, Irene. *Confucianism: The Dynamics of Tradition.* New York: Macmillan, 1986.

Ebrey, Patricia. *Chu Hsi's Family Rituals: A Twelfth-Century Chinese Manual for the Performance of Cappings, Weddings, Funerals, and Ancestral Rites.* Princeton: Princeton University Press, 1991.

Fung Yu-lan. *A History of Chinese Philosophy.* Translated by Derk Bodde. Princeton: Princeton University Press, 1952.

Geertz, Clifford. *The Interpretation of Cultures.* New York: Basic, 1973.

Gernet, Jacques. *A History of Chinese Civilization.* Translated by J.R. Foster and Charles Hartman. Cambridge: Cambridge University Press, 1996.

Graham, A.C. *Disputers of the Tao: Philosophical Argument in Ancient China.* La Salle, IL: Open Court, 1989.

Graham, A.C., trans. *Chuang-tzu: The Seven Inner Chapters and Other Writings from the Book Chuang-tzu.* Boston: Allen & Unwin, 1981.

Hansen, Valerie. *Changing Gods in Medieval China, 1127–1276.* Princeton: Princeton University Press, 1990.

Hawkes, David. *The Songs of the South: An Ancient Chinese Anthology of Poems by Qu Yuan and Other Poets.* New York: Penguin, 1985.

Huang Liu-hung. *A Complete Book Concerning Happiness and Benevolence: A Manual for Local Magistrates in Seventeenth Century China.* Edited and translated by Djang Chu. Tucson: University of Arizona Press, 1984.

Jensen, Lionel. *Manufacturing Confucianism: Chinese Traditions and Universal Civilization.* Durham, NC: Duke University Press, 1997.

Jordan, David K. *Gods, Ghosts, and Ancestors: Folk Religion in a Taiwanese Village.* Berkeley: University of California Press, 1972.

Kaizuka, Shigeki. *Confucius.* Translated from the Japanese by Geoffrey Bownas. New York, Macmillan, 1956.

Kaltenmark, Max. *Lao Tzu and Taoism.* Translated from the French by Roger Greaves. Stanford, CA: Stanford University Press, 1969.

Karlgren, Bernard. *Grammata Serica Recensa.* Edited by Tor Ulving. *Diction-ary of Old & Middle Chinese: Bernard Karlgren's "Grammata Serica Re-censa" Alphabetically Arranged.* Philadelphia: Coronet, 1997.

Keightley, David N. *Sources of Shang History: The Oracle-Bone Inscriptions of Bronze Age China.* Berkeley: University of California Press, 1978.

Knoblock, John. *Xun-zi: A Translation and Study of the Complete Works.* 3 vols. Stanford, CA: Stanford University Press, 1988–94.

Kohn, Livia, ed. in cooperation with Yoshinobu Sakade. *Taoist Meditation and Longevity Techniques.* Ann Arbor: Center for Chinese Studies, University of Michigan, 1989.

LaFargue, Michael, trans. *The Tao of the Tao Te Ching: A Translation and Com-mentary.* Albany: State University of New York Press, 1992.

Lau, D.C., trans. *Lao Tzu: Tao Te Ching.* New York: Penguin, 1963.

Lau, D.C., trans. *Mencius.* New York: Penguin, 1970.

Maspero, Henri. *China in Antiquity.* Translated by Frank A. Kierman, Jr. Am-herst: University of Massachusetts Press, 1978.

Neville, Robert Cummings. *Boston Confucianism: Portable Tradition in the Late-Modern World.* Albany: State University of New York Press, 2000.

Pas, Julian. *The Turning of the Tide: Religion in China Today.* New York: Oxford University Press, 1989.

Robinet, Isabelle. *Taoism: Growth of a Religion.* Translated from the French by Phyllis Brooks. Stanford, CA: Stanford University Press, 1997.

Schipper, Kristofer. *The Taoist Body.* Translated from the French by Karen C. Duval. Berkeley: University of California Press, 1993.

Shryock, John. *The Origin and Development of the State Cult of Confucius.* New York: Century, 1932. Reprint, New York: Paragon, 1966.

Smith, Wilfred Cantwell. *Faith and Belief.* Princeton: Princeton University Press, 1979.

Smith, Wilfred Cantwell. *The Meaning and End of Religion.* Minneapolis: For-tress, 1962.

Streng, Frederick. *Understanding Religious Life.* Encino, CA: Dickenson, 1976.

Tu, Wei-ming. *Confucian Thought: Selfhood as Creative Transformation.* Al-bany: State University of New York Press, 1985.

Tu, Wei-ming. *Neo-Confucian Thought in Action: Wang Yang-ming's Youth (1472–1509).* Berkeley: University of California Press, 1976.

Wakeman, Frederic, and C.A. Grant, eds. *Conflict and Control in Late Impe-rial China.* Berkeley: University of California Press, 1975.

Ware, James R. *Alchemy, Medicine, Religion in the China of A.D. 320: The Nei p'ien of Ko Hung (Pao-p'u tzu).* New York: Dover, 1966.

Watson, Burton, trans. *Chuang Tzu: Basic Writings.* New York: Columbia University Press, 1964.

Weller, Robert P. *Unities and Diversities in Chinese Religion.* Seattle: University of Washington Press, 1987.

Wong, Eva. *The Shambhala Guide to Taoism.* Boston: Shambhala, 1997.

Yang, C. K. *Religion in Chinese Society.* Berkeley: University of California Press, 1961.

Yao, Xinzhong. *An Introduction to Confucianism.* Cambridge: Cambridge University Press, 2000.

INDEX

About the Authors

EMILY TAITZ is an independent scholar and author of *The Jews of Medieval France: The Community of Champagne* (Greenwood, 1994) and numerous essays on Judaism and the coauthor of *Remarkable Jewish Women: Rebels, Rabbis and Other Women from Biblical Times to the Present* (2002), among other works.

RANDALL L. NADEAU is Associate Professor of East Asian Religions at Trinity University, San Antonio, Texas.

JOHN M. THOMPSON teaches in the Department of Philosophy and Religious Studies, Christopher Newport University, Newport News, Virginia.

LEE W. BAILEY is Associate Professor of Philosophy and Religion at Ithaca College.

ZAYN R. KASSAM is Associate Professor of Religious Studies and Chair of the Religious Studies Department, Pomona College.

STEVEN J. ROSEN is an independent scholar and prolific writer on Hinduism.

FOR REFERENCE

Do Not Take From This Room